*Preschool Children
in Troubled Families*

WILEY SERIES ON
STUDIES IN CHILD PSYCHIATRY

Series Editor
Michael Rutter
Institute of Psychiatry
London

Longitudinal Studies in Child Psychology and Psychiatry
Practical Lessons from Research Experience
Edited by A.R. Nicol

Treatment of Autistic Children
Patricia Howlin and Michael Rutter

Childhood Epilepsies: Neuropsychological, Psychosocial
and Intervention Aspects
Edited by Bruce P. Hermann and Michael Seidenberg

Life Experiences, Development and Childhood Psychopathology
Ian M. Goodyer

Precursors and Causes in Development and
Psychopathology
Edited by Dale F. Hay and Adrian Angold

Preschool Children in Troubled Families
Approaches to Intervention and Support
Rory Nicol, David Stretch and
Trian Fundudis

Preschool Children in Troubled Families

Approaches to Intervention and Support

Rory Nicol
David Stretch
University of Leicester, UK

Trian Fundudis
University of Newcastle upon Tyne, UK

JOHN WILEY & SONS
Chichester · New York · Brisbane · Toronto · Singapore

Other Wiley Editorial Offices

John Wiley & Sons, Inc., 605 Third Avenue,
New York, NY 10158-0012, USA

Jacaranda Wiley Ltd, G.P.O. Box 859, Brisbane,
Queensland 4001, Australia

John Wiley & Sons (Canada) Ltd, 22 Worcester Road,
Rexdale, Ontario M9W 1L1, Canada

John Wiley & Sons (SEA) Pte Ltd, 37 Jalan Pemimpin #05-04,
Block B, Union Industrial Building, Singapore 2057

Library of Congress Cataloging-in-Publication Data

Nicol, A.R. (Arthur Rory)
    Preschool children in troubled families : approaches to intervention and support / Rory
Nicol, David Stretch, Trian Fundudis.
        p.   cm. — (Wiley series on studies in child psychiatry)
    Includes bibliographical references and index.
    ISBN 0-471-93868-8
    1. Preschool children—Mental health services—Evaluation.
2. Mentally ill children—Family relationships.   3. Problem families—Mental health.   4.
Family psychotherapy.   I. Stretch, David.   II. Fundudis, Trian.   III. Title.   IV. Series.
RJ507.P35N53   1993
362.2'0425'0833—dc20   92–37834
                                                                                   CIP

British Library Cataloguing in Publication Data

A catalogue record for this book is available from the British Library

ISBN 0-471-93868-8

Typeset in 10/12pt Times by Photo·graphics, Honiton, Devon
Printed and bound in Great Britain by Biddles Ltd, Guildford, Surrey

Contents

Series Preface

During recent years there has been a tremendous growth of research in both child development and child psychiatry. Research findings are beginning to modify clinical practice but to a considerable extent the fields of child development and child psychiatry have remained surprisingly separate, with regrettably little cross-fertilization. Much developmental research has not concerned itself with clinical issues, and studies of clinical syndromes have all too often been made within the narrow confines of a pathological condition approach with scant regard to developmental matters. This situation is rapidly changing but the results of clinical-developmental studies are often reported only by means of scattered papers and scientific journals. This series aims to bridge the gap between child development and clinical psychiatry by presenting reports of new findings, new ideas, and new approaches in a book form that may be available to a wider readership.

The series includes reviews of specific topics, multi-authored volumes on a common theme, and accounts of specific pieces of research. However, in all cases, the aim is to provide a clear, readable and interesting account of scientific findings in a style that makes explicit their relevance to clincial practice or social policy. It is hoped that the series will be of interest to both clinicians and researchers in the fields of child psychiatry, child psychology, psychiatric social work, social paediatrics, and education—in short, all concerned with growing children and their problems.

Until relatively recently, many people have regarded the emotional and behavioural problems of preschool children as of little significance, in the belief that most were just transient 'growing up' difficulties. Longitudinal studies have shown just how mistaken that belief is. Not only do such problems involve suffering at the time but also a substantial proportion constitute the early beginnings of the persistent or recurrent psychiatric disorders of later age periods. This book provides a thoughtful bringing together of the concepts and research findings on preschool problems, the emphasis being on the ways in which they arise in the family and broader social context in which young children grow up. The evidence from previous studies of prevention and intervention is considered in relation to the planning of the authors' own ambitious and systematic evaluation of three treatment methods—special health visiting, family therapy and mother and toddler groups—which are compared with a no-intervention control group. The investigation involved a special concern to assess the effects on parents as well as on children. The findings are in many respects sobering but the implications are brought together and well integrated in a series of practical recommendations with respect to both service planning and future research.

MICHAEL RUTTER

Preface

This book is about the difficulties encountered by mothers and toddlers in the preschool years, and the effectiveness of professional help. We report a major research project which consists of three approaches to intervention: intensive health visiting, family therapy, and mother and toddler groups. The core of the book is a trial of how these approaches affect child disorder, mother's mental health, child development and the quality of the marriage. In the early chapters, we place the study into the context of current thinking and research, considering, to start off with, some issues in child and family development that acted as a backdrop to our own thinking. In Chapter 2 we focus on the main variables of the study and consider how psychopathology may develop over this period and bring together evidence on its outcome. In doing so, we build the case for intervention both by looking at how problems get into the saddle, how this relates to the development of the child and family generally and in turn what effects these problems have on development. In Chapter 3 we describe approaches to helping preschoolers and the contexts in which these have been tried, leading to studies of effectiveness of interventions which is the subject of Chapter 4. This enables us to present our own project, which we describe in the following four chapters. In Chapters 9, 10 and 11 we present the research findings and open discussion of the practical and academic implications of the work.

There are two aspects of our approach which should be mentioned at this early stage. The first is that both in our research intervention and in the pages that follow the child is viewed at every point in the context of the family and the surrounding world. The theme we favour relates to the concept of adaption. As the child develops, increasing demands are made for finely tuned adaption to his or her family and general social environment. Incontinence is tolerated in the 9 month old but not the 9 year old. A more extended example will help to illustrate the process. Before the age of 5 in the United Kingdom, children have to cope for the first time with school. In adaptive terms, school means being, often for the first time, one of a crowd. It means competition and coping with authority. New demands are put on the child's ability to make friends. It means being judged on what you can do rather than for who you are. For some children, the style of discipline at school will be very unfamiliar, as will the idea of sustained attention to a topic and of formal learning. Aggression, which in some cases was adaptive at home, will not be tolerated in the classroom. These issues challenge the adaptive capacity of the child, and many children show signs of stress at this time (Faull and Nicol 1986). Individual differences in children mean that some children cope better than others.

These are themes that we shall be taking up in the early chapters of this book. For the time being, it is important to note that adaption refers to a totality. Inevitably, the measures we use, if taken each on their own, describe only little bits of this totality. We also use some concepts that may seem to be breaking down reality as a whole into artificial parts. This is unavoidable if we are to capture these parts in a reliable way and we ask you, our readers, to bear with us and judge for yourselves whether we have made a useful contribution to understanding the reality which is ultimately the important end point of all research work. Some of the ideas we shall use are psychiatric disorder in parents and children and marital discord as our basis for measurement. As a generic term, we shall refer to "disturbance" in these areas. Psychiatric disorder is defined as a problem of emotions, behaviour, relationships or cognition that is of sufficient severity and duration to cause distress, disability or disadvantage in an adult or child (Cantwell 1988). Measurement of marital problems will be based on interview evidence of discord and quarrelling in the family (Quinton, Rutter and Rowlands 1976). It is equally important to consider the proper cognitive development of the child. We base this on the performance on adaptions of well-validated psychological tests. In the chapters that follow, we shall adopt a second generic term: "delay". The difference between "disturbance" and "delay" is that the former indicates that development has gone off track, whereas the latter indicates that it is slowed up. Mental retardation as such will not be discussed in this book, but within the range of normal intelligence there are vast differences in rates of development which are socially and clinically significant. In recent years, the importance of describing human relationships has become clear, that is what goes on between people rather than describing the people themselves (Hinde 1979). This new emphasis is of great importance to the evaluation of psychological treatments. It is reflected most obviously in our work in the measures of the marital relationship.

The second aspect of our approach is an emphasis on so-called secondary prevention. The idea here is that children and families are identified who show vulnerability or early signs of disorder. Intervention is then offered at this early stage rather than waiting, head in sand, for full-blown disorder to emerge at a stage where treatment may be much more difficult. The vulnerability may be in the form of medical or neurological disability; it may be shown by family or social difficulty or early signs of failure or retardation in development. In what follows these themes will recur.

There is a third term which will be used in this book to cover professionals in the mental health field who undertake assessment and treatment of children which may include any of a wide range of observational techniques, theoretical approaches and intervention techniques. To cover this we shall use the term "the clinician" and the adjective "clinical". This term is selected for its convenience. A clinician, in our meaning, doesn't just work in a clinic, but may offer a service in any setting, including the home of the child and family.

Chapter 9, on the outcome of our own study, presents particular difficulties in presentation since the statistical techniques used are necessarily complex. The risk is that one might make the results accessible to the non-mathematical reader but, in doing so, fail to describe the technique used adequately, while a full mathematical treatment could render the presentation incomprehensible to the very readership who will, it is hoped, find the study of benefit in their own practice. A compromise is necessary, and what we have done is to provide a simple introduction to the principle involved, followed by the results which are set out in a way that we hope will be accessible to everybody. A more technical presentation is available in Appendices 1 and 2.

The work described here was the co-operative effort of a large team, and it is not possible to mention all those who made a contribution, but some stand out. Mrs Glenda Brown and Mrs Margaret Rickelton collaborated in developing the health visiting programme as well as carrying it out. Mr Michael Koziarski and Mrs Susan Hodgson similarly assisted in developing and implementing the family therapy programme. All four helped develop the mother and toddler group programme.

We are most grateful for the wise guidance of our steering committee, consisting of Professor Israel Kolvin (Chairman), Professor Donald Court, Dr Isla Gillie (Community Physician Child Health), Mrs Christine Brown (Unit General Manager, Community Unit) and Mrs Margaret Davidson (Nursing Officer, Community Unit). We are also grateful to Professor Sir Michael Rutter for his helpful suggestions in writing this book.

The study was supported by grants from the Rowntree Trust, the Department of the Environment and the Department of Health and Social Security.

Chapter 1

The Development of the Young Child and Family

The early years are marked by an extraordinary rate of change at every level: the individual child, the relationships of the child to others and at a higher level, in the family as a social system. This rapid change in such immature individuals gives rise to a seductive possibility for the mental health worker: are these rapidly changing systems more susceptible to influence by therapists or teachers than at a later stage? This second issue has to be addressed in its own right. It is the central question of this book. In the first two chapters, we shall lay the problem before the reader, first sketching in some of the relevant issues of normal child and family development and then describing the development of psychopathology in the preschool years. We then move on to look at various types of interventions in the literature so far and, in Chapter 4, their effectiveness.

Even in the modern era of supposedly more fluid roles in family life, it is still mothers who are central to child care. In the past, the mother–child dyad has been the centre-piece of investigation. The picture is now changing rapidly as therapists and researchers begin to consider not only the contribution of other family members, but also the family as a whole as a discrete social entity placed in a broader social network. The concept of the family life cycle is clarifying in bringing these parts together and adding a time dimension.

THE FAMILY LIFE CYCLE

This introduces the important idea that mother and toddler, father and siblings, as well as the wider group of peers, exert many possible mutual influences and that the family can be described not only as an entity in its own right, but also as one with its own characteristic pattern of change through time. Clinicians use the concept of the family as a social system which progresses through stages: young couples, families with young children, families with adolescents, empty nests and older couples (Aldous 1978). Different aspects of family life can be described and a variety of concepts have been developed to identify key components. These can help us to describe the family systematically (Epstein and Bishop 1981; Olson and McCubbin 1983). Issues such as roles undertaken by family members, the flexibility of the family in the face of changes, the quality of psychological support offered to family members by each other and family cohesion have been identified by clinicians as important dimensions of family life. These clinical concepts will be explored at a practical level in Chapter 7.

More recently, the academic research community have made moves towards measuring relationships rather than individuals and using multiple measures: interviews, questionnaires and direct observation to capture the different facets of reality. As Schaffer (1984) tells us, the framework from which the observer is operating is a central guide as to what is actually observed. A child crying can be looked on as a "symptom" which, put together with an excess of similar episodes, may suggest that he or she has an emotional problem. It may be linked to some aspect of the environment, for example separation from mother, in which case it can still be seen as the individual child's problem of separation anxiety. The major step is taken when the mother's behaviour is also measured in a sequence of interactions between the two, for example she may tearfully exhort the child to separate from her while clutching him or her to her bosom. As soon as the mother's contribution is included in the observations, it is possible to collect data relevant to describing the relationship between the mother and child as opposed to just the child as an individual, despite the fact that the observations on the child's behaviour are unchanged. The next stage might be to collect data on the marital relationship as well. This might be the starting-point for hypotheses about the family's functioning and the meaning, in a family context, of the child's crying episodes. It is important to assess where the individual and relationship frameworks meet, and which will be useful in a given research situation.

Returning to the theme of married couple to parents, we shall start by considering the changes in the early years and social factors that may influence them. We need then to focus in on some of the psychological changes in the developing child and the way these influence the developing relationship.

COUPLE TO YOUNG PARENTS

Different writers have offered different views on pregnancy and birth: is it a serene state (Deutch 1947), or a critical, even crisis point in the woman's development (Bibring 1959; Engfer 1988; Puckering 1989)? Most likely, the experience depends on the circumstances. A planned pregnancy for a woman adequately resourced and supported is very different from that of an isolated teenager with no support or income (Wolkind and Zajicek 1985). Zajicek (1981), from a longitudinal interview study, reported that

8% of pregnant women in a working-class sample were negative about their pregnancy at registration for antenatal care, as were 16% at seven months. These general feelings were focused on specific issues such as restrictions, and having to give up work. Dissatisfaction tended to disappear with quickening, and where it persisted, there was evidence that the women did not use their husbands or mothers as confidants, and that they had more neurotic symptoms (Pilowsky and Sharp 1971).

Role change

How does the arrival of a child actually affect the daily activities of family members? There often seems to be a sharper segregation of the roles between the husband and wife. For example, Olson, Lavee and McCubbin (1988), using a theoretical model of the family called the circumflex model, compared families at different stages of the life cycle on dimensions of adaptability and cohesion, dimensions which they consider to be the key to understanding family function. In a nation-wide survey in the USA, using a family questionnaire (FACES III), these authors report a reduction in adaptability in families with young children compared with families at the pre-childbearing stage. This could possibly reflect a differentiation of roles between husband and wife at this time. What is more certain is that this segregation has more implications for the mother. For example, in a US questionnaire survey of 1618 white couples, Rexroat and Shehan (1987) compared the time spent in housework and paid employment in various stages of the life cycle, from young couple to preschool children through to empty nests. This showed that with the onset of childbearing, the housework and total work-load of women shot up from 17.8 to 29.3 hours per week, whereas the change for husbands was hardly perceptible. This change was also reflected in the total work-time of women compared with men, in that the women's work-hours were much higher.

Role satisfaction

It is surprising that in view of this common and enormous work-load, the morale of women, particularly those in employment, remains as high as it does. This was shown, for example, in a small-scale study by Pistang (1984), who examined the effect of involvement in work before the start of childbearing on morale and self-esteem after the birth of the first child. It was found that mothers who had been very involved with their work showed greater irritability and depression if they did not work after their baby. Previous work involvement was not related to post-partum morale if the mother went back to work after her baby.

Community questionnaire studies (Russell 1974; Hobbs and Cole 1976) suggest that while women may worry about their appearance and complain of exhaustion, fatigue and loss of sleep, both parents, if marital adjustment was good as measured by the Locke-Wallace scale (1959), reported pleasure in the child. The authors concluded that the change of role was not a major issue in the transition to parenthood; good communication within the marriage, which led to planning and preparation for parenthood, was more important. Another key predictor of a smooth passage to parenthood was a temperamentally easy baby. Hobbs and Cole (1976), replicating previous work, also confirmed that most couples negotiated the transition to parenthood without undue distress. Those most successful in this respect showed greater cohesiveness in the marital relationship and had been married for some time. Engfer (1988), however, showed a significant decline in the quality of marriage between 4 and 43 months post-partum. Shereshefsky and Yarrow (1973) found that good maternal adaption in the neonatal period was associated with a husband who was prepared to take on added tasks, who did not compete with the baby for nurturing from the mother and who tolerated disruption of established routines. Oakley (1974), however, in an exploration of young mothers' attitudes to housework, points out that at that time, male participation was still rare and that young mothers reported drudgery and boredom.

To summarize, couple to parents means much more change for the wife than the husband and may be accompanied by a new demarcation of roles in the family. In general there is little evidence of change from traditional roles but despite this, the arrival of a baby is helped by a good marital relationship and a sharing of chores.

Different background factors

Our portrait of the family life cycle so far has been a rather cosy one, a sort of middle-class ideal with little relationship to the big bad world "out there". Real families, of course, vary enormously in their circumstances and in very important ways. These variations can be considered under two headings: acute changes in circumstances, often called life events, and ongoing circumstances in which the family lives. There is, of course, no clear demarcation between these two, although the experience for the child and family may be very different when faced with a sudden adversity (or piece of luck) as compared with chronic adversity.

Financial and economic hardship

An important feature of the move to parenthood is the effect it is likely to have on the couple's material prosperity. At the turn of the century, the early reformers such as Booth and Rowntree recognized that exacerbations of poverty were linked with periods of the life cycle (Rutter and Madge 1976), the early years of childbearing being a time of particular financial stringency. The level of poverty in a society depends entirely on how it is defined, and there has been a tendency in recent years to modify this definition according to convenience. This has been made easier in Britain as, unlike many other countries, such as the United States, there is no official poverty line. No one would argue that absolute poverty, that is below the level of any form of subsistence, is now relatively rare in industrial countries, although not unknown. More relevant is relative poverty, where people are denied access to what is generally regarded as a reasonable standard and quality of life and opportunities for the society in question (Archbishop of Canterbury's Commission on Urban Priority Areas 1985). This level of poverty is particularly relevant where, as in the present book, we are intent on addressing the quality of life and the chances it gives to or withholds from families and children.

By the end of the 1950s there was a widespread perception that poverty had been conquered. This was the era of Prime Minister Harold Macmillan's slogan "you've never had it so good". The 1980s and 1990s have been very different in Britain and there have been major increases in the level of relative poverty in society (Oppenheim 1990). Reasons for this are the reappearance of mass unemployment, tax changes favouring the better off, an increase in the proportion of temporary and part-time, low-paid labour and a rise in the number of single parents. The trend has been reinforced by a government with a political philosophy which sees inequality as an economic energizer. The energizer has certainly been provided in liberal quantities, whatever one's assessment of the results. The targeting of benefits to where they are most needed (means testing) often results in handouts not being claimed in circumstances which are considered by the poor as demeaning. Through the mid-1980s, when the study to be reported in this book was taking place, the first increase in inequality and growth of poverty since the Second World War was under way. In 1987, 19% of the population were living at or below 50% of the average national income, compared with 9% in 1979. Over the same period, the poorest tenth of the population saw their income rise by just 0.1% in real terms as against 23% as the average rise of the population (Oppenheim 1990). By 1992, the poorest families had suffered a cut of 6% in income and one-quarter of Britain's children were living in poverty (Delamothe 1992). Economic hardship is usually a condition that remains with children throughout their formative years and often persists across generations (Rutter and Madge 1976; Kolvin et al 1990). There is much research evidence of its effect on physical health. The main common childhood causes of death, accidents and respiratory disease, are associated with conditions of economic hardship (Townsend and Davidson 1982) as are indices of mental health such as suicide. Concerning child mental health, straight poverty is an area where the research remains curiously silent. The concentration is rather on the correlates of economic hardship. The reason may be that calculation of income can be surprisingly complicated and, in Britain at any rate, more taboo than asking parents about their sex lives.

The closest marker to actual economic hardship that is commonly used is social class. It is not, however, synonymous. Social class is measured in terms of some index of job status rather than income. However, a lot of important findings have come out of looking at social class differences and we must now turn to this theme.

Roles and social class differences

This is an important issue for us since the relationship between roles, social support and depression has been found to be so dependent on social class (Brown and Harris 1978). Oakley (1974) found social class differences in attitudes to housework: women who had previously had lower-status jobs expressed more satisfaction in housework and were more likely to identify themselves as housewives; however, they were generally more ambivalent about their mothering role with its attendant unrelieved responsibility for children. Boulton (1983), in a small interview study, looked for social class differences in attitudes of young mothers. She described the change in women's lives when they become the sole caretaker of children and economically dependent on their husbands. She found that working-class mothers gained much psychological support if their husbands were helpful, whereas this was less obvious for middle-class mothers. In a cross-sectional study in an urban population, Brown, Ni Bhrolchain and Harris (1975) found that working-class women with a child under 6 years old reported a far lower rate of supportive relationships than either childless young women or older women. This was not true of middle-class women. It is an observation that is likely to be influenced by which particular group of working-class women are interviewed.

The value of wider network support should not be dismissed; for example, Abernathy (1973), in an investigation of the social network, showed that women in tightly knit networks whose relatives and friends saw each other independently reported feeling more comfortable in performing maternal roles. This was particularly true when they saw their mothers often.

The picture is that working-class women, perhaps where resources are limited, are particularly vulnerable to lack of support in the change from couple to parent. Social support is an environmental phenomenon that one would think was relatively easy to correct. This finding of lack of social support as a factor in psychopathology is reported in numerous studies. It is the finding, more than any other, that underpinned our own thinking in developing the interventions to be described later in this book. In particular, in the mothers' group regime, the aim was to provide peer support for isolated, and possibly self-isolating, mothers.

With development towards school age, social institutions such as child-minders, playgroups and nursery school become more important in the child's life. We shall return to this in Chapter 3, meanwhile we must pause to consider some broader concepts.

Unemployment

Like financial and economic hardship, unemployment is to a large extent a consequence of the economic condition of society. It can strike a family in a variety of ways, for example as a bolt from the blue in an otherwise prosperous family or as a chronic condition, perhaps broken by periods of low-skilled and low-paid work. The former situation will stretch the coping of the family and may precipitate economic hardship and mental health problems. Chronic unemployment carries its own toll of morbidity associated with chronic disadvantage and poverty. It is also true that when jobs are scare, the axe falls most heavily on those who are disadvantaged in other ways such as those with minimal education and with physical disability or mental ill health, particularly personality disorder (Rutter and Madge 1976; Kolvin et al 1990).

Separation and divorce

Currently something over one-third of marriages end in divorce, a very high proportion of these occurring early in the marriage, meaning that young children are often involved (Richards 1984). Recently, the rate of divorce has stabilized after steep rises in the 1960s and 1970s (Elliott and Richards 1991). We shall return in Chapter 2 to some of the emotional consequences of separation and divorce. It is a situation that can also bring about profound changes in the family situation, meaning that the children are in the care of a single parent who may have to struggle for the first time to make ends meet; divorce can lead to a move of house and major changes in the experience of parenting as the custodial parent struggles to cope.

Illness, bereavement and handicap in the family

Van Eerdewegh et al (1982) showed that by middle childhood the bereaved can show an intense level of grief, although it may be relatively short lived. In younger children, it is likely that the indirect effects of the loss, for example the emotional reaction of other members of the family, will be more influential, although surprisingly little is known about this important topic.

A second theme is that of chronic disability and handicap. There has been a recent and very desirable attempt to decrease the stigma and improve civil rights and an ordinary life for physically disabled and mentally retarded people. With this has gone an increase in the responsibilities incurred. For example, with an increase in the sexual activity of this group and on many occasions marriages, what are the prospects of mentally retarded people being able to parent children? Several studies have addressed this topic (see Gath 1988 for a review). Not surprisingly, as we have seen so often already, other conditions commonly have an influence. With good support, if available and accepted, mentally retarded people can do a good job. However, they may be vulnerable to exploitation, particularly as, with the rest of society so ambivalent about their sexuality, they seldom get the help in understanding sexual and intimate relationships that they need.

Severely handicapped people are far less likely to reproduce than those that are mildly so. In the case of mildly handicapped people, under-stimulation and adversity have often contributed to the parents' limited intellect. In turn, these other adverse early experiences may contribute to parents' difficulties in bringing up their children.

Multiple deprivation and disadvantage

In our listing of what can go wrong with this early stage of the life cycle it will have become obvious that misfortunes seldom visit families singly. Divorce often begets loneliness and financial stringency for the custodial parent; loss of a job is accompanied by loss of income, anomie and depression. A follow up study of 847 children in a poor northern British city from 1952 to 1980 analysed how these problems intertwine with each other and showed the strength of continuities in deprivation (Kolvin et al 1990). Work reported there showed, for example, that the number of problems was a powerful indicator of the gravity of a family's predicament as well as the nature of the actual problems under study. Rutter and Madge (1976) addressed the issue of the overlap between problems. Social problems in the general population group in certain families far more than one would expect by chance (Wedge and Prosser 1973). Also, depending on the individual problem under discussion, children's and mothers' disturbance are linked with social problems above chance level. There are also, of course, many families where one or other type of disadvantage exist on their own.

Evidence has accumulated over many years that multiple disadvantages can have a cumulative effect which is greater than the individual elements that make up the total picture. This goes for both "social factors" (such as unemployment, poverty, divorce, etc) and "biological factors" (such as prematurity and head injury). A good example is found in follow ups of children who have had difficulties in the neonatal period. Typically, these children are far more likely to suffer handicaps if they are being brought up in social disadvantage in addition to their early medical difficulties (Sameroff and Chandler 1975).

Is deprivation an unfortunate social by-product? Many would give the condition a more active social role. *The Concise Oxford Dictionary* defines deprivation as a taking away – an active process, rather than simple lack of something valued. This active meaning emphasizes the conception of deprivation as relative. The deprived person can be seen as a social necessity, for example as part of a pool of unemployed labour, or to do dirty jobs (Brown and Madge 1982). Closely related to this is the concept of powerlessness – a lack of personal ascendancy, or of an inability to do or act. Life happens to the powerless while the powerful have a means to mould their destiny to their liking and advantage. The status of powerlessness has profound psychological implications; we discuss it more fully in Chapter 4. Finally there is the more inclusive term of disadvantage. This is closely related to the other two terms but is oriented in meaning more to the future: a restriction of access to opportunities and generally valued goods and services available generally in the community. This is a key notion, particularly in the case of children who have their whole life ahead of them.

The three conditions of deprivation, powerlessness and disadvantage are, in practice, closely linked. In our own work, we considered it as essential that we accorded this social condition of multiple disadvantage a central place in our prediction of the ways that families might respond to the offer of professional help. We explain how we did this in Chapter 5.

Protective factors

Some might see this book as having got off to a rather gloomy start with poverty and powerlessness having grabbed centre stage. It is timely, therefore, to comment that the types of social adversity we have described by no means always result in poor outcomes. It is one of the greatest tributes to the human spirit that even under the most adverse of conditions many children and families seem to maintain hope and optimism and achieve a good outcome. Even among the multiply deprived in the Newcastle study (Kolvin et al 1990), there was a major move out of deprivation over the 30 years of the study. We shall identify some of the protective factors that can mitigate the hardships of early experience when we come to look at the effects in Chapter 2 (page 47).

Of the "givens" in the couple-to-parent stage of the family life cycle, the fastest rate of change is in the individual and social development of the child. We shall now turn our attention to the changes that take place, with particular reference to the second year of life, because this represents the run up to the preschool period which is when our intervention study took place.

DEVELOPMENT OF THE CHILD AS A SOCIAL BEING

Developmental stages and individual differences

In studying the extraordinarily complicated process of child development in the early years it has been customary to make one of two simplifications. First, development has been studied among groups of children as if they were all the same and developed through the same stages over the early years. Second, the individual differences between children have been studied with relatively little interest in the particular stage in development that the children are in at the time. Both strategies have yielded invaluable information to the extent that there are now calls to bridge the gap between the two (Scarr 1992). In this account, however, we must start by considering developmental stages and individual differences separately.

The child's developing capacities have, since Piaget's pioneering work, been seen as developing in stages. There has been a great deal of debate about whether these stages represent small steps in what is essentially a continuity of individual development or whether there are sequential reorganizations of behaviour which occur rapidly at key points in the early years in such a way that little can be predicted from the child's individuality at one stage which is relevant to subsequent stages (Kagan 1982). While extreme generalizations are not likely to lead very far, the idea of stages in development does help one to focus on the junction points where there is rapid change and to describe and understand the processes involved. McCall, Eichorn and Hogarty (1977), using scores from tests conducted on children in an early longitudinal study of development, the Berkeley Growth Study, identified four major discontinuities at 2, 7, 13 and 21 months. At each of these stages new abilities and behavioural characteristics seemed to appear for the first time. There is reasonable consensus that such stages exist, and roughly, the chronological ages at which they occur. Most important for our purposes is the different demands that these stages make on the infant–caretaker relationship. Schaffer (1984) gives a useful summary of how these stages may affect the developing relationship of the baby with the carer. We shall summarize the first four stages and concentrate in more detail on the fifth, since this is most relevant to toddlers, the main theme of this book.

First, in the immediate post-birth period, the child arrives in the world pre-programmed for social interaction. He or she is attracted by the sound of the voice and the brightness of the eyes and will pay attention to these qualities in the mother. Nevertheless, the first need is for the carer to assist in the regulation of the biological needs of the baby such as feeding, sleeping and arousal regulation and harmonize these functions to environment demands. This means that the caretaker has to detect inner states of the infant and soothe or stimulate appropriately.

Second, from two months, the child becomes a social being. The regulation of mutual attention and responsiveness in face-to-face situations becomes a central theme for the first time. The baby's competence at this stage is very limited and it is the carer who takes responsibility for the development of the interaction, often by attributing motivations to the child that cannot exist at this stage.

Third, at five months, the child develops hand–eye co-ordination: the world of objects, and incorporating these into social interactions, becomes important. At this stage, however, the flexibility of the children's explorations is limited by the fact that they can pay attention only to a single task at a time.

Fourth, from 8 to 10 months a very major advance occurs, with the child able for the first time to synthesize activities that formerly he or she could address only separately. This seems to be based on a capacity to recall mental representations from memory so that different events can be separated in the child's mind and linked into clusters and strings. Ends and means can thus be separated, allowing some appreciation of causality to develop. From here on, there is a more symmetrical relationship with the caregiver, with some awareness by the child that both his or her behaviour and that of the caregiver have conscious intent. Clinically, the most prominent characteristic of this stage is the wariness of strangers and distress at being separated from a familiar carer.

The fifth stage begins at around the middle of the second year. Actions can, for the first time, now be represented in the child's mind in symbolic form. This leads to two major changes that concern us: the beginnings of the development of language and of a sense of self. Both profoundly influence the child as a social being.

Children begin to develop the use of single words at around the first birthday; however, at this stage they are little more than an extension of the concrete object. These words often have idiosyncratic meanings and articulation. The change comes when the child is able to use the word when the object is not present and begins to develop new ways of using language to express him or her self. From this point on conversations can be sustained in which the child makes a creative contribution. This has been confirmed by studies which have observed the conversation of young children among themselves, thus ruling out the possibility that the adult carer is in fact provoking interaction of which the child would not otherwise be capable.

Studies of 2½ year olds, for example, have shown that they are capable of brief conversations in which each child listens to the other and adjusts his or her response accordingly (Keenan 1974).

Representational abilities also allow children, for the first time, to conceive of a sense of self which enables them to stand apart and observe their own behaviour. The implications of this might be expected to be extensive but have been difficult to establish because measurement of self-reflection is difficult in young children, who have not yet developed the sort of advanced capacity for self-expression that is needed. Instead, experiments have been designed which record and interpret children's emotional expressions when confronted with different circumstances. Here are some examples which seem relevant to psychopathology.

Kagan (1982) reported a series of studies to demonstrate that children towards the end of the second year of life develop a sense of standards for the first time. Several observations are relevant. First of all, children at this age notice and reject imperfect or damaged toys and differentiate them from familiar toys and also new play objects. For the first time, they show a new sense of social inhibition and embarrassment if they flout a rule laid down by a parent. Dunn (1987), for example, reports that children of this age will conceal behaviour that they know will elicit disapproval. For example, 2 year olds will hide from their mothers if they want to pick their nose. Further, this characteristic bears some relationship to the sense of conscience six years later (Kochanska 1991). Around the second birthday, the child shows a new sense of having developed an ability to put him or herself in the place of others. In one study of 2 year olds in naturalistic settings, the children showed a new tendency to comfort any victim of misfortune. At the same time, they develop the capacity to tease and hurt, drawing attention to rules of behaviour when it is in their interest to do so but not otherwise. This shows that empathic judgements are from this stage a capacity that can be used for good or ill. These phenomena suggest that toddlers are able to hold an internal image of what is right, to relate it to themselves and react to deviations from a moral norm. The implications for psychopathology of this work are great, but perhaps the most useful findings will come from studies which begin to look at why the superegos of different people develop to such different end products.

A second example is anxiety over possible failure. This phenomenon has potential implications for the fear of failure that is so handicapping in later life. Kagan and colleagues observed that when children approaching their second birthday were shown a task geared to the limits of their capacity, they displayed all the signs of anxiety, even if they are not explicitly asked to repeat the task. Unfamiliarity with the toys and with the experimenter were excluded as possible causes and the author concluded that fear of failure was a likely cause. What is in some doubt is whether a 2 year old is able to recognize failure in the normally accepted sense applicable to an adult. Stipek et al (1992) studied self-evaluation in 2 to 5 year olds, using prescribed tasks. The children who failed the task set showed signs of negative affect such as turning away and hunching up their shoulders at the age of 2 but not before. Since the effect was less marked with mothers, the investigators considered that while the children were aware of failure, they were reacting to a supposition that they had done something wrong, that invoked the disapproval of the experimenter. Considerably later, at $4\frac{1}{2}$ years, the children seemed by their facial expressions to be reacting to a truly internalized standard. We must hope that this and similar important work will eventually shed light on why some people seem to go through life in anticipation of personal failure.

Individual differences

So far we have assumed that all children go through these stages of development in the same way. In fact this is far from the case; individuals differ in almost any way one could think of: emotionality, demonstrativeness, shyness, verbal articulateness, moodiness, and so on. Our second theme is to look at the great effort that has been expended in the examination of individual differences in development. The reasons for this huge investment have been diverse: for example, the clinician is interested in why some children seem to develop so effortlessly while others get into such difficulties with their emotions, behaviour or family relationships. Developmental psychologists see the study of individual differences as a way of increasing understanding of fundamental questions of brain–behaviour relationships in the process of development (Hinde 1989). In response to these different aims of research, different concepts of development have been proposed. Rothbart (1989: 63) for example, with a view to understanding brain–behaviour relationships, sees temperament as a composite system governing individual aspects of reactivity and regulation, often with a component of consciousness. Thomas, Chess and Birch (1968), approaching the matter from a clinical point of view, defined temperament as the "how" of behaviour, as opposed to "how well?" (ability) and "why?" (motivation). The nine Thomas, Chess and Birch categories were derived from clinical experience. As such, their system is more all embracing and descriptive, but compared with the psychobiologists, a bit of a mixed bag theoretically. Thus there are descriptions of motor activity such as regularity and rhythmicity, of task engagement such as adaptability and approach/withdrawal, of threshold of responsiveness such as emotionality intensity of response and mood, and of task persistence: distractibility and attention span. What the various formulations have in common is that they describe predispositions to certain behavioural styles which seem to correlate together.

This brings us to the fact that there is powerful evidence that those aspects of behaviour that are commonly defined as temperament cannot be attributed to environmental and experiential influences alone. We shall touch briefly on just some of the strands of inquiry that have contributed to this conclusion. First, there is anatomical work, linking temperament and body build (Sheldon and Stevens 1942). Here individuals with a soft rounded body (endomorphs), prone to obesity, were said to be even tempered, slow and tolerant. Muscular types (mesomorphs) were seen as outgoing, vigorous and prone to risk-taking, while ectomorphs, who were thin and fragile, were introverted, sensitive and self-conscious. Studies have linked body type with teacher reports of behaviour in young children as well as self-reports of adolescents. Delinquency has also been linked positively with mesomorphy and negatively with ectomorphy (Rothbart 1989). It is true, of course, that these correlations may be because stocky, physically powerful youngsters find it easier to get up to delinquent exploits.

A second broad approach is psychophysiological in the tradition of Pavlov. By careful study of sensory thresholds and conditionability, authors such as Nebylitsyn (1972) have developed a typology based on the so-called strength of the nervous system. A strong nervous system is one which continues to condition at strong stimulus levels in the laboratory but which has high sensory thresholds, whereas a weak system is one which develops so-called "protective inhibition" at high levels of stimulus, where the system moves into a protective state but where there are also low thresholds to sensory stimuli. The clinical implications of this and similar work are not immediately obvious but potentially very great. The psycho-physiological approach exemplified by Eysenck started from the other end, with the development of a self-report questionnaire that characterized individuals according to their degree of extroversion and nervousness or neuroticism. From this rather slender basis in behaviour, links were postulated with levels of cortical stimulation and inhibition such that extroverts had lower levels of stimulatory tone and therefore tended to be more stimulus and excitement seeking. Since the evidence is behavioural, the theory does not bridge the psycho-physiological divide, indeed where electroencephalographic studies have been used to compare introverts and extroverts, results have been mixed. Gray (1982), in a more developed theory of the relationship between extroversion and brain activation and inhibition, has shown that anti-anxiety drugs act as if they interfere with a brain inhibition system which is responsible for the fact that behaviour is inhibited in the presence of punishment. Thus when a behaviour (for example aggressive behaviour) is punished or ceases to be rewarded (ie extinction), it will continue for longer if the subject has had an anti-anxiety drug. A second line of evidence comes again from electrophysiological studies of the brain where the response at the cerebral cortex is monitored to a visual or auditory stimulus (an evoked potential). The form of this evoked potential changes as the strength of the stimulus is increased and the form of this change is different in different individuals. Associations have been found between these responses to evoked potentials and degree of extroversion. These differences are in keeping with predictions from Pavlov's typology of the "strong" nervous system as being associated with extroversion. This and similar work has considerable clinical implications; for example Patterson (1980) has shown that parents of non-problem children are able to stop undesirable behaviour, whereas when parents of antisocial children attempt to do so, the behaviour may actually and paradoxically increase. The theories of Gray and others suggest that it may not be sufficient to look for the explanation entirely in parental mis-management of the child: there may be constitutional factors at work as well.

Finally it is important to record the substantial genetic component that has been found in individual differences in temperament. The approaches to genetic investigation that have been brought to bear on temperamental attributes include studies which compare identical and non-identical twins and those which compare environmental and genetic influences on children who have been adopted. In both cases, the principle is that the inheritance and environmental influence can be looked at separately, whereas in studies of ordinary family upbringing the two are mixed up. From these studies, there is general agreement that there is a genetic component to temperamental similarities and differences between children. The degree of genetic influence varies from one temperamental attribute to another and it may be, indeed it is likely, that there are some family environments that facilitate the emergence of a particular partly inherited factor, for example high activity. One example from a longitudinal study of twins (Goldsmith and Gottesman 1981) will illustrate the point. Over 100 pairs of identical twins were compared with over 200 pairs of fraternal twins. Temperamental qualities of all the children involved were assessed at 8 months, 4 and 8 years. Correlations between the temperamental ratings of each pair were calculated and it was found consistently that the correlations were closer for the identical compared with the non-identical twins. This was true at all three ages for activity and at the two older ages for attention. There were a number of other traits which showed differences at one or other age. These pointers to genetic aspects of temperament open important issues that offer pointers for future research. We will now return to the psychological and clinical spheres and describe these further.

The New York Longitudinal Study (Thomas, Chess and Birch 1968) of 133 middle-class children was the first attempt to examine the effect of the child's behavioural individuality on development. Other under-privileged, disabled and ethnic groups have since been studied as well. Based on their longitudinal studies and clinical insights, Thomas and Chess (1977) developed a threefold classification from their original nine temperamental traits. Easy children are not over-active, they are regular in their sleep and eating patterns, they approach new people and situations positively and adapt quickly. They are positive in mood and respond mildly and equitably. Their concentration and attention span are good. Difficult children show the opposite of these characteristics – active, irregular, etc. The slow to warm up child is regular, mild in response but with frequent negative responses and slow adaptability. Thomas and Chess (1977) stress that temperament cannot be understood in isolation from the child's environment; again, it is a predisposition to behave according to a certain style, not the behaviour itself. Within this interactionist framework, it is the "goodness of fit" between the child's temperament and the parenting techniques of the caretaker that is seen as the vital ingredient. Where the fit is poor, the relationship is in jeopardy and behaviour and emotional problems may link with maternal irritability and rejection to form vicious cycles so that the relationship deteriorates.

Thomas and Chess (1981) give examples of how temperament and environment may interact. For example, in the highly timetabled US culture, sleep irregularity can set off major problems, whereas among Puerto Rican families, irregular sleep was tolerated. As clinicians, Thomas and Chess have been able to give fascinating case examples to support their concept of goodness of fit, both in the context of these cultural differences and in the context of individual family systems and caregivers. The problem with this approach is that it is essentially wise after the event; attempts to predict goodness of fit in different situations or with different caregiver and childhood temperamental characteristics have proved more difficult, although there do seem to be demonstrable effects of extremes of child temperament on the caregiver (Bates 1989: 322). The matter poses major methodological problems because it is the response of the dyad of child and caregiver that is at issue, and this may respond in ways that are difficult to model with statistical techniques. The outcome of the search for goodness of fit must remain uncertain but in the meantime, it has proved a clinical concept of the greatest importance as all parents quickly see that their children are temperamentally different from each other. They also respond with relief to the idea that their difficulties are a result of a problem in the relationship with their child, not a reproach on their assumed incompetence as parents.

Attributes such as emotionality and activity levels have very different qualities and social implications in the newborn as compared with the 3 year old, let alone the adolescent. We must now join the two strands we started off with – developmental stages and individual differences – and examine some of the evidence for individual differences through the developmental process.

The path from early infancy to the preschool years is marked by increasing adaption to the environment and autonomy. Different aspects of individuality are caught up in the developmental process in different ways. Two examples will illustrate how this happens. First, vulnerability to irritability and subsequent difficulty in soothing can be tested by direct observational assessment at birth. This has been shown to predict negative emotional tone at 9 months and a variety of indicators of negativity at 24 months again by direct observation. There appears to be a direct continuity. For approach/withdrawal, however, the picture is different (Rothbart 1989). Again, it can be readily measured in the newborn period. However, in the second half of the first year a new set of concerns comes into play as the child develops a new wariness of strange people and objects. Once this wariness has become established, the readiness of the individual to approach or withdraw becomes a more consistent individual characteristic. The persistence of different traits is likely to be different.

There is in some quarters a misconception that biological or genetic components to behaviour mean that the behaviour is unmodifiable by the environment, whether due to change in the environment, or different settings within a single total environment, for example home and school. This is not the case. Still less does a genetic component imply that the behaviour is fixed from birth. Some genes gain expression only much later on. Finally, there is nothing about a genetic component to causation which precludes therapeutic intervention, whether this be psychological or with drug treatment (Hill Goldsmith 1989). This is illustrated in the case of depression where it is just those more severe cases with a genetic loading which seem to respond best to both pharmacological and psychological therapies (Elkin et al 1989).

In terms of prevention also, individual differences and their roots have major implications. Werner (1985), whose important work we shall mention again in Chapter 2, found that children who were "cuddly", "good natured" and "even tempered" at 1 year of age were more resilient in the face of the sort of social adversities described earlier in this chapter than were children who did not have these characteristics.

Finally a word about our own work, to be reported later in this book. In the evaluation of treatment, one is attempting to measure potential therapeutic change in a child who, as we have seen, is already undergoing complex and quite rapid changes anyway as part of the developmental process. In Chapter 9 we shall present ways in which the difficulties that this creates can be overcome.

THE INDIVIDUAL AND THE RELATIONSHIP

We have examined some of the rapid changes that occur in early years, both in the family and in the individual child. In doing so, we have had cause to consider the processes involved from the point of view of the interpersonal relationships involved, and also from the characteristics of the individual people. Both perspectives are valid and complementary, but we must pause for a moment to consider the point at which the two meet.

Studying social interaction and relationships

The parent–child relationship has always attracted interest: it is unique. In the content of the contribution by the participants, in the sense of obligation and in the power balance, it is an asymmetrical but far from a one-way relationship. It is unique also in the sense of intimacy involved, both in terms of the frequency and quality of interactions and their meaning for the participants. It is a long-standing relationship, which survives even parenting breakdown as shown by the feelings of adopted children. Most important in the public mind are its implications as a model for successful future relationships, social competence, human well-being and happiness in all its many forms. This is the reason behind the enormous volume of research on the nature of the relationship itself, on its immediate effects, on the roots of parenting behaviour in the previous generation, and the implications of parenting for generations to come (Rutter and Madge 1976).

A distinction must be drawn between interpersonal interactions and the relationship that may exist between them. An interaction has a beginning and end point: it is expressed in interpersonal behaviour, whether this is a glance across a crowded room or a feeding session between mother and child. An interaction can occur where there is no relationship, for example at a supermarket checkout. A relationship, on the other hand, implies that at some time there must have been an interaction between the two people, but it exists apart, in the memories of those concerned. The fact that there is a relationship will influence subsequent interactions. However, relationships can survive for long periods without interactions as long as common experiences and memories are shared. An example is in the expression "we hadn't met for twenty years, yet we carried on as if it was yesterday".

Given the number of changes that occur in the development of the individual child, together with the individual differences that we have just discussed, it will be no surprise to find that describing relationships in the early years has proved extremely difficult. The most fully explored example is that of parent–child attachment. We have already mentioned some of the interactional demands that are made on the mother at different stages and in association with different temperaments of the child. Are they pleasurable and absorbing to both mother and infant or is there listlessness and lack of spontaneity? Is there a calm and consensual atmosphere or are there continual confrontations and control episodes? The clinician will be interested in something that lies behind these behaviours and that seems to characterize the general quality of the relationship, perhaps as some memory or mental representation carried by mother and child which is governed by many influences: stage of development, temperament, memories of this relationship and past relationships. Once again, however, we come up against the fact that any description must be a psychological construct. Unlike an interaction, no one can actually see a relationship as so defined. We can see only its consequences acted out in the external world. In response to this, researchers have looked for a reliable and valid way of measuring the mother–child relationship, the usual way being the so-called Strange Situation classification. This takes the form of a laboratory situation in which there are seven three-minute episodes involving separation and reunion with mother or attachment figure. The reaction of the child, particularly to the reunion, is carefully observed (see Campos et al 1983 for a useful summary). Three reactions to reunion have been described. In type B (secure) the child shows relaxed pleasure at reunion; in type A (insecure avoidant) the child seems to ignore and avoid the mother on reunion; in type C (ambivalent) the child becomes clingy and resistant, suggesting internal conflict at reunion. This procedure has been found by many researchers to reflect important attributes of the history and state of the mother–child relationship and indeed psychopathology in the mother (De Mulder and Radke-Yarrow 1991). However, there must remain some uncertainty about what exactly the test is measuring. The judgements are made on a very narrow base (during a reunion only), in an artificial environment and the experiment calls upon the mother to behave in a way that would be most unlikely in ordinary life (Schaffer 1984). There are other ways of assessing the quality of the mother–child relationship – for example, the number of confrontations or demonstrations of affection – but can these index, in the way many have hoped, an internal representation of the relationship? Is it helpful to consider the developing relationship in this way? We shall return to attempts to describe the relationship in the case of maternal psychopathology in Chapter 2.

A summary of the methodology that can be used and what we can expect from it

In the account so far, we have concentrated on findings of various studies but of fundamental importance is how the evidence was gathered. Three strategies have been used.

To study those who are the participants in the situation or relationship

Ways of assessing the individual are, in practice, very similar to those of interpersonal relationships, the difference being rather what is actually observed and how the data are used. Again, definition of what is actually to be measured is of basic importance.

Mental health problems have been defined in several ways. Three of these are relevant here, since they were used in the study to be reported later in this book.

The first approach is defined in terms of the statistically unusual. A large number of questionnaires, which can be completed by the child, parent, peers or teacher, have been developed (see Barkley 1988 for a review). This approach provides a lot of information very easily, but the problem is that unusualness does not necessarily mean that the behaviour is a problem. Red hair, for example, is comparatively unusual but is not seen as a problem unless you believe that it goes with a hot temper!

The second approach is to assess both the symptoms and the degree of distress and handicap they cause. Since the information that is relevant is individual to each person, a much more flexible approach than is possible in an ordinary questionnaire is needed. This can best be done by interview techniques which, while maintaining a central structure, allow the interviewer to explore individual and unique areas of problems that would otherwise be missed. This is called the clinical-diagnostic approach (Rutter, Tizard and Whitmore 1970). It can be applied to any aspect of experience, not just the development of psychiatric problems: for example, in the present study, such a technique was used to study the quality of the parental marriage.

The third approach makes use of the social response to the individual problem. For example, one might use the fact that the mother has attended her family doctor complaining of nervous symptoms or that the child has been referred to a child guidance clinic as evidence that they have psychiatric disturbance. This is often a very convenient method of case identification, but it does rely on the presence of appropriate services and whether they are used or not. In turn, this will depend on the attitude of the population to such services and their own perception of their problems as requiring medical attention. In a variation of this approach, we used the likelihood of attending for medical help as an index of severity in the study reported later in this book. The advantage of studying the individual rather than the relationship in itself is that it allows the separate factors to be considered relatively independently. For example, if one is interested in the relationship of maternal mental illness to disturbance in the child, these different phenomena can be measured separately and the strength of the association between them can be determined. However, a very heavy price would be paid if this was the only way in which interpersonal phenomena were investigated. However cleverly the questionnaire is constructed or however skilful the interviewer, it can give only a very indirect and general assessment of the interaction under study. In fact, the idea that interpersonal behaviour is at the root of much psychiatric disturbance can all too easily be overlooked with the attention purely on personal psychopathology.

To study the feelings and attitudes of the individuals involved in the relationship

This approach is that used in many productive studies of adults with schizophrenia (Leff and Vaughn 1985) and with children at all ages, including preschool (Richman, Stevenson and Graham 1982). Other techniques have been less used in research work, for example the Bene Anthony Family Relations Test (Bene and Anthony 1957). These useful methods have been criticized because parents have a poor memory for common events, because people have a very special perception of their own part in any interaction, and because there may be different understanding of the meaning of words between the parent and the interviewer. These problems can be minimized by careful piloting, timing, and the training of interviewers to be systematically sensitive to the *sous-ententres* of the parents' responses (eg Quinton and Rutter 1988). However, patients and parents are relatively inexpensive research collaborators, they can report behaviour that is not usually displayed in public, report long time-spans and observe in many social situations. These approaches have proved very productive, are relatively economical and do allow the testing of interpersonal theories and perspectives as opposed to the very restrictive approaches allowed when individually focused interviewing and questionnaires are used on their own.

To study the social interactions themselves as the central aim

However, this has occurred only since the late 1970s (see eg Hinde 1979). The key difference from individual-based approaches is that the behaviour of both parties is recorded at one time and in such a way that the behaviours can be related to each other. Again, it is all important that one starts out with a clear idea of what is being looked for and some theory or principle of how the relationships work. For example, an extremely productive approach has been that of social learning theory, where observations of strings of interaction have linked behaviour using behavioural theory. Other research has attempted to identify non-verbal cues that might reflect feeling states associated with interaction in very young children (see Campos et al 1983 for a summary). Another approach is to observe the relationship in a laboratory situation: the Strange Situation test described above is a good example.

Important as these advances are, they too have problems. Time sampling can record public behaviour only in a setting which must to some extent be artificial, although this can be minimized by carrying out the observations in the home. They would be a poor measure of unspoken intentions or long-term plans. While video recording and computer analysis have done much to assist in unravelling the complexity of detailed interaction, the techniques remain expensive and laborious. Another difficulty arises where behaviour problems are intermittent, such as in conduct disturbance. Here misbehaviour is linked to characteristic family patterns of disturbance which occur in intermittent bursts (Patterson 1982). Nevertheless, these techniques have become essential to the investigation of family interaction. Direct observation can be in the form of field observation in natural settings, such as the home or classroom, or in laboratory tasks.

In conclusion, no single method for studying the child and family is clearly superior to others: each has its advantages and problems and, most important, has a strong tendency to carry its own theoretical assumptions. Combinations of methods are likely to be most useful, exploiting the strengths and minimizing the weakness of each approach (Maccoby and Martin 1983).

The development of psychiatric disorder

The first theme in this chapter concerned the world surrounding the young child and the changes associated with the developing family life cycle. We went on to consider how different are the experiences of different children, depending on their social circumstances. The second theme was the developmental stages of the child and the challenges that these may bring to upbringing. Again, there are marked individual differences between children in their responses to the environment in the shape of temperament.

What is surprising is that there seem to be so few links between these two main themes: the environment and the process of normal development. Scarr (1992) in a wide-ranging review has recently argued that within fairly broad boundaries of "good enough" parenting, the child is little influenced by the parent's style. It has been accepted for many years that issues such as when to toilet train and start the child on solid food make little difference. It is only when the parenting becomes clearly dysfunctional that disturbance may result. The situation is, of course, not as simple as that; for example, the children of divorced parents are more likely to get divorced themselves. Can this be counted as "disturbance"? It can certainly lead to a high level of distress. Each life path is likely to show its own areas of vulnerability with long-term implications. One area where the meeting of individual development and the immediate environment has been recognized for many years is in the area of temperament. The longitudinal study of Thomas, Chess and Birch (1968) was somewhat inconclusive in showing that negative mood, intense affective expression and irregularity predicted later psychiatric disorder. However, Earls and Jung (1987), in a community study, followed up children from ages 2 to 3 and showed highly significant associations between low adaptability and high intensity at 2 years and behaviour problems at 3. The study was somewhat unusual in not showing associations with environmental variables such as marital discord and maternal depression. The Thomas, Chess and Birch thesis is that if recognized early and handled appropriately, temperamental attributes can be prevented from becoming more serious handicapping disorders. Thus children who adapt slowly can be helped not to develop full-blown emotional disorders by parents who understand that their child must be moved slowly into new situations. High levels of negativism can similarly be handled by firmness and understanding, together with an awareness that refusals to co-operate should not be turned into a dramatic incident where the behaviour sequence will receive secondary reinforcement. This secondary preventive approach is of the greatest relevance to the clinician in the primary care situation, and to the work to be reported in later chapters of this book.

We have referred also to pervasive social disadvantage and its links with disturbance. First, there is the weight of multiple disadvantage to consider, but of the individual indices of social problems the relationship of marital problems to child disturbance carries pride of place, in that good trusting marital relationships impinge helpfully at so many points in the family life cycle. We have already seen this in normal development and will find so again throughout Chapter 2.

SUMMARY

In this chapter we have introduced the theme of the family life cycle and, in particular, the period of early parenthood. We have examined some of the problems that may affect the young family. We have looked in detail at the social development of the infant and, in particular, the toddler through this stage, in terms of stages of development, individual differences and the development of the relationship with the parents. We have examined some of the methodology with which these phenomena have been studied.

Chapter 2

Psychopathology in the Preschool Years

We now have to focus on more problematic issues, starting with those that we chose for our study and developing the theme outwards to consider first the contribution of other individuals in the immediate environment. We will then take in the family life cycle perspective of the child and its parents.

PROBLEMS IN PRESCHOOL CHILDREN

Research in both Britain and the USA shows that disturbance in preschool children is common. Richman, Stevenson and Graham (1982), in a well-known study, found a rate of 22.3% behaviour problems in an outer London borough. Rates are dependent on the methodology used (eg Larson, Pless and Miettinen 1988), but US research, using the same questionnaire, has shown similar rates (Earls 1980; Cornely and Bromet 1986). That disturbance develops over the preschool years has been confirmed using two distinct methodologies. Jenkins, Bax and Hart (1984) surveyed an under-5 population by interviewing parents of children at 6 weeks, 6 months, 1 year, 18 months, 2, 3 and $4\frac{1}{2}$ years. Below 3 years the prevalence of problems identified by the doctor was never over 10% or by mother 13%. At 3 years the rate rose to 27% identified by the doctor and 23% defined by the mother. By $4\frac{1}{2}$, the rate had fallen again. The most common problems were management difficulties, particularly temper tantrums and eating problems, which persisted more than did sleep problems. Coming from a quite different direction, and using a time sampling method which we shall describe in more detail below, Patterson (1982) also found high rates of troublesome behaviour in the preschool years in 44 normal families. The high frequency of problems at this age makes it difficult to decide when intervention is needed and what type of intervention might be helpful.

There are important sex differences in the pattern of behaviour difficulties, with boys being more likely to show restlessness and sphincter control problems (Richman, Stevenson and Graham 1982) and negativism (Patterson 1982).

One should not expect the problems of preschool children to be all of one type, any more than one would at any other age. Setting aside rare conditions such as autism which will not concern us, the more common problems have only recently been analysed by several groups of workers. The picture that has emerged is reasonably consistent between different studies but the clustering of different symptoms is not as simple as was found in the studies of older children (eg Hewitt and Jenkins 1949). Wolkind and Everitt (1974), using a modification of the Richman Scale, analysed the scores of 131 children attending nursery school. They found two clusters, one concerned sleeping and eating problems with fears and habits whereas the other consisted of conduct problems and aggression. Other workers have found similar groupings (eg Kohn and Rosman 1973; Behar and Stringfield 1974; Richman, Stevenson and Graham 1982). Achenbach, Edelbrock and Howell (1987), administering a questionnaire to the parents of 398 children aged 2 and 3, identified clusters of social withdrawal, depression, sleep problems, somatic problems and aggressive and destructive behaviour. The first two of these hung together as an internalizing cluster and the final pair as an externalizing cluster. These clusters, which do not of course necessarily reflect meaningful clinical entities, seem to contain the components of the disorders of middle childhood; indeed Richman, Stevenson and Graham (1982) found continuities between nervousness and emotional disorder and restlessness and conduct disorder at 8 years. It may be that the preschool clusters reflect a mixture of developmental delays of early childhood mixed in with problems that were to become more prominent later on. Many studies (eg Richman, Stevenson and Graham 1982) have found links between preschool behaviour problems and developmental delays, particularly language delays. We shall now consider these.

Developmental delays

As described in Chapter 1, the developmental process in early childhood can be seen as a series of steps which are passed in a more or less predictable sequence. Some variations on the theme carry no particular clinical significance, for example some infants crawl while others shuffle along on their bottoms. The bottom shufflers learn to walk rather later but are in no other way delayed.

In other cases, delays have more serious implications. These are of two types: generalized delays, where the whole sequence is slowed, and specific delays, where one aspect of development drops behind in a normal sequence which is otherwise largely unchanged. Generalized and specific delays can, of course, coexist and often do. At the age of 3, the most important specific delay is that of language.

Both general and specific developmental delays can be linked to child disturbance and the distinction between disturbance and delay is, in fact, less clear cut than implied so far. For example, children vary enormously in their levels of attention and activity. One explanation has been that very active children, in this particular aspect, behave like younger children, yet this high activity level can very easily be redefined as "disturbance" by parents who find the behaviour difficult to tolerate.

Concerning general delay, longitudinal study of IQ indicates high correlations between children at successive years (Hindley and Owen 1978). These continuities refer, of course, to IQ differences between children and do not necessarily mean that the IQ of an individual child cannot be boosted by educational intervention (Ramey, Yeates and Short 1984).

Returning to language problems, it is important to understand that this can be a symptom of a range of clinical disorders (Bishop and Rosenbloom 1987). The commoner problems include a variety of specific developmental speech and language disorders and environmental deprivation. Environmental deprivation seems to be a product of a lack of social interaction, and has been found in the context of family neglect (Allen and Oliver 1982), institutional upbringing (Provence and Lipton 1962) and in large families. A variety of deficits of comprehension and central cognitive processing have been found in children who were previously thought to have simple delays in the acquisition of expressive language (Bishop 1979). The causative links between language delay and disturbance are probably multiple (Rutter and Lord 1987); in the case of expressive disorders, they remain obscure.

The clinician may wonder whether the most useful approach is to tackle the developmental problem, the emotional or behavioural problem, or whether it is necessary to address both at once if any relief is to be achieved.

Mothers

High rates of psychiatric disorders (Richman, Stevenson and Graham 1982; Cornely and Bromet 1986), mental distress (Moss and Plewis 1977) and ill health (Larson, Pless and Miettinen 1988) have been found in mothers of disturbed preschool children.

Richman, Stevenson and Graham (1982) found a morbidity rate of 24.4% in mothers who did not have a disturbed 3 year old and nearly 40% in the mothers who did. Parental marriages were more discordant in families with a disturbed toddler. Of factors from outside the family, it was those which reflected disturbed social relationships, such as quarrels with neighbours or lack of support, such as attendance at the hospital emergency department as opposed to more regular care (Larson, Pless and Miettinen 1988) that distinguished groups of children with psychiatric disorder from those without. Much of the current work has focused on depression in the mother as the key problem, the issue being to try and unravel the effects of genetic transmission from those of the environment. Dodge (1990) lists the childhood disorders that have been associated with maternal depression: depressive disorder, subclinical depressive symptoms, aggressive behaviour, anxiety, behavioural and somatic symptoms, attentional problems, difficult temperament, insecure attachment, emotional dysregulation and social incompetence; many of these are not mutually exclusive. We return later in this chapter to the possible environmental mechanisms. Meanwhile, it should be noted that depression is certainly not the only psychiatric disorder that may have effects on children. Thus Goodman and Brumley (1990) found that schizophrenia affected mother–child behaviour more than depression did; Quinton and Rutter (1985) found that personality disorder had a greater effect. Maternal depression is linked with substance misuse and, very strongly, with marital difficulties: it may be these difficulties rather than the depression which lie closer to the mechanism of transmission.

Marriage

The marital relationship is without doubt a most important one in the rearing of a young child. A number of longitudinal studies have examined family relationships antedating the onset of antisocial behaviour in children (see Rutter and Giller 1983 for review). There is good agreement that as well as parental criminality and harsh, inconsistent or neglectful parenting, marital conflict is an almost universal accompaniment of some types of childhood disturbance. Again, at least in principle, it should be possible to correct marital and family discord and indeed we tried to do so, particularly in the family therapy regime that will be described in Chapter 7.

Divorce

As mentioned in Chapter 1, divorce is now a common social phenomenon, and is not uncommon in the young family. Wallerstein and Kelly (1980) undertook a detailed clinical study of the reactions of children, including preschool children, to their parents' divorce. They found a high level of distress, including fear of abandonment, anger, regression and bewilderment. Two years later, the situation had tended to improve; however, there continued to be particular difficulties for boys when the mother had custody. While the affectionate relationship between mother and son was well preserved, it was mixed with anger and confrontation. Later, this tended to generalize into conduct disorder. School work suffered also. Girls showed better adjustment initially, but tended to be given responsibility early and to mature precociously. Sibling relationships also tended to be more conflict ridden than in intact families (Hetherington 1988). Recent studies based on large longitudinal samples have suggested that the school underachievement and behaviour problems commonly precede the divorce. This raises the question of whether it is the divorce itself, or the poor relationships of which it is part that represent the difficulty. Good post-divorce adjustment is associated with a better outcome for the children.

Mothers as women

We can now turn the tables and look at the problem from the point of view of the mothers as women. Community studies of adult psychiatric disorder have revealed high rates in women (Shepherd et al 1966) and more recently, particularly high rates in working-class mothers of young children as compared with young women without children. The characteristics of the children themselves are not recorded in these studies (Brown and Harris 1978). How do these high rates develop? Brown and Harris's primary interest was the effect of life events. It was noted that the majority of depressions followed a life event, but that, life events being common, it is relatively unusual for a life event to be followed by depression. This leads to the question: why are some women vulnerable to depression under these circumstances while others are not? In their major study, Brown and Harris (1978) looked separately at five life stages according to whether the women had children and, if so, the ages of the children. Of interest here is the group with children under 6: this was the group with the highest incidence of psychiatric disorder, at 31 per cent. No prevalence is given for depression, although as a subset of psychiatric disorder, the rate will have been somewhat lower. Women are even more likely to be depressed if in addition to a child under 6, they have a large family. The differences in prevalence from young women without children were striking. The environmentally sensitive clinician will feel that to prescribe antidepressants for these common and devastating difficulties would be to address only part of the problem at best.

Fathers

Research on the effects of psychopathology in fathers has had a rather different emphasis from that of mothers in that there has been less interest in the effects of depression and other internalized psychiatric disorder. However, many follow up studies have confirmed the strong association of criminality in the father with that in the child. The association appears to go well beyond criminality per se in that there are also associations of conduct disorders in children and other paternal difficulties such as excessive drinking, poor work record and frequent unemployment (Robins 1966; West 1982). Father absence and poor identification with father have also been linked to difficulties for the child. Although conduct disorders are said to emerge in middle childhood (West 1982), the roots of the disturbance can be detected at an early stage in the form of marital problems and temperamental difficulties. This is the stage at which secondary intervention may be appropriate.

Moral development of boys has emerged with reasonable consistency as a casualty of father absence, both in overt behaviour, such as aggressiveness and in tests of internalization of a moral structure, a sense of guilt and moral judgement (Hoffman 1981). In all such univariate associations, the causal relationship is far from obvious. It may, for example, be the effect of discord preceding father absence or the extra stress on the family operating indirectly. Hoffman's study controlled for income and intelligence.

Fathers and mothers differ in their approach to sons and daughters in that fathers are more concerned about sex role typing, particularly during the toddler years and for boys. Concerning father absence, Hetherington, Cox and Cox (1979) showed that two years after divorce with custody to mother, boys showed less masculine play preferences than controls compared with two-parent families.

All in all there seem, as might be expected, to be a host of ways in which problems in mothers and fathers, and in particular the relationship between them, influence child development, problems that must be taken into account if intervention is to have any hope of success.

Siblings

The presence of siblings on the mental health of the child has several facets, and is a fast developing field of study. Sibling rivalry and aggression is a common problem faced in families and has traditionally been seen as an irritant, almost a natural occurrence without wider implications. Recent work has shown that across a wide age band, but including preschool children (Dunn 1988), this is not so. Dunn and Munn (1986), for example, in a direct observation study, showed that the incidence of teasing, bossiness, conciliation, physical aggression and reasoned argument in conflict by second-born children correlated with the behaviour shown by the older siblings at an earlier point in childhood. There is some evidence that difficulties with siblings are linked to broader behaviour problems but, as with all the links identified in this section, causal relationships are likely to be complex: it could be that the peer difficulties are a function of broader behaviour disturbance, that they result in some way from other family disturbance or that the behaviour of an older sibling does indeed model the behaviour of a younger one, as suggested by Patterson (1986). A key role is, we know, played by the parents. If the mother treats the siblings differently, negative behaviour between the siblings is found (Dunn 1988). This work has pointed up a number of ways in which parents can be advised about how to prevent, and at a later point manage, sibling rivalry. For example, discussing the day-to-day care of the younger child with the older one, and asking his or her advice may be a good ploy even if the advice given is a little immature!

Large families have long been associated with poor scholastic achievement and behaviour difficulties. Wagner, Schubert and Schubert (1985) draw attention to the importance of spacing of children. Children in sibships spaced less than two years apart showed lower IQ and verbal ability. The effect was more pronounced for larger sibships and boys were more affected. There was also more sibling rivalry in families with closely spaced children. If we link this with the effect on the mother of a large family of very young children, there are clear and important lessons for preventive mental health.

Peers

Poor relationships with peers has been found to be associated with psychopathology in numerous studies. What has been lacking is an understanding of how these children fail so badly and how their problems with peers relate to their other difficulties. Price and Dodge (1989) marshal both the correlational and some experimental evidence to support an idea that peer rejection is a response to socially aggressive behaviour by the rejected child. This then leads to labelling of the child by peers, selective attention, and a vicious cycle gets in train, maintaining the behaviour. A variety of strategies have been used to explore the various elements of the model. In experimental playgroups, Coie and Kupersmidt (1983) observed peers who had been selected as popular, neglected and rejected. The rejected children showed more aggression and socially inappropriate behaviour than the other groups. Once the child is labelled, such appropriate prosocial behaviours as they may have are discounted by other children, while negative or aggressive behaviours are seen as stable attributes of the child. The opposite set of attributes are given to popular children (Hymel 1986). The next step is that these attributes are translated into rejecting behaviour by the other children so that the child's expectation of rejection is all too often confirmed. Thus a stereotype of the child develops in the peer group. The question for the therapist is: where do we break the cycle? Can we exploit the child's often pathetic wish to improve relationships with other children to therapeutic ends? We return to this theme in Chapter 3.

In our effort to identify the involvement of others in preschool problems, we have come across clues as to where intervention may alter events. What is difficult to define is individual causal relationships, let alone individual people, such as mother, father or siblings as "the cause of the problem". This is because individuals are only part of the story; we have already considered the importance of relationships and how these relationships develop. We need also to discuss how they can go wrong in these crucial early years. This framework continues our theme of considering all family members as having important parts in the development of the child.

We can now turn to considering the development of disturbance in the context of the family life cycle, a theme we introduced in Chapter 1.

THE DEVELOPMENT OF DISTURBANCE

Psychiatric disorder in pregnancy and the puerperium

Psychiatric disorder has many roots: in the constitution, in the life history and in the current situation of the individual. It also has implications for parenting which we shall explore after the next two sections in which we look at the disorders themselves.

Three types of disorder have been identified: at the extremes of severity are puerperal psychosis, severe but uncommon and mild, transient and common post-partum blues. Between the two come antenatal and postnatal depressions. These disorders are common and often persistent and their implications for the development of the young child and family merit close examination. Is depression more common at this time? Has it got unique features? Are the roots and precipitates of the disorder different from other depressions? The better studies have compared prevalence before and after birth, using standard interviews. Most have found a modest increase in depression in the postnatal period (Cox, Connor and Kendell 1982; Watson 1984; Kumar and Robson 1984; Cooper et al 1988). The Kumar and Robson study of married, mostly middle-class primiparae included a calculation of the inception rate at intervals through pregnancy and postnatally. They found that different women developed depression during these two periods, and that the associations were somewhat different. For example, a poor relationship with maternal grandmother was associated with postnatal but not antenatal depression. Watson et al (1984), however, in a more deprived population, found more continuity through parturition. These findings become more significant if it can be shown that the antenatal and postnatal periods have a particularly high risk of depression. Comparisons with non-pregnant populations have suggested that there is no dramatic difference, although this method is not likely to identify small differences in prevalence (Cooper et al 1988; O'Hara and Zekoski 1988). Of studies using a control group, Cox (1976), in Africa, found a higher rate of morbidity in the pregnant women as did Rees and Lutkins (1971) in the UK. O'Hara and Zekoski (1988) and O'Hara et al (1990) have reported a controlled study on women identified during pregnancy and followed up through the puerperium. They found similar prevalence rates between pregnant women and non-pregnant controls, although there was an increase in depressive symptoms in the childbearing women in later pregnancy and after the birth.

The matter remains in some doubt and perhaps the situation varies with the social circumstances of the mother. Minor affective disorder does not seem to be particularly common after birth.

Turning to the possibility of unique features, Pitt (1968), who looked specifically for depression with onset in later pregnancy or the puerperium, detected atypical features of a type usually associated with neurotic depression. This finding has not been confirmed using standard interviews (Cooper et al 1988). Many studies have found that sufferers have a history of psychiatric disorder (Paykel et al 1980; Watson et al 1984). In the Paykel et al (1980) study, the disorder had the same relationship to life events, social stress and lack of support as did depression at any other times of life; indeed specifically pregnancy-related life events were not associated with the onset of depression. As with depression at any life stage, marital problems have been found to be a common association of depression at this time in many studies (Kumar and Robson 1978; Paykel et al 1980; Watson et al 1984).

Psychiatric disorder in mothers of 1 to 5 year olds

In our study of disturbance in the preschool period, it is the long-term implications of perinatal problems that concern us. Depression early in the parenting phase is often short lived (Cooper et al 1988) but Pitt (1968) found that one-third persisted through the first year, while Nott (1987) in a community study of 200 post-partum women found a peak in inception and prevalence at 3 and 9 months which tailed off at 15 months.

Kumar and Robson (1984) followed up their sample of 119 primiparae at four years, and report prevalence of neurotic disturbance at four years compared with antenatally and postnatally. The results show very few new cases and, indeed, a low prevalence rate at four years. Social class was not associated with depression in this predominantly middle-class sample. Looking at frequency of consultation, there was a modest peak at one year post-partum, and a steady, undramatic rate thereafter. The study of a more deprived population, from East London, does give an indication of a high inception and prevalence rate at 42 months post-partum (Wolkind, Zajicek and Ghodsian 1980). Depression that appeared at 4 months post-partum was particularly persistent.

As well as the development of new depression, and its persistence, there is the question of lingering ill effects through associated difficulties. Marital difficulties, for example, may persist and continue to wreak havoc in the family (Nettelbladt, Uddenberg and Englesson 1985) even though the depression has lifted. Loss of sexual interest (Kendell et al 1976; Kumar, Brant and Robson 1981) is an association of puerperal disorder and may sour the marital relationship in the neonatal phase. The sample sizes of these studies have tended to be small and comparison is difficult: although they have been carefully executed population studies, the base populations differ in undetermined ways.

To summarize, non-psychotic depression in and around pregnancy is little different from other depression, either in prevalence or type; indeed, it is doubtful whether there is any increase in inception postnatally. The extensive studies of motherhood and mental illness have not helped us to understand why mothers of young children, as found by Brown and Harris (1978), are so vulnerable. Studies of non-psychotic disorder in pregnancy have not thrown light on how the high levels of disorder in the mothers of preschool children developed. This careful research gives precious little guidance to the clinician confronted with a distressed mother but it may be that the linkages of depression with other vulnerability factors can be of more help.

For this reason, it could be helpful to look for specific differences between different populations. The groups studied (eg by Brown and Harris 1978) had many more vulnerability factors. We shall now look at vulnerability factors in greater detail, particularly current vulnerabilities: lack of social support and the presence of young children.

VULNERABILITY FACTORS

Supportive relationships

Building on the work already mentioned (Brown, Ni Bhrolchain and Harris 1975), there has been a large amount of work on supportive relationships. This has led in two directions. The first of these has been to pinpoint the key aspects of support. Brown, Harris and Bifulco (1986) have examined the contributions of social support and self-esteem in the development of depression. In this prospective study of 400 largely working-class women with children living at home, measures of self-esteem and "social support" were used to predict the risk of depression in the year following an adverse life event. Actual support received at the time of the crisis in the follow up year was also measured. Self-esteem was correlated quite highly with some of the measures of support. Support was refined into the idea of the core tie. This was defined as a husband, lover or someone named as very close at first contact. Although low self-esteem and indices of lack of support from a core tie at first interview were associated with a greatly increased risk of subsequent depression once a stressor occurred, it was lack of active support from a core tie at the time of the crisis that was the vital link. It seems probable that mothers of young children are particularly isolated and exposed in the early years.

The second direction has been to explore over time how the lack of support arose in the first place. Andrews and Brown (1988) identify a group of women who have particular difficulty in maintaining supportive relationships in association with very poor experiences in their family of origin. The problem is that, along with most studies that address this issue (Dunn and McGuire 1992), this study starts with the adult problem and follows back to the childhood antecedents. This approach cannot be used to assess the strength of continuities.

Effect of and on children

There is another possible mechanism in the maintenance of depression in the young mother. This is that, when it does occur, it is prolonged by the stress associated with rearing a young child. This would be augmented if, in turn, the child were to become disturbed, thus contributing to a vicious cycle of deteriorating relationships within the family.

We start by looking for continuities over the early years, involving mother and child disturbance. Uddenberg and Englesson (1978) followed up 69 mothers who had been assessed post-partum when their child was $4\frac{1}{2}$ years. The children took part in structured play, including an adoption of the Bene Anthony Family Relations Test (Bene and Anthony 1957). The disturbed mothers reported more frequent difficulties with their role and with the child at follow up and the children, through the test, indicated a more negative perception of the mothering that they were receiving. There was no measure, however, that might allow one to judge whether the children were overtly disturbed or not. Wrate et al (1985) followed up 91 mothers and their 3 year olds. They had prenatal and postnatal information about the mothers' mental state. Only one mother was currently clinically depressed; there was no relationship between child disturbance at the age of 3 years and depression in the post-partum period. Curiously, a higher rate of symptoms was found among children whose mothers had mild as opposed to severe symptoms of disorder post-partum. This group of mildly symptomatic women were more likely to be primigravidae, to have discontinued breastfeeding early, to be more anxious about their baby, uncertain about the marital role and to have suffered separations in their own childhood. It should be noted that the child disturbance at 3 years was very mild. Caplan et al (1989) followed up 92 mothers and children from the Kumar and Robson (1984) sample. There were links of child disorder with current but not with postnatal depression. Similarly, a follow up of 70 families where the mother had been assessed for depression after birth showed no correlation between child disturbance at the age of $4\frac{1}{2}$ and post-partum depression (Philipps and O'Hara 1991). Marital disharmony during pregnancy and parental psychiatric disorder were associated with child behaviour problems at follow up. In the 100 or so primiparous women from East London studied by Ghodsian, Zajicek and Wolkind (1984) maternal depression was more persistent over time than in the other studies. Follow up when the child was 14 months showed no association with child disturbance, whereas at 27 and 42 months there was an association between mother's depression, both current and at an earlier follow up, and child disturbance. The association between mother's depression at 14 months and child disturbance at 42 months persisted even when the effect of current depression was taken into account. Not surprisingly, other social variables were important in the continuities between depression and child behaviour. Thus frequency of physical punishment, irritability between mother and her partner and social isolation were associated, but did not account entirely for the links between 14 month depression and 42 month child disorder.

To sum up, current maternal disorder is associated with child disorder while, except for the Ghodsian, Zajicek and Wolkind (1984) study, past disorder has little effect. There is therefore little evidence for a process of deteriorating relationships in the mother–child dyad that maintains disorder. In the Ghodsian, Zajicek and Wolkind study on a deprived group of mothers, the continuities occurred in the context of other social factors.

From this point, the issue of the relationship between maternal depression and child disorder can be developed in two ways. First, it is possible to be far more specific about what maternal and interactive behaviours are involved, and what child difficulties arise from whatever is wrong with the interaction. Second, the wider social context is of the greatest importance as shown by the Ghodsian, Zajicek and Wolkind (1984) study.

Taking the issue of specific behaviours first, there are now several areas where short-term longitudinal studies have shown continuities. Following from previous studies which suggested a link between maternal depression, avoidant type behaviour in the Stranger Situation test and passive, withdrawn behaviour in the preschool years, Rubin et al (1991) compared depressed with non-depressed mothers and their children. At 2 years of age, a Stranger Situation test was carried out. Three years later at age 5, the children returned to the research centre for a period of observation in a free play situation. The study showed that the children of the depressed mothers were far more passive and less imaginative in their play than the children of the well mothers when observed three years later. The association of depression with passivity was stronger than that of distressed behaviour at separation. One possibility is that the effect is a cross-sectional one rather than being longitudinal as the mothers' mental state was not re-examined at the 5 year old follow up. This study and others do, however, make the point that children may be handicapped in ways that would not be readily detectable by relatively crude and global questionnaire reports.

We turn now to the theme of the wider family, and indeed the wider social system. It is possible that depression is maintained by a number of influences which may, through unfortunate chance and timing, maintain depression and negative relationships. Recent work on siblings illustrates the point. Dunn and Kendrick (1982) found that the appearance of a younger sibling has profound effects on the relationship between the mother and the older child. Most older siblings showed an increase in demands for attention and naughtiness. Some became withdrawn, others more clinging and aggressive. Sleep and toileting problems increased. There were also more positive changes indicating maturation in about half the sample. These changes were complemented by less attention, less initiation of interaction and more confrontations from mother. The temperament of the older siblings measured before birth was related to their reaction to the birth. The older siblings of mothers who were depressed were more likely to be withdrawn. It can be seen that processes may be set in train that can influence not only the sibling relationships but also the mother's mental state. Understanding of the sequences of events and their timing should lead us to understand sensitive points in development at which preventive intervention could be helpful.

The nature of relationships and of difficulties

We have described a multitude of observations on psychopathology in the early years of the family life cycle. It is important now to develop this theme in the shape of theories that offer insights into how relationships work and how they are regulated. These themes have major implications for psychopathology. Five will be discussed: arousal regulation and sequencing, the management of control episodes, the result of modelling and reinforcement, affective communication and an organizational/relationship perspective.

Arousal regulation and sequencing

All social learning requires that the child is in a state of receptive alertness, as opposed to sleep or distress. A potent idea is that in the early months, one of the caretaker's functions is to help regulate the arousal of infants to bring them to the quiet alert state, and to provide a platform from whence infants can develop this function for themselves (Schaffer 1984). A number of studies show the potential effects of disruption of parent–child interaction. The early work was carried out on an experimental basis. Tronick et al (1978) studied the effect on the infant, aged up to 4 months, of the mother presenting an immobile face instead of her usual reactive, responsive one. At first, the child attempted to elicit a response, then became wary, and finally turned away. The effect, moreover, persisted into later interactions where the child maintained a degree of wariness as if "once bitten, twice shy". In later studies, Cohn and Tronick (1989) have taken their investigation into real life psychopathology. They studied 13 mothers and their 6–7 month old infants from multiproblem families. The mothers' interactive style was very variable but quite different from that in studies of well-functioning families. Two styles were found: disengaged and over-intrusive. The infants responded to these styles in the first case with negative expressions of fussing and crying, and in the second by disengagement, looking away with a glazed expression. Some mothers in the group engaged in normal interaction. There was little of the positive interaction and affective flow found in normal child–caretaker pairs. The children's play and exploratory behaviour was also diminished. These children were very young and the relevance to the toddler stage may be seen as somewhat indirect; however, Mills et al (1985) studied poor depressed mothers with 2–3 year old children. They developed direct observation codes with particular reference to points where mother and child interaction meshed together in a three component exchange of joint activity. This was called a link. In their study of depressed mothers of 2–3 year old children, these workers found that for depressed mothers, fewer such interactions were responded to by the child, particularly if the child was disturbed. The depressed mother did seem able to respond to the child. The chronically depressed group showed the linking problem most markedly, and seemed to get little pleasure from their child, who was often disturbed. In other cases depression had little relationship to the interaction; indeed the mothers seemed to enjoy their children and to be specially sensitive. There is little doubt that some depressed mothers do have difficulties in interaction with their children but others do not (see also Field et al 1990).

The management of control episodes

The most noticeable characteristic of 3 year old children is that they test the boundaries of their independence. A major skill for the parent thus becomes the ability to manage conflict with the child. Kochanska et al (1987) compared depressed mothers with a non-depressed group in a laboratory designed as an apartment where prolonged direct observations could be made. In situations where the mother's attempts to control the child were met with resistance, affectively disordered mothers were more likely to avoid confrontation by dropping their demands on the child.

The result of modelling and reinforcement

For a generation, starting with the work of Bandura and Walters (1963), the main guiding theory in the field was Social Learning Theory. This gave rise to a large amount of research of clinical relevance. The greatest contribution has been in the understanding of conduct disorders where the work of the Oregon Social Learning Centre has been particularly distinguished. A major breakthrough was the development of a direct observation instrument to study family interaction in natural settings. The chief characteristic of this instrument was the identification of behaviours that had a punishing quality. In more technical language, behaviours that reduced the probability of repetition of the other person's preceding behaviour. These were called coercive behaviours, and could be enacted by either caretaker or child, indeed by any member of the relationship. Examples include hitting, whining, humiliating, shouting at, etc. The investigators found that these behaviours were present as a part of normal family life, particularly with 3 year old children, but that they were very much more common in the families of aggressive children. Patterson (1982) proposes that a number of learning situations arise in these families, including modelling of the aggression of other family members and random positive reinforcement of aggression through incompetent parenting. The main mechanism, however, is negative reinforcement, that is behaviours are reinforced because they result in the relief of pain, rather than because they result in a reward. A typical example would be a mother nagging and shouting at a child. The child hits a younger sibling, who cries, the mother's attention is distracted, the nagging ends: the child's response to the punishing nagging is to deliver punishment in return. This is the element of the coercive system (Patterson 1976), in which family interaction, instead of encouraging learning through the trading of rewards and social reinforcement, becomes a market-place for the trading of punishments. This process is highly relevant to the case of the depressed mother where a period of irritability and withdrawal may set in train a cycle of coercion which may outlive the mother's dysphoria.

Affective communication

For many years, the study of human behaviour seemed to include a sort of desiccation process, where all feelings and human passions had to be extracted before a theory or methodology could be declared safe for science. Fortunately, this trend, which by default gave such opportunities for the pedlars of soft pseudoscience, has come to an end. Methodological advances, in particular the measurement of facial expression as a means of studying emotion, mean that emotion has come centre stage as an organizer of relationships rather than being seen as a peripheral and rather embarrassing set of phenomena (Campos et al 1983).

The communication of affective states – joy, anger, anxiety, etc – are potent regulators of the behaviour of others, for example an infant faced with a visual cliff task will cross the cliff if encouraged by mother but will not do so if mother looks anxious. Cohn and Tronick (1989), in the research programme already referred to, got mothers to role play a depressed state and found that this had a profound effect on 3 month old babies. There was increase in gaze avoidance, protest behaviour and crying. Full development of emotional responsiveness and empathy develops well before the toddler period. Denham (1989) made direct observations of normal mothers and their children. There were correlations between mother's emotional expressions and those of the child, and to the child's capacity to cope when mother was absent. Radke-Yarrow, Richters and Elbert Wilson (1988) in a naturalistic study found considerable stability and reciprosity in the negative emotions expressed by mothers, their 3 year olds, and older siblings. In families with a depressed mother, there was more likelihood of a high level of negative expressed emotion. These ideas and findings represent an elaboration and advance on simple arousal regulation concepts. They merit further development and application to the field of psychopathology.

Organizational/relationship perspective

This is the most highly elaborated theme to develop recently (Sroufe and Fleeson 1988). To summarize: relationships can be understood only as a whole in their own right, they exhibit coherence and continuity, that individuals have an internal representation based on relationships they have had, and internal images of relationships are carried forward and act as a model for future relationships. Sroufe and Fleeson (1988) illustrate the principles by an investigation of seductive behaviour between mothers and their sons. This is a distinctive relationship style and the important point is that if present, a number of other aspects of the family system can be predicted: that the mother will have had a relationship with her father where she was exploited, and that she will have a relationship with a daughter characterized by exclusion and rejection. A second example is that of Teti and Abland (1989). They showed that securely attached older siblings were more likely to respond to younger siblings' distress by caregiving than were less secure older siblings. Infant attachment occurred to an older sibling only if the older sibling was securely attached. This type of analysis seems likely to yield rich results and increase our understanding of the relationship between individual problems and family systems across the range of psychopathology in the future.

Clinical studies

Many of the studies of interaction in families with a disturbed member have taken a more empirical approach, looking for those variables among a broad range which predicted disturbance. Crowell, Feldman and Ginsberg

(1988) compared groups of clinic and non-clinic preschoolers during a period of controlled mother–child interaction. This consisted of a period of problem-solving play and a separation exercise. The clinic mothers were significantly less supportive of the children when they were in difficulties with tasks and less affection was shown. The affect of the children was found to be subdued. There were no differences in the response to the Stranger test.

Conclusion

The mechanisms presented in the above discussion represent a variety of possible mechanisms that might explain the links between maternal depression and child psychopathology. They are not mutually exclusive. More than one of the models might quite reasonably explain a particular piece of interaction. It is unlikely, as we have seen, that any of them are specific to depression in the mother. Even if the key disorder is depression the story does not end there. "Depression" as an entity is based on less secure foundations, and is more heterogeneous in manifestation than many physical diseases (Rutter 1990); there is strong evidence that depressed women have a more than average chance of having suffered adverse childhood experiences which may influence their childrearing capacity independently of their current mood state. This is well shown in the study by Stein et al (1991). Women who had suffered puerperal depression were compared with a control group on a variety of interaction tasks with their 19 month old offspring. As expected, the depressed women showed deficits in interaction, but the important point was that this was also true of those women who had been depressed, particularly if they had family problems. The clinical state was only part of the problem.

There are, moreover, other levels, apart from moment-by-moment interaction, at which depression in the mother affects the child. Dodge (1990), for example, identifies the reduced amount of time that the ill and disabled mother is able to spend with her child and the impoverishment of the child's experience that must result from an inert and preoccupied mother who is unable to take the child on outings and generally do fun things.

This section cannot be concluded without returning to the importance of genetic and constitutional factors. In a recent study, Fendrich, Warner and Weissman (1990) examined family difficulties in two groups of children (between ages 6 and 23 months), one with depressed mothers and one without. While the scores of family adversity were high in the depressed group, the relationship between adversity and child psychopathology was very different for the group with depressed mothers when they were compared with the group without depressed mothers. As shown in many studies, conduct disorder was associated with family adversity whether or not the mother was depressed. For depression and anxiety disorder in the child the picture was different. In the group who had depressed mothers, there was no relationship between these child diagnoses and level of family adversity while in the non-mother-depressed group, there were strong associations. At the very least, this suggests that different factors are in play in the pathogenesis of depression where there is a strong family history. Genetic factors must be strong candidates in any attempted explanation.

It is probable that different mechanisms are at work in the transmission process at different stages of child and family development. Here again more precise knowledge should open the way to developing more effective treatment strategies.

THE OUTCOME OF DISORDER IN THE TODDLER YEARS

The study of disturbance, its causes and management is important for two reasons: first, there is distress in families and children at the time the disturbance is identified. Second, while we must insist that children be considered persons in their own right and their suffering alleviated, the long-term significance of disturbance, particularly in childhood, also excites concern. There are a number of questions that are relevant to our own treatment study; the findings are not generally reassuring to those who believe that preschool disorder is essentially a benign deviation from normal development and that children will "just grow out of it".

Do children who are disturbed in the preschool years continue to be so?

Global disturbance

In the Waltham Forest study (Richman, Stevenson and Graham 1982) two groups were compared, a disturbed and a non-disturbed group. Follow up surveys were undertaken at 4 and at 8 years of age. It is mostly the follow up at 8 years of age that will concern us here. The disturbed group still showed a higher rate of disturbance at 8, although the continuity was less marked than at 4 years of age. Minde and Minde (1977) and Garrison and Earls (1985) with small samples and over shorter time-spans came to similar conclusions. Disorder was more persistent in boys.

A higher rate of disturbance was also manifest at school. In the Waltham Forest study 8 year old follow up, particularly in the case of boys, there was an excess of both neurotic and antisocial deviance in those who had shown disturbance at age 3. Conduct behaviour problems were particularly persistent where the severity of disorder at 3 had been high. These home-to-school findings were not confirmed in the small follow ups of Colman, Wolkind and Ashley (1977) and Garrison and Earls (1985), where the behaviour of children who were disturbed at home was no different in the school situation from non-disturbed control children. Lerner, Trupin and Douglas (1985), in a study of children who attended preschool at ages 3–5, found that 18 of the 20 children who had moderate or severe disorder at age 3, went on to develop psychiatric disorder in middle childhood or adolescence.

In the Waltham Forest study, the disturbed group at 3 years had a significantly greater level of general developmental delay; this persisted at 8 years when compared with the control group, particularly in boys. Similarly, there were a significantly greater number of poor marriages in the disturbed group which also persisted to 8 year old follow up. The mothers had more psychiatric problems. On the other hand, within the disturbed group the presence of marital problems, low maternal warmth or depression when the child was 3 years old did not augur a worse outcome at 8 years. Among the initially non-disturbed group, however, the presence of these features at age 3 did predict worse outcome at follow up when the child was 8 years old.

The disturbed 3 year olds thus showed more disturbance at 8, both at home and school. They also showed more developmental delay, and were subject to more family problems as well. Richman, Stevenson and Graham (1982) calculate that only 36% of the children who were identified as disturbed at 8 years had been so at 3; however, these were a group who had had many problems over a crucial period of their development. In addition, and equally important, family problems at age 3 was a sign that the child was at risk. Add to this the suffering in the intervening period, and attempts at intervention at 3 years seems amply justified.

These findings, taken together, suggested to us that a broad approach to secondary prevention was what was needed, taking into account not only the child disturbance itself, but also the risk factors of family problems.

Individual indicators of disturbance

Follow up of individual problems is important because such problems are often the target of treatment in the primary care setting, rather than a concept of global disturbance.

Sleep problems. Kataria, Swanson and Trevathan (1987) found a marked level of persistence in sleep problems that presented in primary care and well baby clinics in the USA. Of 60 children aged between 15 and 48 months, 25 had sleep disturbances. There was a significant association between sleep problems and stress factors in the environment, particularly maternal absence, depressed mood and illness or accident in the family. Of the 25 children with sleep problems, 21 continued to have them three years later, and an increasing number of mothers recognized that the sleep problem itself gave rise to significant family stress. Zuckerman, Stevenson and Bailey (1987) studied British mothers from three general practitioner lists and found that at 8 months, 5% reported severe disruption of family life by sleep problems. At 3 years, 41% of these continued to report problems; this persistence was associated with wider disturbance in that the mothers report depressed feelings and the children exhibited tantrums and behaviour problems in addition to their sleeping difficulties. Taking an older cohort, Klackenberg (1982) studied a community sample in Sweden. At 4 years there was a high level of sleep problems. The rate decreased at the follow ups which were undertaken at 8, 12 and 16 years and while these were still high the persistence of sleep difficulty in any individual child was not great. The Waltham Forest study came to rather similar conclusions over shorter time-spans: although sleep problems were common, particularly in the preschool follow ups at 3 and 4 years, it was only in a minority of cases that the same children had persistent sleep-related problems.

Poor appetite and faddy eating. In the Waltham Forest study, these showed much more continuity between 3, 4 and 8 years of age than did the sleep problems.

Wetting and soiling. As one might expect, these are far less common at 8 years than at 3 years, although there was a persistence of 22% of those identified at 3 in the disturbed group.

Restlessness and over-activity. With maturation, the level of restlessness and over-activity reduces and attention improves, but particular importance has been attached to over-activity in preschool children as an early sign of psychopathology in the form of attention deficit disorder. In the Richman, Stevenson and Graham (1982) study, restlessness at age 3 was strongly associated with the development of later conduct disorder in those children who were disturbed at the age of 3. This association was much stronger in boys, who in addition showed more restlessness than did girls at the outset. There were thus two tendencies in 3 year old boys that made hyperactivity in middle childhood more likely than in girls: the higher prevalence at the earlier age and the fact that when hyperactivity did occur in boys it was more persistent. The Dunedin, New Zealand, study (McGee et al 1991) was based on a large community cohort: 2% of the children were found to have pervasive hyperactivity and a slightly larger group to be difficult to manage at home only. The pervasively hyperactive group had very poor language skills and developmental delays. Both this and the difficult-to-manage group showed a high level of family adversity. Four groups were selected: the hyperactive and difficult-to-manage-at-home groups, the rest of the study population and a group matched on developmental retardation but not hyperactive. Follow up was carried out at intervals for 15 years. Among the hyperactive but not the difficult-to-manage group, a very high rate of psychiatric disorder of various types developed. The cognitive problems continued and these were similar to those of the developmentally retarded group. There were a relatively high number of girls among the hyperactive group and the girls showed particular problems in perceptual motor skills.

In a clinic-based study, Campbell (1987) and Campbell and Ewing (1990) also found that activity in general decreases as the preschooler moves into middle childhood. They compared hyperactive children identified at 3 years of age who had improved at 4, 6 and 9 years with those who persisted. There was a normal control group. The persistent group had more severe problems at the outset, poorer relationships with peers and parents, also more antisocial symptoms such as lying and destructiveness.

Nervous problems. These tended not to persist very much except worrying which was very persistent, particularly in the behaviour problem group. Nervousness at age 3 was, however, strongly associated with the development of neurotic disturbance at the age of 8 (Richman, Stevenson and Graham 1982).

Do developmental delays predict future delay and disturbance?

As mentioned earlier in this chapter, given a similar environment, there is a reasonable level of consistency for IQ through childhood, when children are compared with each other. Richman, Stevenson and Graham (1982) found that in boys but not in girls, general developmental delay at 3 was associated with neurotic and conduct disturbance at 8 years.

In retrospective studies (Rutter, Tizard and Whitmore 1970), 10 and 11 year olds with reading difficulty were reported by parents to have had language delays much earlier on. Richman, Stevenson and Graham (1982) compared 22 children who had been language delayed at 3 years with a group matched for age, sex, disturbance and mother's mental state. The language-delayed group were also delayed, for the most part, in general development as well. At age 8, more language-delayed children had persistent disturbance, despite the initial matching, in the home situation. These authors also examined the associations with disturbance at school at the age of 8 (Stevenson, Richman and Graham 1985). At 3 years measures were made of vocabulary and language structure. It was the latter only that showed interesting associations at follow up. For both boys and girls, low structure at 3 years predicted neurotic but, interestingly, not antisocial deviance at age 8. Further, these differences were due to children who were not disturbed at the age of 3 years, but who did have the structural language difficulties. Put another way, if the child was disturbed at 3 years, the chances of deviant behaviour at school at 8 years was high, whatever the initial structural language score. If the child was not disturbed at 3 years, the chances of the child becoming disturbed by 8 years was much higher if structural language difficulties were present.

Do family problems in the preschool years predict later disturbance in the child?

Among the non-disturbed, 22% developed disorders by 8 years old in the Waltham Forest study, the children who become disturbed, tended to come from families with high adversity and poor marriage at 3 years of age (Richman, Stevenson and Graham 1982). By 8 years, it was possible to classify the children who had continued disturbance into those with conduct disorders: characterized by aggression, stealing, destructiveness, and so forth, and those with emotional disorders: characterized by anxiety, fears, unhappiness, etc. As toddlers, the conduct disorder children, who were predominantly boys, had been over-active and restless, while the emotionally disordered children, equally boys and girls, had shown signs of fearfulness and temper tantrums. In both cases, the mothers had been depressed. The disturbed boys had more developmental delays than the non-disturbed boys. Again, this suggests that intervention at age 3 with children who are not yet disturbed might constitute a good preventive measure.

Maternal depression

Depression, at least at a primary care level, is usually seen as a rather mild and self-limiting disorder. However, this popular and optimistic idea is unfortunately a myth. Recent follow ups, notable for the rigour of their methodology (Lee and Murray 1988; Kiloh, Andrews and Neilson 1988), offer a gloomy picture, although as follow ups of hospital outpatients, the original disorders were more severe than would be found in community or primary care surveys.

The community study of Lewinsohn, Zeiss and Duncan (1989) is perhaps more relevant to our theme. These authors report a retrospective study which examined the pattern of relapse following first and subsequent episodes of depression. The sample was drawn substantially on a volunteer basis with most of the subjects over 45 years of age. The probability of relapse showed a different and more gloomy prospect for women compared with men. In the same way, the median period of health before relapse was very much shorter for women, 13.2 years as against 21.6 years. In women, the probability of relapse did not decrease with the passing of years of health, while it did for men. At interview, 46% of patients who had one episode of depression had a second one within the follow up period.

Concerning young mothers, the Waltham Forest study provides invaluable information (Richman, Stevenson and Graham 1982). Depression was identified at 3 years of age and again at 8. The evidence was that there was strong persistence of depression between the two ages. Marital disharmony was persistent between the ages, and there were strong associations between marital disharmony and depression at each age. While there was some association with social class and family stress, these were not so marked or persistent as was the case with marital disharmony.

Looking at the situation from the perspective of the family life cycle, some of the families seemed to have become locked in a system of poor relationships and depression by the time the children were 3 years old.

Long-term effects: some conceptual issues

The account so far illustrates some of the issues that have to be taken into account in unravelling long-term effects of early childhood disturbance. The time has come to identify these and extend them before we are properly equipped to look at the more complex issues of long-term effects.

The first point is that there are interactions between different aspects of early problems. Nature has little respect for the categories that the scientist develops to understand her. For example, delay at 3 years of age is linked with disturbance and continues to be so through the early school years. As with the birth to 3 years research findings described on pages 34–6, the intercorrelations at any given age between disturbance in different family members are stronger than they are between ages. They are also more consistent between studies. However, where there are associations between different delays and disturbances at younger and older ages, they give fascinating glimpses of what the causative mechanisms may be. For example the fact that marital problems at age 3 predict disorder at 8 years of age suggests that the marital problems are causative in some way. Similarly, with structural language delay, this seemed to precede and usher in disturbance at 8 years. The mechanisms behind these phenomena are little understood. They could reflect the fact that the delayed child has difficulty in coping or that some neurological problem underpins both aspects of difficulty.

Through the long time-span of human development, such continuities become attenuated. Unhappy marriages break up or improve; some happy marriages go sour. Children develop in a world which makes continual and different demands on them through development. Loved ones die or depart. In short, there are numerous imponderables that may strongly influence the outcome in adult life and yet which cannot be known in early childhood.

Against this the prospect of finding factors that predict the future may seem a vain search, yet such factors do exist. An example would be the effect of a particularly good relationship which may support the child through a difficult patch. Another example would be the effect of good self-esteem, or of an equitable temperament. The spacing of siblings, so that the parents have some respite from constant childbearing and care has also been shown to be of benefit. A study that demonstrated such protective effects particularly well was that carried out in the island of Kauai, in the Hawaiian Archipelago over the childhood of a post-war cohort. It was found that among the most disadvantaged 10% of this predominantly poor community, there were a number of such protective factors (Werner 1985). More recently, several research groups have begun to look at the pathways through childhood that may, through the interplay of luck and predisposition, lead to good or bad outcome. One way to understand these continuities is to consider development in segments of time. At the outset of each segment, the individual has a pack of cards, some are high in his or her favour, some are against. Many examples could be given. If we consider conduct disorder in middle childhood, then to be a boy at preschool is a poor card. Boys are more likely to be hyperactive and have attention deficits; if they do have these problems they are more likely than girls to develop conduct problems as time goes on. These assemblies of probabilities have been called transactional effects. We will be meeting this idea again in Chapter 4 when we consider the long-term effects of treatment. More precise study will distinguish those boys who are more at risk; by no means all boys carry these vulnerabilities, and of those that do, not all will develop conduct problems (Richman, Stevenson and Graham 1985). At a later stage, deprived children brought up in care may be lucky enough or have the temperamental attributes that enable them to find good experiences at school and to take a hand in planning their own future. For those that do, there is a chance that they will find a route through the difficulties of young adulthood and make a good adjustment against the odds (Rutter, Quinton and Hill 1990).

Finally, one can look backwards from knowledge of the outcome. For example, Brown, Harris and Bifulco (1986), in retrospective studies, explored the finding that depressed women had often suffered a loss in their own childhood. They concluded that there were probably two pathways, which were not independent of each other and which influenced outcome. The data showed that such girls often suffered a lack of care and supervision and hence drifted into difficulties. Early unsupported pregnancy or an immature and unwise choice of love relationship was a common consequence, resulting in the lack of social support that we referred to earlier in this chapter. The second pathway was that of low self-esteem and the development of a set of attitudes based on the assumption of powerlessness and helplessness. We have examined powerlessness as a characteristic of multiple disadvantage, but such attitudes are also part and parcel of the depressive picture.

In considering the sheer weight of adversities confronting some children and families, this painstaking methodology can appear a little too easy. Is it really true that the massive and hopeless seeming problems of poverty and unemployment encountered by some of the families, for example in our own study, can be unravelled in this way? As well as different types of problems and opportunities in the life cycle, it is important to take account of total adversity as a key factor (Kolvin et al 1990). This proved a useful, if rough and ready, construct in our own research.

SUMMARY

In this chapter we have set the scene by introducing the problem of disturbance in early childhood and some of its correlates. We quickly found that it was particularly helpful at this age to consider the family as a social system passing through a family life cycle. This concept of a cycle can also help organize our thoughts when we come to consider the development of psychopathology, although it is essential to consider the contribution of the individual child and of the caretaking relationship. Finally we have looked forward from the preschool stage to school and finally at some of the possible pathways of adulthood which have helped to understand both the roots of maternal depression and the outcome of toddler disturbance.

It is now appropriate to prepare the ground for our own study. In considering the outcome of intervention, it is essential to look at the context in which the intervention is to occur and how this will affect both the delays and disturbance that one hopes to influence through intervention and also other factors that may play an important part in the outcome. In order to do this predictive measures are needed. The description in Chapters 1 and 2 helps us to see what some of these predictors might be. We have already considered temperament and social disadvantage in Chapter 1. In this chapter we have seen that the sex of the child is an important factor in the outcome of child disturbance, as is the developmental level of the child. We have also reinforced the central place of the quality of the marriage.

We finish with an ambitious question: can any of the pathways we have explored in this chapter be influenced by therapy, either for short or long segments or both? This question, central to our own study, will be picked up in Chapters 3 and 4.

Chapter 3

Help for the Preschool Child

At a public meeting, held in the Guild Hall Newcastle on February 25 1825, the Right Worshipful Henry Cramlington Esq mayor, in the chair, it was resolved to establish one or more infant schools, by which the children of the labouring classes, from the ages of two to six years, may, for a small weekly payment by the parents, be not only kept from the danger of accidents, to which at this tender age they are liable without the most watchful care, but, by a judicious interchange of exercise and instruction, may experience a gradual development at once of their bodily and mental powers, and may be prepared for a more beneficial improvement of the means of education provided for children of a more advanced age. (Mackenzie 1827: p. 456)

Mackenzie in this single sentence touches on some of the issues to be tackled 166 years later in this chapter. Although the concept of special need has been somewhat refined since that time, Mackenzie did recognize that poverty falls particularly severely on the young. This brings us back to the theme of secondary prevention: intervention with individuals in a population who show vulnerability or early stages of disorder in order to prevent the development of established disorder at a later stage.

Our task in this chapter is to look at whether and how the rapid development of the early years can be influenced by intervention for those children who need it. The concept of intervention at this age seems a simple one at first, but where does good upbringing end and intervention start? Does a good preschool curriculum constitute intervention? What about high quality day care as against the run of the mill variety? To most parents, promotion of their children's development is among their highest priorities in life, even when there are formidable obstacles. Is this intervention? Definitions based on these themes are too all embracing, yet to restrict intervention simply to counselling in a clinic environment, as one might with adult psychotherapy, is equally unhelpful, since so much can be done as part of the support that society provides for the young family.

For the present purpose, we define intervention as where the child had an identified special need for which a programme or curriculum has been developed.

A MAP OF PRESCHOOL PROVISION

As a platform for the discussion of intervention according to this broad definition, we turn to the supportive network of services for preschool children. We shall not consider situations that imply parenting breakdown such as fostering and children's home care, nor shall we consider intervention for rare psychiatric disorders such as early childhood autism or psychotic disorders. Rather, the theme is common family, child and parenting problems.

In describing preschool provision, the classification of Clarke-Stewart and Fein (1983) offers an integrating framework. With some modification, we developed four main headings which are as follows.

Two input categories	1. Organization and funding
	2. Participant characteristics and the psychosocial milieu in which intervention occurs
Two process categories	3. Theories and values of the intervention
	4. What actually happens in the intervention.

In Chapter 4 we shall spend time on the most important of all the issues, that is the outcome and effectiveness of interventions of various types with relevance to the preschool child.

It is helpful to distinguish those settings which broadly take over parental responsibility, that is stand *in loco parentis*, for periods of time (eg a childminder) from those that do not (eg an outpatients department).

Each of the four headings of the classification throws up its own research issues and in order to further our aim of providing an integrative map of the field, we shall pick these issues up and discuss them as we go along.

ORGANIZATION AND FUNDING

Resources for preschool children may be deployed in many ways, preschool care programmes being only one of them. Other examples would include sex and educational programmes including contraception to tackle the problem of unwanted teenage pregnancy, offering financial support for the family such as financing maternity leave as in the UK (Moss 1991) or maternity and paternity leave as in Sweden (Broberg 1988) or building improved acute paediatric facilities in an effort to reduce the rate of perinatal casualty. However, there has been a tendency since the early 1970s to increased facilities for preschool child care; this is widely true even of countries where there have been otherwise major curbs in public spending (Clark 1988: ch. 3). The reasons are not hard to find, for example more mothers return to work at an earlier stage and there are more single parents than there were in the early 1970s. Funding comes from a variety of sources and where the money comes from does make a difference. In the UK, for example, where preschool provision has not developed as in some other European countries, support may come from educational funding, such as nursery schools and classes, where there will be an emphasis on preschool education. Support from social services sources, either local authority or from the charitable sector, is associated with more flexible hours, geared to the needs of working mothers. This provision is very limited and available only for families in great need. Childminders are a common source of support and approval by the local authority is required, a regulation that is often flouted. Playgroups are an institution that has grown up to fill the gap; this will be described more fully on page 52. In other countries, the administration is different, which probably gives its own colour and emphasis to the resources provided; for example, in the UK childminding is a private contract between mother and childminder, but in Sweden there is state support for home-based care. In France, where school entry is at 6 years, preschool education is offered to all children according to parental wish and 94% of children over 3 attend, as do one-third of children over $2\frac{1}{2}$ years; the funding source is the Ministry of Education (Le Prince 1991). This service is limited to school hours. Facilities that can care for the child through the working day are far less widespread, being available to around 4% of the under 3 year olds and supplied by local and central government. If these are large in size, an educator must be employed for part of the day with the older children. In the UK, there has been some move towards combined centres, offering care and education in the very limited resources available. There is also a scheme for registering childminders in France, and financial advantages accrue from using a registered childminder in what is partly a demand-led system of allowances to parents. In Sweden, where the proportion of children in municipal child care has increased from 3% in 1965 to 45% in 1985, all public preschool provision is under the aegis of the National Board of Health and Welfare and divided between childminders and day care centres, where a trained teacher will be present. Demand in the USA has also increased dramatically since the mid-1970s: in 1977 there were 18 300 day care centres while in 1986 these totalled 62 989, including infant centres for children under 1 year. The true extent of day care has been difficult to estimate in the USA, and much effort is being put into installing regulation in what is predominantly a free enterprise system with no statutory maternity leave. Federal Law 99-457 has made preschool education for preschoolers with special needs mandatory (Cohen 1990). Only 9% of day care centre programmes get direct government funding. The main provision is entrepreneurial, with small often franchised concerns offering day care (Clarke-Stewart and Fein 1983). In practice, regulation is patchy (Phillips 1991). The US facilities that are widely reported are high-quality grant-aided research provision attached to universities. These constitute a tiny proportion of the whole. We shall return to them as a great deal has been learned from them about the effectiveness of preschool provision.

Playgroups

These are 34.1 places per 100 3 and 4 year olds in England, Wales and Scotland combined, making it possibly the most extensive provision in those countries. We pay particular attention to playgroups here since these are part of our theme later in this book. Playgroups are a national institution which started at least partly because of the lack of provision from the state sector. They have voluntary funding, usually with a fee paid by the parents. They are run by a playgroup organizer, who is likely to be a parent, on a non-profit-making basis. Qualifications are incidental rather than mandatory, but the umbrella Preschool Playgroups Association runs special courses. Playgroups normally run in sessions of a few hours a time, a few times a week. They should be registered with the municipal authority social services department. Most playgroups take place in a hall or other public building, but some take place in parents' homes. A survey conducted in 1975 (van der Eyken 1984) suggested that playgroups are much more common than government-funded provision, comprising 70% of the total. The development of playgroups is a relatively recent phenomenon, arising in the 1960s.

As well as these services, it is estimated that in the UK over two-thirds of care is provided by relatives, nannies and au pairs. Surveys by the Preschool Playgroups Association and van der Eyken (1984) suggest that 20–30% of children have no preschool experience at all, and that these are often the most disadvantaged children in other ways (Cohen 1988). In our own work (reported in Chapter 8), we also found that isolated and disadvantaged mothers found it difficult to respond to offers of service, even when they were encouraged to do so.

Support

These main types of provision are supported by a retinue of professionals and experts. The National Health Service provides paediatric and child psychiatric services, and paramedical services such as speech therapy, dietetics, physiotherapy, and so on. Local education departments provide educational psychology and peripatetic teaching services, while social services departments offer social workers and home help. There is a major voluntary component to early family support, for example Homestart and The

Children's Society, Gingerbread groups for single parents and Red Cross toy libraries.

Research issues

He who pays the piper calls the tune, thus educational research tends to be done by university schools of education, health service research by paediatricians, psychiatrists or developmental psychologists working in the health service framework, and so on. Such research dichotomies lead to the development of different research terminologies, different journals and research organizations. In the real world, however, different types of provision may, in empirical terms, have major areas of overlap. For example, all provision that provides an *in loco parentis* service should provide an element of emotional support, stimulation, reinforcement and physical care to small children.

PARTICIPANT CHARACTERISTICS AND THE PSYCHOSOCIAL MILIEU IN WHICH INTERVENTION OCCURS

What are the qualities which the child or family bring to an intervention which influence success or failure? As we have seen in Chapters 1 and 2, the field can be conceptualized at several levels of organization. We worked inwards from a consideration of the family life cycle and relationships within it, then the child as an individual including temperament as behavioural style and as predisposition to behave in certain ways. We considered disturbance in family members and the way this developed throughout the life cycle before focusing in again on interactions and as sets of attributions and predispositions which govern successive interactions. All these, as well as knowledge of the outcome of difficulties, can help in developing a framework for intervention and in deciding where intervention is likely to make a contribution to adaptive psychological development.

While common sense dictates that these considerations should be taken into account in designing intervention programmes, there remains a gulf and something of an atmosphere of suspicion between research and practice. Perhaps one of the reasons is that some links are missing in translating research to practice. One example is that while research deals with probabilities, in clinical practice, the concrete individual clients sit before the clinician with their pressing problems.

A second consideration is that the clinician approaches the individual with difficulties by asking what the specific problems are. Analysing problems is an activity that yields far richer dividends than immediate reference to research findings which fit the individual case only in a general way. For the clinician, here are some questions that could be asked.

Who, if anyone, is concerned about the situation? It may be a parent, or a local child protection agency, a paediatrician or people who have got together as a political pressure group. The expectation could be that something can be done, given resources, or that they "ought" to be doing something or, alternatively, impotent complaining. In short, is anyone prepared to take personal responsibility for change? The attitudes of the problem identifiers are crucial. In a useful analysis, Reid (1979) distinguishes between wants and needs. A "want" is a characteristic of the client. A family may want, and need, help with the mortgage repayments, or they may bring to the situation one of a number of frameworks which we explore on pages 56–60. A "need" is what the clinician articulates. It is more likely that the clinician will see the need for child protection, or for a counselling programme. In many situations wants and needs show depressingly little overlap, a situation where, as Reid says, hope of change is forlorn indeed.

Assuming that client's and clinician's perspectives coincide sufficiently for intervention to be a possibility, there are factors that will determine whether a particular child or family is suitable for a given intervention. For example, it seems unlikely that an over-active, impulse-ridden child will benefit from a highly permissive educational programme, although in a study of group therapy in schools, a rather permissive group therapy approach did seem to help 7 and 11 year old children with conduct disorders as much as those with emotional disorders (Kolvin et al 1981).

Another set of factors, much less well understood but critically important, is whether the parents, child or family feel that they can take advantage of what is on offer. There are almost certainly factors which are less obvious and easy to measure that influence the outcome of intervention. One such is a feeling of personal potency by the parent. Does the mother, for example, feel that what is on offer is an opportunity or yet another criticism and intrusion into her fragile feeling of autonomy? The attitudes that we have identified in Chapter 2 as protective against depression may also represent hopeful indicators should treatment become necessary. Does the father feel that what is going on is a threat to his authority that must be sabotaged at all costs, or as an opportunity for the children? Does the child "take to" a member of staff and thus become engaged in what is going on, and is the mother able to step back and view the resulting progress with pleasure? The therapy or curriculum may offend against deeply held attitudes by the parents about the correct way to bring up children – a route to certain failure. These issues are hard to measure but crucial. They may become manifest only once the programme is underway.

Secondary prevention, a dominant theme in this book, is a rather special case in that intervention has not been triggered by the child or family coming forward with a problem. This has some major implications for how such programmes can be set up, and a lot of ethical issues are raised that we shall consider in the context of our own study (see Chapter 11). Needs, in Reid's (1979) use of the term, are present, but it is less certain that the family want anything.

What we learn about participant characteristics and the way they are viewed will turn on the theories and values of the intervention. If the basic approach is a corrective to social deprivation, assessment of the children coming into the programme will dwell on deficits in environmental stimulation and parenting difficulties. However, if the basic approach is the modification of maladaptive behaviours, the assessment will include an analysis of the reinforcers of maladaptive behaviours in the child's environment. It would not be good practice to find out everything about all the clients who come to a specific programme. For a start, most clients would express their feelings with a vote by their feet, if nothing more!

Faute de mieux, wide differences are found between the users of preschool facilities, whether or not they are planned to cater for a particular need. An example is the comparative study of McGuire and Richman (1986) of the prevalence of behaviour problems in three types of preschool provision. Children in day nurseries had four times as many problems as in nursery schools and ten times as many as in playgroups. This is not surprising when one considers that nursery provision is available for about 1% of the population under 5. As the only agency that offers an alternative care environment to home, it is bound to be used by families with serious difficulties, such as unsupported mothers and families where there is a risk of child abuse. While this area of intervention is better researched than most, there are some yawning gaps.

Research issues

In Chapter 1 some space was set aside to discuss the problems of measurement of behaviour, relationships and psychopathology. Without the development of measurement technology through interview, observation of behaviour and testing in standardized situations, the knowledge that has been built up would not have been possible. The assessment of intervention programmes makes even greater demands on measurement technology since, in addition to the requirement to reflect psychological events or behaviour, there is the need to measure change. Most instruments in child psychology and psychiatry have been developed with the prime purpose of identifying disorder, assessing prevalence or predicting future performance. A good example of the difficulties that this can lead to is the use of the IQ test as an outcome measure for nearly all the educational intervention programmes that will be discussed in Chapter 4. No one can doubt the importance of the IQ test as a measure with great power to predict outcome of development in very general terms. However, its use, not only routinely but also exclusively as a measure of the value of early intervention with deprived children, is highly questionable. We shall take up this theme in more detail in Chapter 4.

THEORIES AND VALUES OF THE INTERVENTION

Having been mystified by the diversity of sources of care, the young parent is likely to be even more confused by the varied philosophies of different services. Clarke-Stewart and Fein (1983) identify several dimensions and categories in which programmes differ: these illuminate clearly the diverse nature of different preschool initiatives. There is a great variation among programmes in the extent to which the underlying values are made explicit, and in how the underlying values influence programme variables (our next major category). Some of the assumptions and values of preschool programmes are as follows.

The "problem"

First, preschool provision is designed to tackle different perceived problems. The same problem, let alone different ones, may look quite different when viewed through different ideological spectacles and this can lead to quite different plans when it comes to intervention. To take an example, with a parenting problem with a young child, a "Homestart" service (see page 68) may give greater emphasis to parental despair and the need for befriending while a clinical psychology service may focus more centrally on the need for behavioural management of a sleep problem in the toddler.

As well as this, there will be variation according to the context, in the degree to which the problems are explicit, in some cases they will be simply assumed: for example a young child needs a playgroup to promote development. If there isn't one, that's a problem. In other cases the problem will be made highly explicit, for example the careful delineation of the features of a depression in developing a cognitive therapy programme for a depressed mother. There are broad categories of problems, which give us some bearings in our map of preschool provision. Many, indeed, most programmes aim to tackle more than one of them, for example a day care programme for poor working mothers should also attempt to provide an enriched environment for children who will often be brought up in poverty. As Clarke-Stewart and Fein (1983) say, assumptions about the nature of the problem will be related to assumptions about an appropriate solution.

Substitute care is needed

The 1970s and 1980s have seen a major change in patterns of family life and of employment. However much politicians talk of the sanctity of family life, more children than ever are now being brought up in one-parent families and by parents who go out to work. Preschool provision in Britain is ill equipped to cope with these changes. At one time day nurseries were provided for such children but their function has now changed to helping families with special needs (see page 51). The gap has to be filled by childminders or relatives, or the mother has to stay at home. This may be the reason why the rates of employment of women in the UK are among the lowest in Europe, with 6% of mothers of under 5 working full time and 28% working part time (Pugh 1988). Similar problems exist in the USA, where there are some 1.4 million children in licensed day care centres, another 1.4 million in group day care and 2.2 million in family day care (1987 figures). In addition, there are unknown numbers of children in unregulated day care facilities, and the numbers are growing (Cohen 1990).

The child needs protection

The subject of child abuse has become the dominant theme in child care and we can do no more than touch on this vast and distressing subject here. In all industrialized countries, concern started with physical abuse, at first only the most severe cases, but soon the destructive effects of long-term, less dramatic abuse became evident. Thus less immediately dramatic physical abuse as well as neglect and emotional abuse began to cause concern. The most recent development has been the understanding of the prevalence of sexual abuse of children. These problems are common. The largest continuous survey of abuse is that conducted by the NSPCC in the UK (Creighton 1988). This shows that rate for all abuse, in particular the 4 year old and younger group, has climbed steadily over the years, from 0.9 per thousand in 1979 to 1.4 per thousand in 1986. The rate for the first year of life is even higher, reaching 1.86 per thousand in 1986. In contrast, the rate of serious or fatal injury fell between 1977 and 1984, and has now steadied. The incidence of sexual abuse is difficult to estimate, figures from child protection registers of about 0.6 per thousand are likely to be a considerable underestimate. Specialist teams and child protection committees exist in each district in the United Kingdom to monitor the detection and management of this problem, and the difficulties of detection and manage-ment all too often lead to appearances in the national press. No professional who works with children can afford to be ignorant about the problem of child abuse and its detection.

Maternal depression

Maternal depression is a central theme of this book: we have discussed at some length the status of this disorder and its linkage with parenting problems. The problem of depression has been conceptualized in many different ways, but some of these have proved more useful in the development of effective intervention than have others. Some of the more useful approaches have been depression as a neurohumoral disorder (eg Morris and Beck 1974), depression as a disorder of interpersonal relating (eg Klerman et al 1984) and depression as a disorder of thinking (Beck et al 1979). A new set of problems arises when it comes to treatment, since it is not clear whether it is best to treat the depression per se or to focus on the parenting problems that may arise partly from the mother's unhappiness and lack of energy to care for her child. In Chapters 6 to 8 we explore three methods of approaching this problem, using professional intervention with techniques such as behaviour modification and family therapy. At this point it is important to emphasize that these are only three among many approaches.

The child has a psychiatric disorder

The formal definition of psychiatric disorder is a broad and sweeping one, as outlined in the preface to this book. The Court Report (1976) on the future of child health in England and Wales is one of many that recommended that child psychiatry services should be available to a range of children's facilities. What this implies is a clinical approach allied to the definition in the introduction to this book. Basically, the approach is a broad one which starts with an attempt to understand the child's problem from many angles, including development, physical health, family and social history. Clinical practice from a multidisciplinary standpoint should be able to work in several of the theoretical frameworks described in this section. Such frameworks might include a biological approach, which looks at the brain mechanisms that must ultimately contribute to psychological disorders, and at disturbances in the individual child's mind: the basis for individual psychotherapy and psychoanalysis. Four approaches will be described here in somewhat more detail as they have relevance to secondary prevention. These are the concept of problems being linked to difficulties in the child's wider social system (leading to mental health consultation), problems as maladaptive learned behaviours (leading to behaviour therapy), problems as related to faulty perceptions and beliefs (leading to cognitive therapy) and problems arising as a part of a faulty family social system (the basis for family therapy). We shall return to them under the heading of nature of intervention below.

Lack of stimulation leading to developmental delay

This very basic concept underlies the development of much preschool education. It is closely identified with the view that the development of intelligence is influenced by the environment (Hunt 1961), rather than being predominantly hereditary. The argument about the hereditary versus environmental nature of intelligence has raged over decades, but (as we shall see below) intelligence, as rated by intelligence tests, is only indirectly related to school success (Schweinhart and Weikart 1980). We shall have much to say about preschool education in Chapter 4.

Another intervention, less intensive, that has grown out of the idea of understimulation is the use of a toy library. In their studies of the developmental potential of home environments, Bradley and Caldwell (1984) emphasize the significance of a range of toys in the home. This may lead to the idea that the availability of toys could be a great help, hence the value of toy libraries. This provision may need, of course, to be accompanied by parental education in the importance of play in early childhood.

Lack of opportunities for socialization

Compared with their great grandparents, the experience of the young child today must be a lonely one. Families are small, roads are busy and dangerous, and their extended family may live far away. Parents feel the need to offer their children an opportunity to play with other children; indeed, there is plenty of evidence that the quality of peer relationships is linked to wider emotional adjustment (Bukowski and Hoza 1989). A preschool playgroup may answer this need, although the evidence is that such experience does not necessarily make the child more sociable (Osborn and Milbank 1987). There is also the question of how the child goes about trying to establish relationships when the opportunity does arise.

The child will start school at a disadvantage

We shall leave aside the children of ambitious middle-class parents, who feel that early instruction will give their child a competitive edge, and focus on the other extreme. Disadvantaged children may benefit from preparation for entrance to the infants school. For our purpose, education in the strict sense may seem somewhat peripheral to our sphere of interest. In Chapter 2 we reviewed the evidence that this is not so. Rather, developmental educational and emotional problems are closely linked. The idea of preparing the child for school is at the centre of the Headstart initiative, although the actual transition from preschool to the school system is an aspect that has often been neglected (Bricker and Veltman 1990: 381).

Lack of family power

The utter helplessness that many parents show in relation to their children's impulsivity, demandingness and aggression often seems to reflect their general experience of having little control over their lives in general. Such parents don't have the opportunity to make things happen: things happen to them. The promotion of parental competence over a broader scope than just in the parenting role can thus be seen as of crucial importance. The Milwaukee study (Garber and Heber 1981) showed how such a problem might be tackled. Very deprived teenage mothers were encouraged to train for a job or skilled trade. The important idea here was to promote empowerment of the individual and a feeling of competence and autonomy. We describe this important outcome study below.

The desired outcome of intervention

This second theme under the heading of theories and values of the intervention is fundamental but often passes unexamined. Programmes may set out to achieve some idealized attainment of good (eg cleanliness is next to godliness); to attempt to achieve some normative standard (eg to bring deprived preschoolers up to the developmental milestones of their non-deprived peers) or to attain the child's own potential in some parameter, whether intellectual, expressive, in sociability or on the sports field. The aim may be to provide a nurturant soil in which the child can grow and self-actualize (a horticultural analogy) or the intervention may be backed by some emancipation ethic, as in empowerment programmes. The goal may be the attainment or maintenance of physical or emotional health (a medical analogy). Sociologists may see so-called "deviant" behaviour as merely the child's attempt to survive in a subculture of violence and crime, an adaptive response to social conditions which they are powerless to change. Finally, a strong motivating force in child programmes has been to prevent problems developing in adult life. This has been seen as an analogy to inoculation by some but derided as such by many. It is unlikely, for example, that a brief intervention will have much lasting effect in the presence of pervasive adversity in the social environment.

As mentioned in the introduction to this book, we favour the concept of adaption through the developmental process as a way of understanding the developing relationship between the child and the family and social environment. Brief therapies fit very well with this concept of progressive adaption during the life cycle. We do not offer intervention in an attempt to remodel the personality, or to work some miracle. It seems both less arrogant and more realistic to see intervention as aiming to offer help with simple discrete and down-to-earth problems and to do so in such a way as to give a helping hand in the ongoing process of adaption.

The nature of the theories and values underlying intervention

In a recent review, Kazdin (1988) enumerated 230 alternative psychosocial treatments as a conservative estimate, and that did not include educational approaches. Each of these carries more or less explicit assumptions about what children and families are and what makes them tick. This will include assumptions about child development and the way that family and social influences work. Here we shall dwell at greater length on that very small proportion that have relevance to our own work.

Intervention in the wider social network: mental health consultation

Emotional and behaviour problems in children are common and there is no hope of child psychiatric clinics being able to see all children and families who have such problems. It is very doubtful that they should do so even if this were possible. An alternative approach is for the mental health worker to develop a working relationship with other professionals (consultees) who have direct contact with the child (Caplan 1964; 1970). This is called mental health consultation and it is very widely used. The assumption is that through such a relationship, the mental health professional can bring his or her skill to bear on a problem.

Turning to some of the practical issues, the consultant and consultee should meet regularly as professional peers with different areas of expertise. The responsibility remains with the consultee who has freedom to disregard the consultant's suggestions. The discussion can cover a variety of areas: direct discussion of the clientele, in this case parents and young children, the consultee's work situation and colleagues, and the consultee's attitudes and feelings about the clientele and workplace (Steinberg and Yule 1985). It is important that the consultation process does not become personal therapy on the one hand, or simple advice-giving on the other. The aim is to widen the consultees' perspectives and problem-solving ability and to ensure that their emotional involvement with their professional situation does not distort their perception of the child and family problems. The concept of consultation is very relevant to the approaches described in this book, as, at least in the cases of health visiting and playgroups, the primary helpers are not mental health professionals in the strict sense. As such, it will be important, in evaluating our project, to examine how much the findings can be generalized to ordinary practice. In his important writings, Caplan (1970) emphasizes the need for the consultant to be sensitive to the working environment of the consultee, and to negotiate entry to the situation from the highest level, while making it clear that the consultation is outside the normal channels of supervision and line management of the consultee's organization. Consultation is a difficult process requiring training and effort.

Some of the potential pitfalls revolve around the constraints of the working environment, thus consultation cannot flourish in a setting of authoritarian line management. Another difficulty can arise if the consultee's training is so poor or their perception so different from that of the consultant, that communication becomes almost impossible.

Correction of maladaptive learned behaviours

What is going on in the mind of the child who seems to be behaving irrationally, who resists toilet training or who cannot settle to sleep at night? This question often underlies the assumptions that go with intervention programmes. It is not, however, a problem for the set of techniques and the approach linked to behavioural psychology. Here the internal workings of the mind are considered as unknowable and attention is centred instead on the behaviour of the child, and, in particular, the relationship of this behaviour to the immediate environment. There is not space here to provide an adequate description of behavioural psychotherapy. There are many good texts on the subject (Herbert 1987, for example, gives a very clear account of both principles and practice). All we can do is to offer a framework here and in the next section assess the progress that has been made in evaluating techniques relevant to preschool children. This brief introduction draws heavily on Herbert (1987: ch. 5).

Behaviour can be modified by three basic procedures: those that increase a particular behaviour (response increment), those that facilitate the acquisition of a new behaviour (response acquisition) and those that eliminate or reduce an unwanted behaviour (response decrement). Each of these may be relevant to the preschool child.

Response increment. To a significant extent behaviour is determined by what the child has learned to be the consequences of that behaviour. If the result is a reward, the behaviour will be more likely to recur in the future. If it is the decrease in punishment (so-called negative reinforcement) then again the behaviour is more likely to recur. An example will illustrate the principles.

A neglected child in a large family gets more attention when he lights fires in his bedroom: the likelihood of his lighting further fires is thus increased. He is rewarded for undesired behaviour. Treatment may consist of finding other ways in which the child may gain attention from the parent, for example they work together at learning to light fires in the right place, so that the child gets more attention in a positive way. It is not always understood that it is the analysis of these natural processes that lies at the heart of the approach. Treatment consists of a rearrangement of rewards and punishments to encourage wanted and discourage unwanted behaviours, not the adding on, in an indiscriminate way, of standard rewards. However attractive these are made to be for the child, they are unlikely to make much difference on their own. The approach is called contingency management.

The young child with limited understanding and language may have difficulty in differentiating when a particular behaviour is appropriate. This is particularly true when family communication is unclear and inconsistent or, as happens so often, the parental control communication carries with it a message of expected defeat. Sharpening up communication is essential as part of training in new responses. The technical term is stimulus control.

Response acquisition. Before behaviour can be encouraged, it has to be learned in the first place. Two processes can be identified: observational learning and shaping.

Observational learning is where a child copies a role model. Much work has shown that role models are typically people who have high status, such as parents for the young child (Bandura and Walters 1963). Thus a child who witnesses parental discord or even marital violence will learn these undesirable behaviours vicariously. It is the reverse of "don't do what I do, do as I say" that works in practice.

Shaping is where a behaviour is developed gradually by successive approximation. The development of accurate articulation in speech may be a good example. New, more differentiated behaviour develops out of simpler, more immature responses. Both observational learning and shaping probably occur in normal upbringing. They can also be put to good account in therapy.

Response decrement. A whole range of techniques has developed for the reduction or elimination of unwanted behaviour. A key theme is that there is little use in reducing behaviour, for example by punishment, if an alternative is not given. Thus care must be taken that punishment (technically interventions which are associated with a reduction in behaviour) of one behaviour is accompanied by reward (or an intervention that is associated with an increase in behaviour) of an alternative behaviour.

Punishment can be arranged by reduction of positive reinforcement, such as by isolating a child – so-called time out or by extinction – blocking positive reinforcement. Very brief periods of time out can be useful with young children and the art of therapy can be demonstrated by finding ways of operating time out under domestic conditions.

Another very important approach with preschool children is the rearrangement of stimuli so that the triggering of unwanted behaviour is avoided in the first place, for example if the child breaks his olders brother's models through innocent interference, keep the models out of his way.

Again, perhaps the most important issue to understand in the development of behavioural programmes is that the child is living in a world of natural rewards and punishments. It is these that we have referred to in Chapter 2 where we described a behavioural model of parent–child interaction. This uses several of the principles described here: modelling, reinforcement (particularly negative reinforcement) and punishment. We shall take up the theme again below.

Cognitive behavioural approaches

A more recent and very fertile development in behaviour therapy has been to consider the effects of knowledge and styles of thinking. The observations of Spivack, Platt and Shure (1976), that maladjusted children tend to generate fewer alternative solutions to interpersonal problems, focus on ends and goals rather than the means of attaining them, see fewer consequences associated with their own behaviour and fail to recognize the causes of other people, laid much of the groundwork for this approach in very young children. Several groups of researchers have developed treatment programmes based on these principles, but the Shure and Spivack group have made contributions in the case of preschool children (see Chapter 4).

Modification of a faulty family social system

This set of techniques, family therapy, picks up a theme that ran through Chapters 1 and 2. This is, that in the world of relationships and psychosocial development, it is seldom appropriate to speak of causes in a simple way. Rather, any event in a family, be it a tragedy such as loss of life or livelihood, or a happy occasion such as a birth, will affect the relationships in the family and influence behaviour in all family members. Secondary repercussions in the family will occur with feedback of supportive or maladaptive influences. Individual families have their own character which can be detected at interview. Qualities of communication, involvement or enmeshment and the clarity of roles taken by family members describe the family as a whole, not the people in it. These characteristics can be observed to be linked to family psychopathology. Using a range of techniques, the family therapist attempts to identify unhelpful ways of relating in families and to alter them (see eg Minuchin 1974; Epstein and Bishop 1981). We shall return to the important topic of family assessment and therapy in Chapter 7.

We shall finish this section with one further important point. So far we have talked about the explicit values of different programmes; it is also important to identify implicit or hidden values. These may be counter to the aims of the setting. For example, there may be an implicit assumption that a "certain type of parent" is bad for the child and should be excluded from help. The self-indulgent view that "this type of family cannot benefit from our type of help" is equally unhelpful and unethical.

Voluntary organizations and intervention

This is a convenient point at which to note the important contribution made by volunteers to preschool support. The largest of these in the UK is the Homestart project. This started in the city of Leicester from experience in child guidance and work in playgroups, as described on page 52. Experience of US programmes such as the DARCEE project had shown that underprivileged parents often lacked the confidence and self-esteem to act as authoritative teachers and guides for their children. The aims of Homestart (van der Eyken 1982: 3) emphasize encouragement of self-help and a focus on the parent, with the use of volunteers who are themselves parents in a "mum-to-mum" relationship which includes a lot of practical help. Building up the parent's self-confidence is a central component of the approach, leading on to work through the parent to increase communication between parent and child and thus promote development. The approach takes a long-term developmental view with each volunteer taking on up to three families. Involvement starts with a ten-week training programme. This programme has been very successful with 138 schemes now in operation in Britain and abroad. A pilot evaluation (van der Eyken 1982) showed how much such a theme is valued in the community. A similar, more recent scheme, the Newpin project in South London, was also shown to be of value (Pound and Mills 1985).

Research issues

The battle of ideologies

The history of psychotherapy is one of passionate battles between the proponents of different therapeutic approaches. Within psychoanalysis, there were major disagreements from an early stage between the Kleinian and the Freudian schools (Grosskurth 1985). Later, schisms opened up between behaviour therapists and dynamic psychotherapists which seemed unbridgeable for many years. More recently, a sobering truth has emerged from comparative studies of outcome of behavioural vs psychodynamic therapies, which is that objective evidence of difference in effectiveness between these various approaches has been difficult to detect. This has contributed to a healthy rapprochement and broadening of thinking which has allowed the development of hybrid approaches such as cognitive therapy.

Yalom (1985: 3), writing about adult group therapy, presents an entirely different menu of key factors notable for the fact that they are not tied to any particular therapeutic dogma. These include such things as instilling renewed hope, mobilizing altruism, helping the patient to see that they are not the only one with puzzling and painful problems, helping the patient to recognize that at times life is unfair and unjust and that one must take ultimate responsibility for one's own life. Evaluation based on ideological dogmas, or indeed simply on the mechanics of child development and therapeutic technology, do not address these phenomena.

WHAT ACTUALLY HAPPENS IN THE INTERVENTION

As we have just described, the therapist or specialist teacher go about their work with a sense of mission and an ideology. How closely does this link up with what actually goes on in the intervention rather than with the ideological superstructure? Clarke-Stewart and Fein (1983) list the setting of the programme, its goals, intensity, size, the target of the intervention and the curriculum emphasis. To this we can add the detailed interaction that actually occurs and, most fascinating and tantalizing of all, the actual processes that may be the "magic bullet" of effectiveness at a psychological level. Assuming that this is a useful way of looking at the issue, these matters are closely related to the theory and values of the enterprise in both directions. The underlying mission of the organization will affect the setting on the ground, and in turn, a well-managed setting will raise morale and encourage examination of ideology and ethical issues. There is a need, however, for more finely tuned observations in assessing what actually goes on in a programme. What amount and quality of social interaction is actually given to parent and child in the child and family centre? How closely is this geared to the underlying philosophy of the establishment? Are the staff equipped and trained to do the job? Is there a prescriptive programme in operation and if so how close is the reality to the prescription? How much time do the staff spend talking to each other rather than interacting with the children? The clarity of the programme and the degree in which aims and procedures are followed are likely to be important. In various settings, attempts have been made to measure these qualities. These techniques have been used for some time with *in loco parentis* settings, for example Rutter et al (1979) in the secondary school; Moos (1975) in a variety of correctional establishments; King, Raynes and Tizard (1971) in homes and hospitals for mentally handicapped people. The observation of what actually goes on must be clearly separated from the philosophy of the establishment, that is it must not be influenced by what is supposed to be going on. Nevertheless, observational systems must have clear principles about what is being looked for. A good example is the Patterson observational system referred to above: here there is a clear idea that various types of reinforcing and aversive interactions are the object of study.

In intervention research, measurement and monitoring of programme variables has proved to be one of the most difficult and expensive tasks, yet it is one of the most important. A brilliantly successful intervention in town *A* is not much help to others if, when they try to introduce it in town *B*, they suddenly realize that nobody knows what it is! A treatment programme can be almost entirely prescribed, making observational checks on whether it is sticking to prescribed principles at least a clearer task. Many, however, would find that this violates the very basis of work with children, which includes relating to them as individuals.

Several studies of preschool educational programmes have tried to compare different curricula. Miller and Dyer (1975) compared published descriptions of four contrasting preschool curricula for deprived children and generated a series of dimensions on which they could be compared and their differences defined. Observations were made of the curricula in action and the four methods fell into two pairs: those with a fast-paced didactic approach (the Bereiter Engelman and DARCEE programmes) and a slower paced, more child-centred approach (including the Montessori and traditional approaches). Immediately after treatment, the Bereiter Engelman children were achieving better, while at sixth and seventh grades, the children from the Montessori programme showed greater progress on a number of reading and arithmetic tests. For our purposes, this and similar projects (see Palmer and Anderson 1981 for review), provided an example that we needed to follow.

Therapist effects

Long ago, therapists began to ask: which is more important, the theoretical baggage attached to therapy, or the person-to-person encounter of the therapy itself? Since there is such general agreement that the relationship between therapist or teacher and client lies at the core of therapy, the question had sharp relevance. It does not appear to have been addressed in preschool programmes, but there is evidence from psychotherapy research. Here attention has focused on therapists' styles, in particular the warmth and genuineness that they brought to the therapeutic interaction. This was found to have an effect on the outcome in client-centred therapy with adults (Truax and Carkhuff 1967), although evidence has been mixed (Mitchell, Bozarth and Krauft 1977). In a study of group therapy in schools (Kolvin et al 1981), it was found that qualities of openness, extroversion and assertiveness were associated with good outcome. Directiveness and activity of the therapists may be other important qualities, as may the level of training and experience, although here again, evidence is mixed (Lambert, Shapiro and Bergin 1986). This is not an area that has attracted interest in work with preschool children, but it is clearly important.

SUMMARY

Examination of preschool programmes under these four headings helps us to see the areas where the research is weakest. In general, the input variables – the funding of the programmes and the characteristics of the parents and children – are well researched, although there is little known in the crucial area of encouraging involvement of the child and family in the intervention. The process variables – the assumptions and values and the characteristics of the programme – are usually vague and implicit rather than clear and explicit. These are important topics for research, but the research needed is difficult and expensive. Process research is of little value unless it is linked to the most important area of all, which is research into the outcome of interventions. It is now time to move on to this most difficult and complex area to examine what progress has been made into investigating what interventions are effective.

Chapter 4

Evaluation Research on Provision for Preschool Children

In this chapter, we shall carry forward the broad view of intervention and examine its impact on a number of aspects of child development: the need for care in the early years, clinically significant disorder in child and mother, and the problems of extremes of dysfunctional parenting manifesting in child abuse. We shall consider family approaches before moving on to the contribution of early educational and developmental programmes.

In the past, there has been a tendency for researchers in the fields of social care, health and education to have different concerns in their research. Thus educational research has focused almost exclusively on IQ and achievement tests, while in child psychiatry there has been a concentration on issues of syndrome delineation, classification and the natural history and distribution of disorder. At some points in this account, therefore, we have felt that we are gathering what crumbs we can from the richly furnished tables of research covering related areas. The fact remains that programmes set up to promote one aspect of development inevitably affect others, for example preschool programmes set up to boost IQ affect mother–child relationships and child behaviour so that the sooner the boundaries dissolve between disciplines the better. This is already happening in the exciting recent surge forwards in developmental psychology.

First, the definition of intervention was set out in Chapter 3; a planned programme, or curriculum for an identified special need, can be applied here comfortably as well.

CHILD CARE

As families become separated from key intrafamilial supports, and as mothers increasingly return to work (Scarr, Phillips and McCartney 1989), the major issue in practical child development becomes non-family non-domestic day care. The issue of day care is important to this discussion because families in difficulties and with inadequate support are especially likely to call on and need such services. The field is one of high emotion and dogmatic, if sometimes unsupported, opinion. It involves fundamental issues that affect all children, including the debate as to whether they are best brought up by one constant parent figure, preferably the mother, or whether a broader concept of secure care is equally valid. Closely attached to this is the equally emotive issue of the role of women in society and the labour market. For these reasons, the actual evidence of effects on child development is of crucial importance. The evidence in fact is in good agreement that good quality group day care for children in itself does not have adverse effects. The problem is that, as shown by surveys of care, for example in Britain (e.g. van der Eyken 1984), quality has all too often left a lot to be desired. The children were often from families who were under stress and had emotional problems of a degree that merited highly skilled care, yet staff were undertrained, often very young and there was a high rate of absenteeism and high staff turnover. In comparison studies it was, as one might expect, the quality of the care provided that mattered in the longer run. For example, in one recent study (Howes 1988) the preschool experience of 87 children was rated for age of entry, quality, stability and structure. Family variables were also collected and, at first grade (7 years of age), the children were assessed for academic achievement, school skills and behaviour. In the resulting analysis, family variables were controlled. When this was done, school skills and a low rate of behaviour problems in both boys and girls were predicted by high quality care and by stable child-care arrangements. Good academic skills were predicted by stable child-care arrangements for girls and by both stable child-care arrangements and high quality care for boys. Very recently, attention has focused on the growing phenomenon of day care for very young children. In the USA, where there is no statutory system of maternity leave, group day care for children in their first year has become very common. Using measures of attachment which focused on the behaviour of the child at reunion (see Chapter 1, page 19), it has been shown that children who have over 20 hours of day care in their first year show high levels of insecure attachment. Also, follow up studies have shown high levels of aggression and non-compliance in such children in the first and second grade (7 and 8 years of age). This has led to grave concern (eg Belsky 1988). These findings are not supported by the Swedish study of Andersson (1992). In a follow up study of children who were admitted to day care in the second half of the first year, their progress was compared with children brought up at home in the early years and also a group entering day care at a later stage. At 8 and 13 years the early care group showed more independence and verbal fluency and better teacher ratings than the other groups. Path analysis suggested that the early care placement itself played a role in the good outcome. In interpreting the results it is necessary to bear in mind the common experience that child care staff are the second most poorly paid group of workers (Phillips 1991), that regulation is weak and that staff turnover is extremely high. Balleyguier (1991) in France has demonstrated the effects of poor care, especially at 9 months old, where babies show major passivity in day care settings. While the findings of disturbance associated with day care should be assessed in the light of other factors such as poor home circumstances and discordant relationships, the community has a grave responsibility to ensure that public facilities are of a standard that will promote child development. The problem is that in order to check quality in a wide basis, administrators need simple quality indicators. This matter has been addressed by Howes, Phillips and Whitebook (1992) in an investigation of a large sample. They found that simple indices, such as carer–child ratio, group size and training of teachers, did correlate with a range of measures of carer–child attachment and social competence.

CLINICAL APPROACHES: GENERAL PRINCIPLES

Is treatment effective?

This fundamental question was seldom asked in the early days of psychotherapy. That treatment was helpful appeared self-evident to clinicians. Eysenck (1952) reviewed the evidence available at that time and concluded that there was no evidence that psychotherapy in general was effective. Levitt (1971) came to the same conclusion following a review of the literature in child psychotherapy. These findings caused great disquiet at the time but also led to a much more serious examination of the issue and progressively better quality research. Reviews of the effectiveness of psychotherapy, such as those of Levitt (1971), have traditionally consisted of a pooling of different studies, often undertaken without control groups, and a comparison with an estimate of the natural history of the disorder where no therapy was given. These early reviews can now be seen to have been very unsatisfactory. Not only were simple design requirements not followed, but also different diagnostic groups, such as emotional disorders and infantile autism, were inadequately identified and differentiated. As we have seen in Chapter 2, the natural history of child disorder through to adult life is very complicated and is sensitive to a number of environmental and constitutional factors. Yet in these studies "natural remission" was expressed in terms of a simple crude percentage rate of recovery, ignoring all these considerations. Despite these many shortcomings, the early reviews were extremely useful in that they alerted us to the fact that psychotherapy was not necessarily effective. There was another way in which these early reviews were important, which was that it exposed the very poor methodology that was being used even in those few attempts at evaluation of the therapy. This was a matter that one would think would galvanize the clinical and scientific community into action, yet over 20 years later, child psychotherapy outcome research is still being given very low priority. Recently, a more sophisticated technique for pooling the results of different studies has evolved, called meta-analysis. Again, the idea originated in adult psychotherapy research, and is seen as a more objective method, since in more descriptive approaches it is possible to derive different conclusions from the same set of studies.

In a meta-analytic review, the results of each study are standardized, that is the difference between the treatment outcome and control outcome is adjusted mathematically so that it is comparable for different studies. This is done by dividing the difference between the outcomes by the standard deviation of the control group, or the combined standard deviation. The result is called the effect size (Kazdin 1988). Meta-analysis started in the adult field and from an early stage yielded results that were reassuring for the practitioners of psychotherapy. Psychotherapy did seem to lead to modest improvement when compared with control groups.

There have been criticisms of the approach from those who saw little virtue in pooling studies, each of which contained serious methodological weaknesses. There was also the problem that studies that yielded positive results were more likely to be published in journals than those which showed no, or even harmful, results. These criticisms are not, of course, about the method itself, but rather the way it is being used. With more discriminating use, meta-analysis is a helpful, indeed the obvious, way of pooling and comparing different studies. In the adult field, a large number of meta-analytic reviews have now been undertaken. Most show that psychotherapy is indeed modestly effective. More encouraging is the fact that the studies which have been most carefully carried out, with more respect for the need for reliable and valid measures and careful experimental design, have shown the most positive results (Lambert, Shapiro and Bergin 1986).

In child therapy also, there have been attempts at meta-analysis. Casey and Berman (1985) analysed 75 studies published between 1952 and 1983 where there was a control or comparison group, where the subjects were aged 13 or less and where the primary focus was the child. Most of the studies were school intervention projects where the subjects and families were not seeking treatment. This is an important consideration since these are probably relatively mild cases and the findings may not apply to the treatment of serious disturbance. Behaviour therapy in some form was the most common technique used, followed by client-centred therapy. Overall, therapy was significantly more effective than controls, the mean effect size was 0.71, a difference deviating from zero at the 5% level of significance.

Weitz et al (1987) carried out a further meta-analysis. They found 108 studies of children and adolescents with which to consider some further questions. Their overall finding was similar to that of Casey and Berman (1985), of significant effectiveness of psychotherapy overall. The effect size was 0.79. Their first question was to compare effectiveness with children and adolescents. They found the effect size with children to be larger, even after adjusting for type of therapy and sex of child (therapy seems generally to be more effective with girls). They also found that children seemed to respond well to less experienced therapists, whereas adolescents responded better to experienced therapists. There was an inverse correlation of age with size effect suggesting that the younger the child, the more effective the therapy.

Which therapy is best?

Casey and Berman's (1985) meta-analysis showed that behaviour therapy was initially more effective than other therapies, but that because the outcome measures used were very close to the treatment techniques, this might be an artifact. When more general and comparable outcome measures were examined, the behaviour and non-behaviour approaches were very similar, with treatment showing an improvement rate of 0.46 standard deviations above the mean of no treatment. Weitz et al (1987) re-examined the Casey and Berman (1985) finding that behaviour and non-behaviour therapy were equally effective. They concluded that the exclusion of outcome measures that reflected the therapeutic process had been too strict, and that there was considerable evidence that behavioural approaches were superior.

Whether the therapy was play or talking, individual or group, child or parent centred made little difference, but there were differences according to the outcome measures examined. Fears, anxiety and cognitive skill measures showed the greatest, personality and self-concept measures the least change, perhaps because these latter are based on theoretical constructs that relate only indirectly to observable behaviours. Effectiveness also varied according to who judged the outcome. Observers, therapists, peers and most of all parents gave favourable measures of outcome whereas teachers and the subjects themselves reported less change. Attempts to assess the effectiveness of therapy for different disorders was hampered by very poor clinical description of the subjects' disorders in individual research studies; indeed the general quality of the underlying research was very variable.

What type of problems?

We have spoken of the importance of classification and of distinguishing between disorders of different sorts. In the preschool years, fearful children with feeding and sleeping problems were distinguished from hyperactive children and aggressive children. In Chapters 1 and 2 we described environmental and intrinsic factors which affect outcome irrespective of treatment; to this must be added the appropriateness of the intervention and a range of other rather intangible factors (described in Chapter 3). For example, as well as the types and the severity of problems, the number of problems faced by a single family is important, as Patterson, Chamberlain and Reid (1982) found in the treatment of antisocial children where there was less success when the children were in multiproblem families.

Direct vs indirect therapy

The question is whether the therapy is offered direct to the child, or via a process of mental health consultation (Caplan 1970). Mental health consultation has become increasingly popular as the demands for mental health services outgrow resources. In a school intervention study (Kolvin et al 1981), group and behavioural therapies were compared with a teacher consultation approach. The results were quite clear in showing that direct approaches to the children were effective and the consultation approach was not effective. In Chapter 3 (page 61) we discussed consultation and how it is relevant to our own study.

In the study described in this book, all the approaches were direct in that the therapists, whether health visitors or social workers, had quite intensive training from the mental health team. However, in community intervention in general, consultation is an essential technique requiring more research.

The length and intensity of the therapy

The overall duration of the therapy is probably not important whereas the intensity with which it is offered may be. In the adult field, it is now generally accepted that length of treatment is not a crucial ingredient. This was shown in the classic study of casework where problem-oriented casework was compared with long-term work, and found to be more effective (Reid and Shyne 1969). Concerning intensity, in a study of psychoanalytically oriented therapy with 6–10 year old children, children seen four times a week were compared with children seen once per week. The more intensively treated children showed greater gains both in personality and in school achievement (Heinicke, Ramsey and Lee 1986).

CLINICAL APPROACHES: PRESCHOOL CHILDREN

A range of treatment approaches are appropriate for the preschool child, which can now be described. One characteristic of young children is that they are dependent in so many ways on those around them; for this reason, when we think of changing the behaviour of a young child, we almost automatically think of his or her milieu of family and preschool. It may be an indication of our state of knowledge about young children, a comment on the fact that it is usually oppositional and externalizing behaviours that elicit parental concern or a response to the developmental level of the young child, but most of the interventions in use have developed from the theories of behaviourist psychology.

Aggression and oppositional behaviour: parent management training

In Chapter 2 a series of approaches to understanding parent–child interaction was presented, including, in particular, how such interaction could be influenced by psychopathological processes. One of these was a behavioural model, called the coercive cycle. Several of the components of learning that have been presented in Chapter 3 (pages 62–4) are involved. First, in a conflict-filled household, there are plenty of opportunities for the child to model on aggressive behaviours and shape skilful aggressive responses. Second, the lack of reinforcement for wanted behaviour – because the parents are too preoccupied or weighed down to respond sensitively – means that the child begins to respond to anything that gets attention as a positive reinforcer: misbehaviour is the obvious example. The third and very powerful origin of problem behaviour is negative reinforcement. The preoccupied and incompetent parent, with a deep conviction that she is powerless to influence even her own child, unwittingly reinforces undesirable behaviours by giving in to the child's aggression, thus reinforcing it.

The most attractive aspect of this theoretical approach is that it has such immediate treatment implications. A large number of evaluative treatment projects have been undertaken. In a review, Kazdin (1988) identifies the principles common to the many variations of parent management training that have developed. Treatment is conducted primarily by the parent, who directly implements several procedures at home. There is usually no direct intervention of the therapist with the child. Parents are trained, often with the help of easy-to-read written material (eg Patterson 1975), to observe and make detailed descriptions of behaviours according to behavioural principles. The treatment sessions consist of continued discussion and instilling the importance of positive reinforcement, and "time out". Most important, the parents are encouraged to try out techniques and then bring the results back for discussion. The therapist uses instructions, modelling, role play and rehearsal to convey how the techniques are implemented. Several outcome studies have been carried out; while these have for the most part been with school-aged children, they are described briefly here as the technique, possibly in a simpler form, has implications for preschoolers and for secondary prevention. The Patterson group have followed a programmatic approach in that as their concepts and techniques have developed, they have checked with outcome studies. The first group of studies used a relatively weak before-to-after treatment comparison design. There was before-to-after improvement in behaviour, and also some evidence that siblings improved as well and that the effects generalized to school behaviour. Follow up using observation and parent reports also showed persistence of the improvement (Patterson and Fleischman 1979). More recently, comparison studies have appeared which again gave encouraging results. The most recent and most satisfactory of these (Patterson, Chamberlain and Reid 1982) used observation and parental report as change measures and random allocation to case and waiting list control groups. On the other hand, the sample sizes were small (total $n = 19$) and, in common with most such studies, there was a drop out rate of over 20%. Treatment was by well-qualified staff who were highly trained in the parent-training technique. The results were that there were significant decreases in rates of aversive behaviour in the treatment but not the control group. The parents also reported satisfaction with the treatment but there was no drop in parent-reported problem behaviours.

Influence of marital distress

Two studies, using direct observation of mother–child interaction as the outcome measure, have taken account of marital distress in evaluating the effectiveness of parent-training programmes. Brody and Forehand (1985) found that if the behaviours were highly specified and treated directly, the fact that treatment occurred in the context of marital problems makes little difference. However, the effects failed to generalize if there were marital problems, whereas they did generalize if the marriage was a happy one. In a similar study, Dadds, Schwartz and Sanders (1987) found again that immediately after intervention, there was improvement whether or not there were marital problems. The difference was that at six month follow up, the behaviour of the distressed families had relapsed, whereas in the non-distressed families it had not. If a component of partner support training was included, however, the outcome of the distressed families was as good as the non-distressed ones.

Sleep problems

Behavioural methods including a bedtime routine with positive reinforcement and either rapid or graduated extinction procedures have been found to be effective in treating sleep disorders in young children (Richman, Stevenson and Graham 1985; Adams and Rickert 1989).

Cognitive problem-solving skills training

Understandably for an approach which taps into cognitive function, much of the research and practice of cognitive behavioural approaches has been with older children (see Kendall and Braswell 1985 for a full review). Interestingly far and away the earliest study, that of Chittenden in 1942 (described by Kendall and Braswell 1985), was on 3–6 year olds, where 71 children were screened; children high on domineering behaviour and low on co-operativeness were assigned to an intervention and matched control group. The treatment group were given individual sessions of structured doll play to teach them to identify disagreements and how to negotiate agreement. At immediate post-treatment follow up, and one month later, there were reductions in domineeringness in the treatment group, although changes towards more co-operativeness were less persistent.

Spivack and Shure (1974) developed a training programme for preschool children in a secondary prevention project. As the children were so young, the prerequisite language had to be taught first, together with the concepts required for the interpersonal problem-solving exercise. These included the ability to consider alternatives, and to own and predict consequences of one's actions. The skills, once developed, had to be placed in the perspective of means to the end of better social relationships rather than the end in itself. A variety of techniques were used in learning, including pictures, story books and puppets. The curriculum was carefully sequenced, and care was needed to elicit appropriate attention from difficult children. Outcome was measured by a test designed specifically to assess the skills that had been taught. Three evaluations were carried out. There was consistently good learning of the programme in that testing after the curriculum was given showed better performance in the treatment group but not the control group. Increased skill was reflected in improved behaviour in the treatment situation. In the third and largest evaluation study, a treatment vs control group design was used; in addition impulsive, inhibited and behaviourally adjusted children were evaluated separately. The results showed that the programme children learned as expected when tested after the intervention. Teacher ratings from ordinary class also showed improvement; this persisted at six month follow up. Anecdotal reports from parents were also favourable.

The same techniques were later applied in a parent treatment programme with preschoolers (Shure and Spivack 1978). Again both impulsive and inhibited children were included, who in addition scored low on tests of interpersonal problem-solving. There was a control group. The treatment mothers were trained in the same curriculum as was used in the school study. They then offered the programme to their children. Results suggested beneficial outcomes for the programme children in alternative and ends–means thinking. Not surprisingly, there were changes in the mothers' perceptions towards improved ends–means thinking and these changes correlated with those of the children. Teachers' reports confirmed that behaviour at school was significantly improved in the treatment group.

Most of the subsequent studies have concerned school aged children.

Here the techniques have been used to help in prevention and in the treatment of established disorder (Gesten et al 1987). There have also, however, been some studies that have brought more refined research designs to the study of prevention in preschool aged children. Vaughn and Ridley (1983), for example, demonstrated improvement in peer-rated interactions and included an attention placebo control group. Fries and Simons (1985) showed gains in both problem-solving and adjustment with low-income rural preschoolers.

Overall, findings of preschool and school based studies have been inconsistent. Some have given negative results, some have shown improvement in scores on focused tests, but not on classroom behaviour while others have shown improvements in behaviour but seemingly unrelated to learning of the interpersonal skills (Olexa and Forman 1984; Gesten et al 1987).

CLINICAL APPROACHES: THE DEPRESSED MOTHER

Depression in mothers (let alone fathers) has seldom appeared as an outcome variable in studies of preschool intervention. Equally, in studies of adult depression, the parenting capacity of the adult is seldom if ever evaluated as an outcome indicator of interest. In view of the widespread interest in maternal depression as a barrier to effective parenting, this is surprising since an enormous amount of research has been devoted to the treatment of depression as an individual problem. The treatment of depression falls into two types: drug treatments and psychological treatments. Commonly used antidepressants have consistently shown effectiveness in clinical trials (Morris and Beck 1974). It is also true, however, that effectiveness is greater for more severe depression, rather than the persistent, less acute disorder that is so common in the community. The evidence for psychotherapy approaches has been less secure. Recently, reports of a major multicentre treatment trial incorporating a drug therapy regime, compared with two psychotherapy approaches and a control group, have started to appear (Elkin et al 1989). The study shares with others a very careful evaluation of symptomatology from a variety of perspectives and a measure of general social functioning. There is not, however, an assessment of effect on caretaking behaviour or other family variables. The general results of this study were hopeful in that with more severe disorder, all the approaches, but particularly the medication, showed some effect. The two psychological approaches were cognitive therapy (Beck et al 1979) and interpersonal therapy (Klerman et al 1984). It was the interpersonal therapy which was associated with statistically and clinically significant gains. The study is a landmark one in the care with which the actual execution of the therapy was monitored and the careful training that went into the development of the two different types of therapy. The full results of the study are not yet available, including the more specific social impairments associated with depression. The effects of treatment on parenting capacity may require separate study, targeted on young mothers.

ABUSIVE PARENTING

Treatment of families who have abused their children is a difficult and uncertain undertaking; this is particularly so for anyone seeking to undertake the evaluation of therapy. None the less, there have been such attempts (see Nicol 1988 for a review). In a comparison of casework with play therapy (Nicol et al 1988), the results were not clear cut. There was a significantly greater decrease in aggressive behaviours associated with casework when the results of all the family were pooled, but when fathers, mothers and children were examined separately, the differences disappeared. Perhaps the most significant finding was that 45% of the subjects dropped out of the study.

Egan (1983) carried out a controlled comparison of two treatments: stress management and child management. There was a waiting list control. Numbers were small, between nine and eleven per treatment condition. The outcome measures were somewhat indirectly related to child abuse, consisting of self-report questionnaires, a role play exercise and a period of observation of a set task in the clinic setting. With these reservations, the results were encouraging, with both treatment techniques showing advantages compared with controls, particularly on the observation measures.

SOCIALIZATION

In Chapter 2 we briefly reviewed the association between peer relationships and adjustment. We noted the important part that peers play in development and the vicious cycle of expectation and confirmation that develops between the rejected child and his or her peers.

This cycle can be broken into, theoretically speaking, at any point; the key issue is that intervention needs to involve the peers as well as the child. Actual evaluation of intervention is less plentiful, especially for preschool children where it is less certain anyway that the process outlined above is relevant. Further, much of the evidence concerns the less grave problem of children who are socially withdrawn rather than rejected by their peers.

Co-operative activities can break down stereotyped attitudes in many situations such as towards ethnic minorities. Furman, Rahe and Hartup (1979) studied two approaches to socially withdrawn preschool children. Three experimental groups were compared. In the first, a structured co-operative task situation was developed with same aged peers; in the second, younger peers were used. The third was a no-treatment control group. The children in the treatment conditions showed marked improvement in interaction, particularly those who had been in mixed age groups.

Another approach tackles the cycle at the point of hostile behaviour by peers. Strain, Shores and Timm (1977) taught two 4 year old children to persist with socially withdrawn peers when rebuffed, and offered rewards for so doing. They confirmed that such children became more responsive. The same changes were found if groups were rewarded for increased social interaction (Greenwood and Hops 1981).

In attempting to modify the rejected child's own behaviour, prosocial models or so-called sociometric stars have been used. This has been shown to increase the rate of prosocial interactions; however, it is less certain that there are long-term changes (Greenwood and Hops 1981).

It is unlikely that one mechanism underlies all the problems of unpopular children, and a single prescription is unlikely to be as effective as intervention based on an appraisal of the problems of a particular child.

FAMILY APPROACHES

Some form of family intervention or support took place in the majority of the interventions described in this chapter. Bronfenbrenner (1974), writing about early intervention, which at that time seemed to lead to temporary effects which disappeared soon after the child entered school, wrote persuasively of the need to include the family in any intervention if there was to be any hope of effectiveness. He saw parent–child relationships as the medium for the most crucial aspects of learning in the early years. Accordingly, he vigorously advocated the need to stimulate parent–child interaction and to foster conditions that would lead to a stable attachment. He quoted the early work of Levenstein (1970) as supporting his ideas. Levenstein developed a programme for the promotion of parent–child interaction around a common activity, and showed impressive early gains in development in the preschool period.

Whether this and similar approaches are called family therapy is largely a matter of definition. Gurman, Kniskern and Pinsof (1986) in the authoritative *Handbook of Psychotherapy and Behavior Change* gave a very broad definition: any psychotherapeutic endeavour that explicitly focuses on altering the interactions between or among family members seeking to improve functioning of the family as a unit or its subsystems, and/or the functioning of individual members of the family. Many of the therapies described in this chapter fall within this definition. A more restrictive definition might include the need to conduct therapy using a systems approach as outlined in Chapter 3 (pages 64–5), including whole family interviews. Within this narrower definition, there are no outcome studies specifically involving preschool children. This is a major gap in research, particularly as the family system in this relatively early stage of family development, might seem to offer particularly interesting opportunities for family change.

EDUCATIONAL PROGRAMMES

The British and US priorities in evaluating preschool provision have been sharply different. In Britain the preoccupation has been with a better organization of services, with pointing up deficiencies, and with naturalistic studies, particularly in the field of the stimulation of language development in home and different preschool settings (Tizard and Hughes 1984). In the USA programme evaluation has been much more of a theme, and so of greater interest to us. Before turning to the US scene, the study of Osborne and Milbank (1987), mentioned several times already, merits description in more detail.

A comparison of various types of provision in Britain

The study arose from an opportunity afforded from the third of three national longitudinal studies, in this case the National Health and Development Study of children born in April 1970. Comprehensive information was gathered from the mother about the child's preschool experience at interview when the child was 5 years old, together with details of the child's home background. At 5 years, health visitors carried out developmental and vocabulary tests and at 10, a battery of tests which covered general ability, vocabulary, reading, mathematics and communication skills. Children's behaviour was assessed by questionnaire by mother at 5 years while at 10 years the teacher completed behaviour and the child self-concept scales. Independently, a national survey was undertaken of preschool provision, which was used to validate the mother's reports; 60% of the children were matched with the preschool institution they had attended. The successfully matched sample was then the subject of the further study.

Not surprisingly, independent (non-state-financed) provision was used more commonly by the more advantaged sections of the population. More seriously, state provision did not fill the gap in that 40% of children in poor neighbourhoods had no preschool experience, compared with 14% of the well-to-do children: a classic case of the ancient dictum "to those that have shall be given".

In a more general analysis, type of neighbourhood of residence, family size and a social index score derived from measures of occupation, education and housing of the parents were found to predict test score results at 10 years. Not surprisingly, therefore, major differences were found in test results at the age of 10 for children who had attended different types of provision in the preschool years. The research strategy was to see whether these differences persisted when statistical adjustments were made to take into account differences in family size, neighbourhood and social index score.

The first finding was that the differences in test scores for children who had had different types of preschool experiences were very large and highly significant, particularly at 10 year testing. They were also large compared with other types of preschool factors, such as family size and social index.

Children who had attended home playgroups, local education authority (LEA) nursery schools and hall playgroups showed good results not only at age 5 in copy designs and vocabulary but also at age 10, in general ability, language, reading, mathematics and communication. Those with no playgroup experience or LEA nursery class did least well. The heavily disadvantaged local authority (LA) day nursery children also did surprisingly well, after appropriate adjustment.

The most deprived 30% of the sample showed somewhat greater benefits from the nursery school and hall playgroups than the most advantaged 30%. There were advantages in the child's own mother being involved in the preschool care: where that occurred the child had better scores on vocabulary at ages 5 and 10, and better reading and maths at 10 years.

Turning to behaviour, the situation was more complex. There was a high degree of correlation at age 5 between nervousness in the child and maternal depression. Also depression was particularly common in mothers of children attending LA day nursery. When this was allowed for statistically, the children at independent day nursery, hall playgroup and LEA nursery school were more likely to be nervous than the no-provision or LA nursery groups. On measures of hyperactivity, conduct disturbance and extroversion, LA day nursery children had the highest scores, well ahead of the other groups.

Osborne and Milbank (1987) undertook a number of validity checks and are confident about their results, particularly in the cognitive sphere. The differences between different types of provision measured more than five years later, and particularly that the differences persist, are indeed impressive. The main problem with this argument is that context of the delays and disturbances of the children are statistically flattened out to give a sort of level playing-field picture. In real life the playing field between the privileged and under-privileged is not level, and it is doubtful if the differences can be corrected by sophisticated statistics. The factors taken into account, moreover, are entirely environmental with a strong emphasis on current environment as opposed to the legacy of the past, even intergenerational influences. Equally, no mention is made of possible genetic differences between the groups. The findings need confirming in a controlled trial. The assumptions and values as well as programme variables of the different provisions, and how these might differ are almost entirely left to speculation.

The basis of Headstart

World-wide, the best known programmes in early education arose around the time of the massive Headstart initiative in the early 1960s. The aims were ambitious, the expectations high and, most important to remember, the depth of deprivation suffered by the children attending the projects was often severe. This was reflected in the profound level of developmental retardation in the study children and by other indicators such as the high percentages of young single mothers. The intervention was to be comprehensive, involving four components: health (nutrition, immunization), social services, parent involvement, and education. Not only parent involvement but also community involvement was to be high, and sensitive to cultural factors (Washington 1985). The subsequent story follows a familiar mood swing that accompanies many innovations: early uncritical euphoria, rejection when the innovation does not live up to inflated expectation, and finally acceptance of the value of the innovation in the right circumstances and in the hands of adequately trained people. Despite changes in political philosophy of succeeding governments, funding for preschool programmes has persisted.

It is clear that only a tiny subsample of programmes have been recorded, let alone evaluated (Palmer and Anderson 1981). Nevertheless, the findings of these few are of interest. Some now have very long-term follow ups while others are more recent, asking more specific questions. The main aim of a preschool programme should be directed at giving the disadvantaged child preparation for the school system, an aim which assumes that the schools that the children move on to are of satisfactory quality. IQ assessment, which, particularly from the second year of life, is depressed in disadvantaged children, has been widely used to make the judgement of readiness for school (Bronfenbrenner 1974). In retrospect, IQ seems a strange criterion to have achieved such prominence as an outcome measure. First, it is a quality that was developed to be predictive of continuity rather than change. Second, it does not measure a discrete area of competence, such as reading or social skill, which one might hope to modify by intervention. In the real world cognitive, let alone other aspects of development, have a broader scope than that measured by IQ tests. Education should develop special talents and take account of the behavioural individuality of the child. Learning readiness cannot be divorced from the acquisition of impulse control and attention span, from capacity to respond to positive adult role models and reinforcement (Patterson 1982). Generosity, co-operativeness and a sense of compassion are also legitimate educational goals (Bronfenbrenner 1974). In short the total adaption of the child to the environment must be kept in view.

Around the time that the Headstart project was set up, a number of high quality demonstration projects with built-in evaluation were developed in different parts of the USA. Early results, as measured by IQ scores, suggested that the children who had been in these programmes showed an immediate increase in IQ compared with no-treatment controls. The benefit persisted through kindergarten, but by second grade (at 8 years of age), the control children had caught up. In so far as they were recorded, other measures of function such as achievement tests and social adjustment seemed to indicate more persistent advantages for the children who had been in a preschool programme compared with the controls but these had not been systematically investigated (Ryan 1974).

The effective components of early education

IQ as an outcome measure

In a recent review, Bryant and Ramey (1987), by comparing 17 studies, tried to tease out the components of successful intervention. All the studies had random allocation and no-treatment control groups. The only measure that could be compared across studies was IQ, which was measured in a variety of ways in the different studies. In eleven of them, intervention started in early infancy; in all but four, the mother and sometimes other family members were centrally involved in the intervention. Using the limited outcome measure of IQ, Bryant and Ramey (1987) explored some possible key components of success of these preschool programmes.

Age

Gains as a result of intervention did not appear in the first year of life; however, intervention seemed equally effective whether started in the second or third year (Ramey, Yeates and Short 1984).

The intensity of programme input

In their review of 17 studies, Bryant and Ramey (1987) demonstrated that the effectiveness of early intervention programmes in raising IQ was proportional to the intensity of the programme, in particular to the direct work with the child. The most successful programme, the Milwaukee project (Garber and Heber 1981), was also the most intensive and merits description in more detail.

Twenty programme children and twenty controls were chosen on the basis of an IQ of below 70 in the mother. The programme had two components: educational and vocational rehabilitation for the mother and an intense, direct educational programme for the child with primary focus on language and problem-solving skills.

The mothers were found to distrust authority; a sense of despair, both social and economic, pervaded their lives. Since absence of a stable breadwinner was so common, occupational training was essential. After this training, the differences from controls remained small but the programme mothers did show advantages in reading, in mean income and in job stability, although they were able to spend more time with their children. In parallel, mothers seemed to engage more often in verbally informative behaviours with their children. The child educational programme started at 3–6 months of age and continued year round until the child was 6 years old. Differences from controls emerged at 18 months and persisted to the final measure when the child was 10 years old. They were particularly marked on measures of language. Garber and Heber (1981) note that some of the children had difficulties of adjustment at school entry. There is an urgent need to attempt a replication of this project which, with such a low power research design in that there were so few subjects, shows such remarkable results. It may be that the key issue was that the intensity of the deprivation induced developmental delay: the intervention may therefore show less spectacular results with other samples.

Home versus central day care intervention

The seemingly ephemeral results of the early programmes stimulated much thought and review of the available findings. We have already mentioned Bronfenbrenner's (1974) influential report, identifying positive motivation and home and family based intervention as two components likely to lead to longer-term effectiveness, in contrast to day care approaches where the parent was more peripheral. The toy demonstrator project of Levenstein (1970) seemed particularly promising. In this the intervention was in the home, and the mothers were well motivated in both the intervention and control groups. There were large gains in the intervention group. More recently, the variety of different approaches that have been tried have tended to blur the distinction between home and centre care. For example, Seitz, Rosenbaum and Apfel (1985) report a ten year follow up which offered individualized care according to a professional appraisal of the wants and needs of the family. This included day care and home intervention. Further, programmes which are almost entirely centralized have shown good results.

The Abecedarian project (Ramey and Haskins 1981), for example, offered full-day day care with an educational programme that emphasized activities that stimulate both the social/emotional and the intellectual/ creative domain of child development. The research design compared purely preschool intervention, additional input in the early school grades, a combination of the two, and a no-intervention control. At risk children were allocated randomly at birth; the programme started by 3 months of age. School achievement after three years in school was consistent in showing that the children who had both programmes did best and almost achieved the performance of average children in the town. The next most effective was the preschool only programme, while the school only programme had a slight but non-significant advantage over at risk control.

In project CARE (Ramey et al 1985; Wasik et al 1990), a preschool day care programme was supplemented by a family education component. Children were chosen for the project at the time of pregnancy, based on an index of multiple deprivation. The day care programme was compared with family education alone and with a no-intervention control. The day care component emphasized activities which stimulate both the emotional and intellectual development of the child. The family education regime consisted of a visit about every ten days at which problem-solving skills were taught, based on the work of Shure and Spivack (1974) described earlier in this chapter. There was random allocation to the three groups in a controlled trial. Drop out from the project was low. The programme started when the children were aged from 6 weeks to 3 months of age. The day care children showed marked developmental gains through the second year compared with an at risk control group and the home visit only condition. They did nearly as well as a general population sample of children in what was a predominantly middle-class environment. The advantages of the day care plus family education group over the family education alone group persisted until 54 months, which is the latest follow up reported. However, the advantages over the control group disappeared. Shure and Spivack attributed the attenuation of the effectiveness of the programme to the fact that towards the end of the second year, parents from the other two groups had started to use community day care facilities. Evaluation of the home environment was carried out using the HOME inventory. This is an interview and direct observation instrument designed to measure the potential of a home environment for promoting child development (Caldwell and Bradley 1979). Both this and a measure of parent attitudes showed no difference between groups. Shure and Spivack comment on the relatively low input to the family education only programme. The overall conclusion from these studies was that success was associated with high intensity of input, rather than with its type.

Home-based programmes

A number of projects have emphasized involvement of mothers in preschool education programmes aimed at increasing cognitive function. This follows the encouraging early findings of Levenstein (1970) and the review of early programmes by Bronfenbrenner (1974). In a review of these studies, Farren (1990) notes that the results are mixed and that of those completed more recently, only the study of Slater (1986) on children at risk showed positive results. This programme was brief and focused on story reading. Farren (1990) notes that extensive, unsolicited home visiting may well be more of a burden than a help for hard-pressed poverty-stricken mothers.

Prematurity

A large number of preschool programmes have concentrated on children who are developmentally at risk because of prematurity. Reproductive difficulty is another factor that is closely tied up with psychosocial disadvantage (Birch and Gussow 1970).

An important eight-centre randomized controlled trial of intervention which included 985 children offered an intervention to children with birthweight under 2500 grams (Infant Health and Development Program 1990). Apart from the very smallest, it is unlikely that the retardation of most of these children could be attributed to neurological damage. The sample was diverse, but at six of the eight sites the proportion of black families was very high. There were three components: weekly then biweekly home visits, centre-based teaching from 12 to 36 months five days per week and bimonthly parent groups. Outcome at 36 months was measured in terms of cognitive development, behavioural problems and health status. Outcome analysis used multiple regression techniques to disentangle effects of initial status and a number of background variables such as parents' education from that of the intervention in contributing to the final outcome. The study showed highly significant differences between the intervention and control groups. The intervention had resulted in improved intellectual development as measured by IQ tests, and a somewhat lower rate of behaviour problems according to mother's report on the Child Behaviour Checklist (Achenbach, Edelbock and Howell 1987). As might be expected, several background variables also predicted outcome, such as maternal education, race and sex of the child. It is interesting that at the site with the least disadvantaged population and the best community services, the case control differences were relatively slight. This reinforces the impression that the results are related to the fact that the children were disadvantaged.

There has been a suspicion that the results of these more successful programmes are related to the fact that they are high-status projects, usually mounted from university departments. Burchinal, Lee and Ramey (1989) examined this possibility in a controlled comparison of a university programme with the much more widespread community programmes. There was also a no-treatment control. They found that the university programme did indeed produce the best results, measured by IQ, but that the community programmes were also associated with considerable advantages, as long as the children attended for at least a year.

Long-term follow up studies

As already mentioned, most of the early Headstart programmes showed initial encouraging effects on IQ but these seemed to disappear by the second grade in school (about 8 years of age), often because the control group children seemed to catch up in their development rather than the preschool intervention children deteriorating. This finding led to pessimism about preschool enrichment programmes, a pessimism which has been somewhat relieved by more recent developments.

Lazar and Darlington (1982) reported a bold project which combined the outcome of the best evaluated programmes. Twelve studies were included in the investigation, the so-called consortium studies. The children involved were followed up at ages 9–19. Outcome measures that could be pooled from these quite independent studies were limited, but there were significant and educationally meaningful differences. The preschool programme children showed substantial advantages in that far fewer were assigned to special class and retention in grade when compared with controls. Tests of educational achievement were significant but tended to diminish and disappeared by the fifth and sixth grades (11 and 12 year old children). In IQ equally, early advantages tended to disappear and at the combined follow up there were no robust case control differences. Achievement orientation and self-concept were also measured at combined follow up. Achievement test showed that younger programme children were more achievement oriented, and that this was true of older girls but not boys. The findings are of rather small and patchy differences, few of the constituent studies could stand on their own in showing significant results. Also, the findings are, of course, post hoc. They do, however, fit a pattern that we have already mentioned in Chapter 2 in the study of the careers of girls brought up in care (Quinton and Rutter 1988). The aim here was to find out how the experience influenced their own parenting capacity. The main finding of the study was that parenting capacity was influenced primarily by the current social support provided for the mother but that the legacy of the past influenced not only the likelihood that the mother was living in a currently supportive environment but also her vulnerability to lack of support, which was very high compared with unsupported mothers who had been brought up in their own homes. One among a number of protective influences was a successful school career with good reports and examination results. Similarly, in the Consortium follow up of Headstart, the older programme girls were more often proud of school achievement and helping at home while the control girls were proud of having babies or reported nothing to be proud of. Mothers in the programme group were not satisfied with their children's school performance. Perhaps the most important lesson from this research is that school competence, as measured by ability to stay in grade in mainstream school was far and away the most impressive finding. As the authors point out, this seems likely to require a combination of social competence, common sense and emotional stability which is unlikely to be reflected in purely cognitive tests, the results of which were less enduring. Royce, Darlington and Murray (1983), in a later report on the Consortium study, found that the programme children more often completed high school and were more likely to find employment.

One of the studies included in the Consortium follow up had particularly low sample attrition and complete data up to late adolescence. This was the Perry Preschool programme. The children came from Ypsilanti, Michigan, were all black and multiply deprived. Measured IQ was between 70 and 85, below the mean for poor black communities; 58 children were taken into preschool programmes of, seemingly rather variable curriculum (Schweinhart and Weikart 1980: 22). There were 65 controls. As in other programmes, there was a major superiority in measured IQ in the preschool years over controls, but this advantage disappeared by the age of 8 years. From then to 14 years, the IQs of experimentals and controls were indistinguishable. When attention is turned to commitment to schooling, however, differences from controls are more persistent. Throughout kindergarten and the early grades (from 5 to 9 years of age), the programme children scored higher on a measure of school motivation, although differences were only marginally significant. At 15, the programme children scored higher on a measure of value placed in schooling, and this finding was confirmed at interview with the parent. The programme children rated themselves much higher in taking time to do homework and in school ability; at 14 years they showed consistent superiority in achievement tests and had spent less time in special education. Classroom conduct of the programme children was better in the 6–9 age range although the statistical significance of this finding was marginal and did not continue into the teenage years. There were, however, a significantly lower number of persistent offenders among the programme group.

At 19 years this programme appeared to have resulted in significantly less delinquency and recidivism, both for serious and for minor offences measured by self-report and official records when compared with controls. The study children were more likely to have graduated from high school and to be working. The girls were less likely to have been pregnant, early unwanted pregnancy being another event that can close off life opportunities, let alone the implications for the unwanted child. The authors see a transactional process (see Chapter 2, page 47) as giving an explanation for the results. The study also had the advantage that there was some control of group differences before the start of the programme.

There was little family input to the Ypsilanti programmes. However, home intervention was a major plank in the Family Development Research Programme (Lally, Mangione and Honig 1988). Trained paraprofessionals carried out home education and liaison with very deprived young mothers who were usually single, black and had failed to complete high school. Five days a week, fifty weeks a year, day care from early infancy was offered and there was a focus on family advocacy. The day care curriculum emphasized good nutrition, co-operation, prosocial skills and interest-led education. Co-operation with other social agencies was important. As time went on, parent organizations, formal and informal, sprang up.

Concerning outcome, there were early gains in IQ which, however, disappeared by age 5. The children seemed advanced in socio-emotional development, but by first grade (7 years of age), this led to more demanding behaviour in school which was often perceived as troublesome.

A comprehensive ten year follow up was undertaken. Of the families who had completed the programme, 79% were successfully traced, together with 73% of the control families. There were major differences between programme and control children in self-image and among parents, in their pride in their children. Positive changes in school were confined to girls. Thus girls showed better grades and better reports on a teacher questionnaire. Lally, Mangione and Honig (1988) point out that it was only in adolescence that these remarkable differences between programme and control children were found. Delinquency was much more common among control group children.

A transactional model

In their monograph, Lazar and Darlington (1982) developed a transactional model. This postulated that the early programme boosted IQ and attainment in the early grades of school which in turn set in train increased motivation and achievement orientation which outlives the cognitive changes. The work of Rist (1971) is brought forward in evidence for this hypothesis. Rist showed that within a very short time of entry into the classroom of the mainstream school, a stratification has occurred, together with self-fulfilling expectations of which children will do well and which will do poorly. In this way, the augmented IQ at school entry is seen as the critical link between the preschool programme and achievement in the adolescent years. As described in Chapter 2 (page 47), the cards were stacked in favour of the children who had had the preschool programme.

Alternative explanations

This transactional model is a fascinating possibility, but IQ seems a rather slender conceptual bridge on which to make the vital crossing from preschool deprivation to adjustment in adolescence and adult life. As we have mentioned, child development has broad scope, and one has an instinctive feeling that much broader aspects of development must be in play in the early school years. We have already seen in the multicentre study of premature children, that disturbance is relieved as much as are developmental delays. In our own study, for example, to be reported in Chapters 5 to 8, we were interested also in child adjustment, state of the marriage and mothers' mental health. Our next question therefore is about evidence for the involvement of a broader set of developmental issues than IQ alone. Two questions can be asked.

1. What other changes, apart from those associated with IQ, occur as a result of preschool programmes?
2. Is there evidence of any other change apart from boosted IQ in the early grades, that could suggest alternative pathways to the improved school performance in high school and early adult life?

Of interest to our inquiry is the effect that the programmes may have had on child behaviour, mother–child relationship, and mother's self-esteem and mental state.

Child behaviour

Gutelius et al (1977) offered support for young single mothers in a programme that started at 7 months of pregnancy. Health care and a cognitive stimulation programme were offered. At follow up, the treatment group performed better than controls on a number of non-standardized behavioural measures, and on measures of behaviour during formal testing of confidence and ability to establish a relationship. Using a parent questionnaire, of undisclosed quality, the treated cases showed less naughtiness and bad temper at 3 years. This infant programme does not tell us about psychological readiness at school entry, but does support the idea that behaviour can be improved by very early intervention. In a more recent study, Lee, Brooks-Gunn and Schuur (1988) demonstrated more direct effects. Disadvantaged children who had been through Headstart programmes were compared with similar children in other school programmes and a no-preschool group. One of the tests used, the Caldwell Preschool Inventory, was specifically designed to tap these broader social and cognitive skills necessary to take advantage of classroom learning. At one year follow up the Headstart group showed gains as measured on this test. More recently, in the multicentre study, the Child Behaviour Checklist showed modest gains as a result of an intensive day care and visiting programme (Infant Health and Development Program 1990). Seitz, Rosenbaum and Apfel (1985), in the ten year follow up of their home-based intervention, found that improvements in behaviour were much more persistent than in development.

A different set of findings has emerged from other programmes, for example Haskins (1985) reviewed the literature and examined relations between child care attendance and later aggressiveness in children attending cognitively oriented intervention programmes or community-based child care programmes. He concluded that child care was related to the programmes' content rather than attendance at a preschool facility per se. He suggested that children attending cognitively oriented programmes may be at risk of negative behaviour.

The mother–child relationship

There is plenty of evidence that the more successful programmes resulted in an improvement of mother–child relationship. In the Abecedarian project (Ramey and Haskins 1981), where the children were in full-time preschool day care, direct observations were made of mother–child interaction at regular intervals in the preschool period. Both these and interview data confirmed that the interaction in the programme group was more rich and stimulating than in the controls as measured by the HOME inventory, and this despite the fact that there was no direct intervention with the mother. It should be added that the control group seemed to be more deprived at the outset in that there were more single parents and lower family income. Similarly, there were some positive effects, despite very small sample sizes, as measured by the HOME inventory in the Family Oriented Home Visiting Programme (Gray and Ruttle 1980). This consisted of a nine months' visiting programme in which there were some thirty visits of between one and one and a half hours each.

Andrews et al (1982) report three loosely linked studies in three southern cities in the USA. In Birmingham, children and mothers attended between the ages of 3–5 months and 3 years. There were increasing amounts of centre-based contact which started with child care and development. The mother then assumed increasing responsibility as a teacher within the centre and thus moved towards her own career development. Subject matter included health, social services and child development. Outcome was measured by a laboratory parent–teacher interaction task and by developmental tests. There was improvement of mother's contact with her child, but interpretation is complicated by the fact that the groups were dissimilar at an early stage in the study. At Houston, mother and child entered a two-year programme at 12 months of age. Cases showed significant differences from controls on some of the interactional measures and Binet IQ at 36 months of age, but again there was little to go on in trying to decide whether the programme and control groups were similar at baseline. At New Orleans, the programme started when the children were 2 months old and continued to age 3 years. In an interaction task, mothers of programme children demonstrated more positive interaction with their child at 2 and 3 years. At 3 years, there were significant gains of the programme group on vocabulary, concept formation and the Stanford–Binet. Follow up at 48 months showed sustained gains in Stanford–Binet at two of the sites.

Slaughter's study (1983) was based on black families in Chicago apartment projects, where 2 year old children and their mothers were allocated to two well-developed programmes and a control group. There was a fairly high level of sample erosion, despite the fact that the sample was made up of volunteers. The programmes were both home based and were the Levenstein Toy Demonstration Project and the Auerbach-Badger Mothers' Discussion Group Programme. The evaluation centred on interaction variables in a controlled situation, where child's and mother's behaviours were measured; there were also IQ tests and tests of mothers' attitudes. The mothers' groups did best, showing several important differences from both the Toy Demonstration programme and controls in the interaction measures for both mother and child as well as for ego development of mother and IQ gains for the child. The Toy Demonstration results were less strong, although they did show some gains over controls. Slaughter (1983) suggests that the results can be seen as showing that the mothers gained mutual support in a culturally appropriate way.

Mothers' economic independence

A number of the studies, for example that of Garber and Heber (1981), included a means of training mothers to encourage economic independence. In some studies this criterion was included among the outcome measures, for example Seitz, Rosenbaum and Apfel (1985) found a much higher level of independence at ten-year follow up. This may be particularly relevant where the mother has not yet completed her education. For example, Gray and Ramsey (1985) were successful, in their small study of teenage mothers, in getting the mothers to complete high school.

SUMMARY

We can now summarize the evidence on intervention according to the main outcome factors that form the theme of this book. Many of the studies that have been described are very small scale, and the first point is that, considering the importance of the evaluation of intervention and the vast expense of psychosocial and educational interventions in preschool children, the resources that have been devoted to this area of research and development can only be described as extremely weak.

Child day care is becoming increasingly important as women return to the labour market with increasing frequency. The matter turns on the quality of the care. While there is no evidence that good quality care is detrimental, poor quality care, which may be quite common, remains unevaluated. There is evidence that children who have extensive day care are more assertive than their peers brought up in a home environment. There are also doubts about the effect of day care for infants in the first year.

The evaluation of child therapy with preschoolers, whether this be for oppositional behaviour or sleep disturbance, is limited almost entirely to behavioural approaches, including both parent skills training and cognitive approaches. There is modest evidence that these are effective, although studies have characteristically been small scale. In some cases it has been necessary to extrapolate from studies of somewhat older children. The findings of the effect on treatment results of marital problems are particularly interesting. The presence of such problems limits the generalization of therapy, but does not preclude effectiveness.

There is no evidence for family therapy using a systems model simply because no studies have been done.

The quite extensive studies of social problem-solving training have been aimed at prevention but there has been some evidence of effectiveness within this framework.

For mothers' depression, there is plenty of evidence for the effectiveness of antidepressant medication and some for psychotherapy interventions for the depressive disorder. What is much less certain is whether these approaches improve parenting capacity. This is somewhat indirectly related to the psychiatric syndrome, as shown by the fact that mothers prone to depression may have difficulties parenting even when they are not depressed.

For delays in development, we have examined the effects of preschool educational programmes and seen that the effects are clear but short term, and that developmental assessments have been rather narrow. Long-term effects seem to have worked by altering the attitudes of the child and parent leading to better performance in senior school grades in a number of areas of motivation and planning. There is evidence of short-term improvements in behaviour and in the mother–child relationship in preschool programmes and, in one case, at ten year follow up.

One point to note is that many of the projects described are either demonstration projects or special projects set up purely for the research. Indeed, the cynic might note that the theory put forward for the long-term success of the Headstart programmes is that it gives the children a competitive edge over their peers in the battle for inadequate resources in the school system. Our interest was in evaluating run-of-the-mill interventions that could be implemented on a wide basis, indeed which were being implemented up and down the country. Our special health visitor and mothers' group approaches fit into this category. The family therapy approach was considerably more specialized and represented an attempt to intervene in the family system in a more thorough going way. We shall now move on to describe the study.

Chapter 5

The Aim and Design of the Research Project and a Description of the Sample

In the first four chapters we have described the problems of mothers and toddlers in the preschool years and examined some attempts to tackle these problems. Our own project arose at a time of great concern at the epidemiological findings that were appearing, around 1980, which showed high distress and psychiatric morbidity in mothers and toddlers at the preschool stage. We recognized that in the absence of research findings, both the debate and attempts to help with the problem would remain sterile and in years to come would be yet another fashion that would all too soon begin to show its "sell by" date. This was the reason for the project that we shall begin to report in this chapter. We shall describe the following areas.

1. The general approach (including the concept and methods of secondary prevention)
2. The study area
3. The hypotheses of the study
4. The study design (including the interviews and questionnaires that were used)
5. Assessment of the mothers, children and families (including the construction of a scale of social adversity)
6. The social circumstances of the study families.

THE GENERAL APPROACH

Community interventions can adopt two basic starting-points. First, there are approaches to the social fabric, which might include schemes to attract capital to the area or to develop training opportunities. The alternative is to approach the problem on a more individual level. If one assumes that even under the most unpromising circumstances, some opportunities exist, one task might be to relieve depression and low self-esteem enough so that people can take advantage of what is available. The three approaches to be described in the chapters to come were adopted because they were different ways of enhancing social support.

The health visitor approach was attractive because it involved using a profession who were familiar and welcomed by young parents. The support was substantially from a professional under normalized circumstances.

The mother and toddler group approach equally was a familiar concept to young mothers (and some house husbands). Here support was offered by a peer group of mothers.

The family therapy approach was less familiar yet, having taken account of the importance of the family system, it seemed important to adopt a technique that would focus on the improvement of the family as a supportive institution. In this chapter we shall look in more detail at the context of our project and at its aims and design.

Secondary prevention

This is a central theme that has surfaced repeatedly; now we have to describe how a secondary prevention project could work in practice. Attention is focused on those cases who show vulnerability or early signs of disorder. The idea is that it should be possible to intervene at an early stage and thus prevent an escalation of the problems (Caplan 1964). There are four ways in which cases may be identified in the type of preschool project to be described here.

In the first approach, one might concentrate on groups of the population at high risk. Studies of children from inner city areas have shown high rates of various types of problems such as emotional disturbance, delinquency and educational difficulties (Rutter and Madge 1976). These findings have led to the establishment of a large number of intervention programmes in inner city areas as well as the setting up of special government-funded projects, the best known of which were the Educational Priority projects (Halsey 1972). The problem with these blanket approach programmes is that even in the most deprived area, there may be many families who are not in need of help and those who do need help, may not always have the same type of problem (although the general provision of resources and training is to be welcomed). Additionally, there are many families in need of help who do not happen to live in deprived areas.

A second approach is to identify cases through attendance at recognized agencies such as the family doctor's surgery. Watts (1982) for example described the important role of the family doctor in the treatment of depression with counselling and sometimes antidepressants. Again the problem is to find out whether or not all the families with the problem actually attend their doctor and to what extent. Watts (1982) estimates that only about 10% do, and the rate for problems with the toddler may be lower. More recent evidence comes from various epidemiological surveys. Summarizing this evidence concerning adult psychiatric disorder, Goldberg and Huxley (1980) estimate that the great majority of patients with a psychiatric problem consult their doctor at some time. However, the use of general practitioner (GP) attendance as a screen would require subjects to attend their doctor at a particular time. Brown and Harris (1978), in their community sample, found that almost half the depressed women had not consulted their doctor. It has long been recognized that GPs differ widely in their "psychological mindedness" and therefore their recognition of psychiatric disorder (Shepherd et al 1966).

The third approach to case identification is typified in everyday practice by the health visitor service. This is a truly preventive approach, actually visiting and assessing the families. Without too much difficulty, it is possible to identify families in difficulties either by clinical identification or, for the purposes of research, by standardized questionnaire. As will be seen, we were able to tap health visitors' knowledge in our study and to evaluate the results. We held back from using the health visitor as our sole source of information since it is a relatively untried technique and we suspected that it may be subject to some of the same biases as would the GP attendance approach.

The fourth approach is the use of questionnaires actually distributed door to door. This was the main approach we used; it is expensive and could be justified in normal practice only if the result was the prevention of particularly severe disease to at least a few children, or a great deal of good to many. In the context of a research project whose aim was to reach as many in the population as possible, it seemed justified.

In summary, identification of families in need of help is important. Many, for various reasons, may not come forward for help but may welcome it if it is offered. This was our rationale for using a screening approach to case identification.

THE STUDY AREA

The study took place in an urban area in north-east England, for the most part in five city wards. There was, over the area as a whole, a mixture of private and council housing and a range of social class groups, mainly skilled and semiskilled working class. Much of the area constituted the traditional heavy engineering and shipbuilding which had made the area famous in the early years of the twentieth century. Recent decline in these industries had led to high levels of unemployment, approaching 20% long-term unemployment in the age group of the study. The area had a very stable population over many generations which meant that there tended to be much neighbourhood and family support, although the combination with

Table 5.1 Summary of hypotheses

---

1. The three interventions differ from each other and from the control in reducing disturbance and delay.
2. There are other social and biological predictors of outcome, for example social adversity and sex of the child.
3. The other predictors (social adversity and sex differences) influence the effects of the various treatments on the various types of disturbance.
4. Independent of treatment, "high-risk" families have a poorer outcome than "low-risk" families.

---

high unemployment meant that fathers often worked away in the south of England, on oil rigs or in the Middle East.

THE HYPOTHESES OF THE STUDY

The four hypotheses of the study are set out in Table 5.1.

THE STUDY DESIGN

The design of the study is outlined in Figure 5.1. At its core is a stratification of the case material based on the General Health Questionnaire (GHQ), Behaviour Checklist (BCL) and Health Visitors Questionnaire (HVQ) scores as recorded at screening. Within this stratification, cases are randomly allocated to the three treatment groups and control. After follow up, the effectiveness of the different approaches for different problems was assessed by comparing change scores on the measures made.

Screen instruments used

The screen had three components: the General Health Questionnaire, Behaviour Checklist and Health Visitors Questionnaire.

The General Health Questionnaire (GHQ)

This was designed (Goldberg 1978) as a self-administered test aimed at detecting psychiatric disorders among respondents in both general practice and community settings. It is not concerned with distinctions between different types of psychiatric disorders but rather with common features of individuals with disorders when compared with those without disorders. In the present study, the 30 item version of the questionnaire was used as a screening instrument. While less efficient than the full 60 item version, it

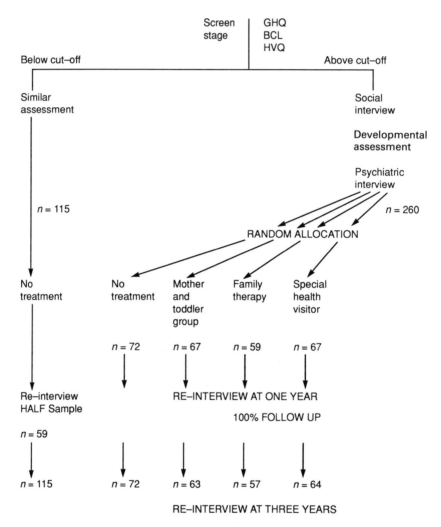

Figure 5.1   Design of study

was considered that because a whole population group was being approached, the shorter version was likely to be more acceptable and more readily and reliably completed. Studies of the GHQ have been carried out on the 60 item version and reliabilities of 0.9 for retest and 0.95 for split-half have been found. It was predicted (Brown and Harris 1978) that the prevalence of psychiatric problems in the population under study would be quite high (over 20%). Since the efficiency of a screen is better when the prevalence rate is higher (Goldberg 1972) this high estimated rate also justified the use of a shorter scale.

The Behaviour Checklist (BCL)

This scale was developed (Richman 1977; Richman, Stevenson and Graham 1982) as a self-report questionnaire on the behaviour of preschool children. It was thus well suited for use as a screening instrument for this project. In adapting the scale for use in this project, two extra "dummy" items, concerning bowel and bladder control and siblings, were added to clarify the meaning of the responses. Before the items on bowel and bladder control we added a clarifying item about whether or not the child was in nappies; before the item on sibling relationships, we added an item on whether the child was an only child or not. The reliability of the BCL on test-retest has been found to be 0.81 under conditions similar to those in the present study (Richman 1977).

Health Visitors Questionnaire (HVQ)

This was designed for the project to tap an independent source of objective information since health visitors (public health nurses) visit the families from infancy onwards. The questionnaire was developed in consultation with two experienced health visitors. Since the questionnaire was developed for this study, its psychometric characteristics were at that time little known; we therefore used it as a supplement to the screen only. As a result, we have found that the questionnaire discriminated usefully between screen positives and negatives (Nicol et al 1987). High scorers on the questionnaire were noted and a special group of high scorers were included as screen positives (see pages 102–3).

The questionnaire asks for some demographic data and has items which tap four areas: mother's verbal complaints (11 items), objective assessment of mother (13 items), observations on child management (10 items) and assessment of child (5 items).

Recruitment to the study

The cut-off scores recommended for the two screen instruments are 4–5 for the GHQ and 10 and above for the BCL. Since we are concerned with a high level of true positive case identification it was decided that we would risk a raised false negative rate and raise the level of cut-offs. If the scores on both questionnaires were raised, a lower combined cut-off was accepted. The cut-offs were as follows:

	GHQ alone	7 or above
	BCL alone	14 or above
Combine score	GHQ	4 or above
	BCL	8 or above
	HVQ	11 or above

Cases scoring above these cut-offs were designated high-risk cases.

Allocation to treatment groups

We aimed to allocate 60 high-risk families to each of the four treatment groups in a stratified design for male and female toddlers separately. In addition, 115 screen negative families were studied. Of these, 72 were retested at one year; the whole group of 115 were retested at three years. The actual numbers chosen, with the projected numbers in brackets, are given in Figure 5.2. There were two sets of twins: one in the at risk control

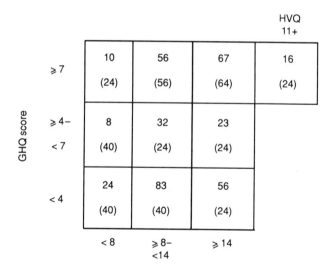

Screen positives and screen negatives are combined and the projected numbers are given in brackets

Figure 5.2 The distribution of families over the nine combinations of levels of screen GHQ and screen BCL

group and one in the family therapy group. In each case the twins were both allocated to the same group. These figures are presented here because, as described later, the fact that cases were selected for the design meant that corrections had to be made in estimating the efficiency of the screen.

The screen was designed to identify mothers and children in need, so we will now turn to the operation of the technique in practice.

The screening programme in practice

Information about the project to the study population and the establishment of consent

The first approach to the families was a personal visit by a social interviewer with the two screening forms. Originally, this approach was accompanied by a letter from the family health visitor, who, in the case of a population of preschoolers, was likely to be well known to the majority of mothers. At a later stage the family health visitors became uncomfortable with this role and the approach was made directly by the research staff. This change did not seem to affect the recruitment of families in a major way. The letter stated that we were a research group attached to the local health authority and that we were carrying out a survey of the health and progress of preschool children. It also stated that part of the project was to offer help to some of the families if this seemed to be needed. The next stage, for those families that were picked for interview, was to reiterate that this was a survey and that the health authority was trying to assess the best way of offering help to families with young children. The message was repeated at the time of the psychiatric assessement and that we would be offering help to some families in order to try and find out if our helping techniques made a difference. The importance of trying something out before it was introduced on a wide basis was stressed, together with the idea that if it proved unhelpful, the money might be better spent another way.

The next approach for those families introduced into one of the treatment programmes was from the professional concerned (ie a special health visitor or social worker) who made an introductory visit to explain what they had to offer and answer any questions. Families were, of course, free to drop out of the study at any stage. Table 5.2 gives information about this drop out.

Numbers selected and procedure

Families with a child born between 1 March 1980 and 31 March 1981 were identified using the inoculation register which is updated regularly by the

Table 5.2   Recruitment to the study at each level of assessment

Number sent questionnaire	949
Questionnaire returned	802
Chosen for baseline interview	459
Social interview completed	403
Psychiatrist assessment	383
Included in treatment	376
First follow up at one year	
(minus one n. control)	320
This represents 100% follow up at first follow up	
Second follow up at three years	
parent interviews	371
school interviews	356

health visitors working in the area. Initially 949 families were approached with the screen questionnaires (GHQ-30 and BCL); the first instance was by a social interviewer who visited the home. If no one was in, the questionnaires were left with an explanatory letter and stamped addressed envelope. The screening programme was undertaken in four phases over one year and at the same time the family health visitors were asked to complete the HVQ on each of these families. Completed questionnaires were received from 774 families and, of these, a total of 428 were identified as at risk. The screen positive families were selected in such a way as to fit into the stratified design described above. Those who were unavailable, refused, or who were about to move (27 families in all) were replaced by other families and 375 families were eventually included in the study, 115 screen negatives and 260 screen positives. Table 5.2 shows the stages of inclusion in the study, and the numbers at each stage.

ASSESSMENT OF THE MOTHERS, CHILDREN AND FAMILIES

An extensive general assessment of the families in the study was carried out. This approach follows the principle developed in Chapter 2 of looking at a network of risk and protective factors as a prelude to intervention. The areas investigated were selected on two criteria:

1. Areas of disturbance and delay that we hoped to modify in treatment, and where we needed, therefore, to measure outcome.
2. Measure of social adversity that might affect outcome, and which, therefore, we needed to take into account in our assessment of outcome. These were particularly relevant to Hypotheses 2 and 3 of the study (see Table 5.1).

Measures of disturbance and delay

Mother's mental state

This was assessed by the Leeds Self Assessment of Depression and Anxiety, which yields four scales: specific and general depression and specific and general anxiety (Snaith, Bridge and Hamilton 1976). These scales showed high agreement with observer ratings of the two conditions. Kearns et al (1982) compared a variety of depression questionnaires and found the Leeds scales to be among the most discriminating. Two further scales were added: inwardly and outwardly directed irritability, scales which arose out of further work of the Leeds group (Snaith et al 1978). The Leeds scales were given at baseline and both follow ups.

Mother's cognitive failures

This scale is a self-report of simple episodes of perceptual, memory and motor failures (Broadbent et al 1982). The scale correlates with scales measuring psychiatric symptoms but is usefully independent of it. It has been found to reflect a single factor; it is not influenced by the intelligence of the respondent. At retest, the scale was stable for quite long time periods.

Psychiatric assessment

Following the general assessment, each mother was visited by a psychiatrist who administered the Clinical Interview Scale (Goldberg et al 1970). Following this, the psychiatrist made a psychiatric diagnosis and a rating of severity of the mother's disorder, if present, and severity of the toddler's disorder. These judgements were based on all the information available. The severity of any psychiatric disorder in the mother was rated according to the assessed need for referral as judged by the overall assessment of the psychiatrist. Elsewhere (Stretch et al 1992) we relate this to the objective scores on the Leeds scales. The levels of severity were: no disorder (0); minor symptoms only (1); requires surveillance at primary care level (2); merits treatment at primary care level (3); merits referral to a psychiatric service (4). These severity levels were significantly discriminated from each other by the Leeds scales. The interview was given at the baseline assessment only.

The child's behaviour

The Behavioural Screening Questionnaire (Richman and Graham 1971) is a semistructured interview widely used in community surveys (see Chapter

2). Twelve types of behaviour problems are covered which were found to be the best discriminator between the general population and children attending psychiatric clinic. The test-retest reliability was $r = 0.81$. The interview was used again at first follow up.

Subgroups identified by the Behavioural Screening Questionnaire

A principal components analysis was carried out to examine for subscores of the behaviour screening questionnaire. These were anxiety problems, relationship and temper problems, attention problems, bowel and bladder problems, sleep problems, and eating problems.

Behavioural interview for infant school children

This standard interview consists of a series of standard questions which are rated on five point scales covering the main symptoms of disturbance in children (Kolvin et al 1975). The version used in the present study was specially designed for infant school children and had been shortened following extensive piloting. Four dimensions have been reported: neuroticism and withdrawal, antisocial acting out, psychosomatic symptoms, and modesty and phobia. For the present study items reflecting hyperactivity were added. This interview was given at the final follow up.

Conner's Teachers Scale

This widely used scale (Conners 1969) has been validated on populations in many countries (eg Taylor and Sandberg 1984). It was given at final follow up when the children were at school.

Prosocial Behaviour Questionnaire

This questionnaire (Weir and Duveen 1981) was designed to tap a wide range of helping behaviours in the classroom. Split-half reliabilities in three samples were all over $r = 0.8$ and test-retest was 0.92. Inter-rater reliability was less satisfactory at 0.58. This measure was also given at final follow up when the children were at school.

Quality of marriage

This was again rated by semistructured interview (Quinton, Rutter and Rowlands 1976). The instrument has been shown to have good inter-rater reliability ($r = 0.82$), and there was also high consistency between the accounts given by husband and wife. A four year follow up showed high predictive validity for later marital breakdown. The instrument yields an overall quality scale and a type scale, which differentiates marital problems associated with quarrelling from those associated with indifference. In the present study we also included subscales of satisfaction with everyday conversation, communication, participation in household activities, care of children and enjoyment in doing things together, and also of irritability, quarrelling and nagging. One of the authors (ARN) undertook training in the administration of the scale and subsequently trained our social interviewers. The marriage rating was given at baseline and both follow ups.

Cognitive and language function of child

The assessments of the toddlers were carried out in their own home by a trained examiner who was "blind" to the child's group allocation (Fundudis et al, in preparation). Owing to the relatively tender ages of the toddlers and the variability of the environments in which each child was being assessed it was important to use measures which would be simple but efficient. These included the following tests.

Stanford–Binet Intelligence Scale. The toddler's Development Quotient (DQ) was estimated by administration of the short form of the Stanford–Binet based on the two tests (picture vocabulary and identifying body parts). The two-test short form has been found to be reliable with children under the age of 6 years (Gordon and Forehand 1972).

Mean sentence length. The sampling of verbal statements of young children in terms of their mean length utterance has been found to be a simple, objective and useful indication of speech development (Fundudis, Kolvin and Garside 1979). In the present study spontaneous and/or elicited verbal remarks by the child at any time during the assessment were noted verbatim by the examiner. The mean number of words of the toddler's three longest statements was used as the index of speech development.

Identifying shapes and objects

The children are shown a series of shapes and asked to match them with identical shapes illustrated in a small booklet placed on the table in front of them.

Observational, social and developmental progress

The toddler's social responsiveness during the course of the assessment was rated by the examiner according to a scale developed for the study. It comprises seven areas of behaviour:

1. use of speech
2. clarity/intelligibility of speech
3. amount of talkativeness
4. amount of motor activity/restlessness
5. degree of social ease
6. level of self-confidence
7. general level of readiness to engage in doing the tasks/co-operation.

Each area is rated on a three point rating scale, 0–2; a total score is also obtained. The scale was used as part of a pilot study and the inter-rater reliability was found to be satisfactory. All these scales were given at baseline and at first follow up.

The Wechsler Preschool and Primary Scale of Intelligence

This standard intelligence test is designed for children aged 4 to 6½. The test consists of 10 scales but a short form was used in this study: Information and Vocabulary Subscales made up a verbal subscale and Picture Completion and Block Design made up a performance subscale. The reliability and validity of the scales are well documented (Anastasi 1982).

Clinical examples of level of severity

We have already mentioned our categorization of severity of disorder into two strata: the level at which therapeutic concern would be raised at primary care level and the level which might trigger referral to a psychiatric clinic. These different levels of severity were reflected, as one might expect, in the severity scores on the interview. A few case examples may help to bring the nature of the problems to life.

Case example: Jones family

Mrs Jones had two children, James being the younger. The older child, Pauline aged 8, had severe asthma, had had a large number of hospital admissions and remained a focus of her parents' anxiety. They had been hoping to improve their housing and move to an area where they could place Pauline in, as they put it, a more suitable school. Their worry was exacerbated by Pauline's complaints of being bullied at her present school.

Mrs Jones was judged to have somewhat low morale but not amounting to significant psychiatric disorder. James's main problem was to do with sleep: he disturbed the household nearly every night. Recently his parents had taken him into their bed, leading to temporary respite. He was also a faddy eater and showed little capacity to concentrate even on activities that obviously interested him. He was fairly dependent and tended to follow his mother around in a rather worried sort of way. The parents had not consulted their GP about James. The mother was judged to have minimal symptoms (1) and the child disorder at primary care level (3).

Case example: Briggs family

The Briggs family consisted of both parents, some grown up children and $2\frac{1}{2}$ year old Cathy. The first impression was that this was a child who had total control of the family. Difficulties in both settling and waking at night added up to a severe sleep problem which had left both parents completely exhausted. Mother, in particular, was exhausted, angry and depressed yet a slave to every whim of her severely hyperactive child. There were also less serious problems of dependency and feeding. The family had not consulted their GP but despite this the mother's disorder was judged to rate attention at primary care level (3) and the child to merit attention in a child psychiatry clinic (4).

Case example: O'Neil family

The O'Neil family was of three children, $2\frac{1}{2}$ year old Jimmy being the youngest. Nine months before the interview, father had lost the job he had held steadily for many years in the shipyard. This caused severe financial strain and mother became anxious and sleepless. She found herself irritable and lacking in energy. Soon her feelings snowballed into a sense of hopelessness and she felt sad most of the time. She found herself becoming deeply resentful of her extended family who she saw as completely unhelpful, although in fact she had not asked for help and it is doubtful if they even knew of her plight. She often gave way to tears. She had consulted her GP, who gave her some tablets which she tried once but gave up because they made her feel worse. She had had no problems with Jimmy apart from some minor tempers from time to time. Mother's rating was of a psychiatric outpatient level of severity (4) and the child minor symptoms only (1).

Case example: Valentine family

The Valentine family had one child, Kerry, the identified patient age $2\frac{1}{2}$. There were major marital problems and mother reported some tension and lack of energy. Kerry had some difficulty settling on some nights and a few food fads which did not, however, interfere with her nutrition. In both cases there were some problems but not at a level judged to merit medical consultation at any level. Mother's rating was (2), child (2).

Measures of social adversity

Home observation for measurement of the environment (HOME)

This semistructured observation and interview schedule has been developed in 0–3 year and 3–6 year versions, the former having 45 items and 6 subscales and the latter 55 items and 8 subscales (Caldwell and Bradley 1979). The aim of this instrument is to provide an assessment of the quality of the cognitive, emotional and social stimulation of the environment available to the child in the home. It is based on observation and interview of the child's parent in the home. Numerous studies have shown that HOME scores correlate consistently with the results of developmental and intelligence tests and also less direct indices of home environment such as measures of occupational status and parental education. For us, the HOME inventory offered a useful measure of the extremely important areas of social interaction in the domestic situation. The reliability and validity of the instruments have been found to be satisfactory. The infant version was given at baseline and the preschool version at first and second follow ups. We intended to use the HOME inventory as an outcome measure but in the event, the scores were too near the ceiling of the test for this to be possible.

Social network

This interesting neighbourliness scale (Wallin 1954) has been used in previous community outcome studies as a background variable (Kolvin et al 1981). For the purpose of this study, the structure of the scale was explored in more detail. The twelve item scale yielded two factors. The first seemed to reflect the number of people that the subject related to, while the second reflected the degree of intimacy of the subject's relationship with neighbours. In each case Kaiser's criterion and the screen test indicated that the subscore had a single underlying factor. This scale was given at baseline, first and second follow up.

Demographic and family measures

A wide range of other information was gathered. This included family size, disturbance in siblings (also measured by the Behaviour Checklist), social class and employment, parents' education, family physical and mental health and behaviour.

The social adversity scale

As outlined in Chapter 1, there is evidence that in considering social disadvantage, it is the weight of the total adversity rather than the individual features of it that represent the most serious problem. Accordingly, we constructed a scale to tap this dimension. In order to distinguish our scale from what it was supposed to reflect, we termed it the adversity scale. Table 5.3 shows the components of this scale.

Table 5.3   Components of the adversity scale

The following are the criteria that score one point on the adversity score. The resulting adversity index is a simple sum. Scores at or above 4 are high adversity and below 4 are low adversity.

1.	Number of children	four or more
2.	Marital state of parents	separated or divorced
3.	Social class of main breadwinner	manual
4.	Social class of second breadwinner	manual
5.	Degree of unemployment	unemployed over six months in last year
6.	Mother's education	left school without any leaving certificate
7.	Father's education	as for mother
8.	Home conditions – physical	damp, crowded, above fourth floor or nowhere to play
9.	Home conditions – housekeeping	dirty
10.	HOME inventory	total score over 61
11.	Father's illness – severity	inpatient episode
12.	Father's illness – duration	over three months
13.	Father's nerves	reports nervous problems
14.	Father – drink or drugs	psychological or physical dependence
15.	Mother's illness – severity	as for father
16.	Mother's illness – duration	as for father
17.	Mother's nerves	as for father
18.	Mother – drink or drugs	as for father
19.	Index child severity of illness	as for father
20.	Marriage quality	serious disruption of marriage (4 or more on the marriage rating)
21.	Total index child behaviour score	any total above screen cut-off
22.	Sibling behaviour problems	any total of over 19
23.	Neighbourliness	score 16 or less
24.	Total rating psychometric score	

The question of temperament

In Chapter 1 we introduced the concept of temperament, and a strong case could be made for introducing it as a background variable in the study. The dictates of resources and our wish to limit the amount of research interviewing meant that we reluctantly had to decide not to study the predictive power of temperament in the study. We were worried about the effects of too extensive research interviewing for two reasons. First, the experience may have been experienced as tiresome by the families that had agreed to help us. Second, there was a possibility that the research interviews themselves might have had a therapeutic effect. This may seem unlikely, but in fact more than one harassed mother said spontaneously that they felt much better after the chance to talk to the research interviewer! In what follows, we have to accept temperament as a random variable.

THE SOCIAL CIRCUMSTANCES OF THE STUDY FAMILIES

Here we give a brief portrait of the study and screen negative control families.

Age

The average age of the mothers was 27.6 years for the study and 28.9 for the control group. Fathers were slightly older: 30 years for the study and 30.9 years for the controls. The average number of children was 1.95 (1.46 under age 5) for the study group and 1.97 (1.37 under age 5) for the controls.

Social class

As might be expected from the description of the area, there was a predominance of working-class families. Of the 115 screen negative control families, 76 (66%) were manual working class and 48 (42%) skilled manual workers. In the study group, of the 260 families, there were 195 (75%) working class. When the social class of the second earner was examined (nearly always the mother) the emphasis was on semiskilled work, with 47 (41%) of the control group and 127 of the study group (49%) registering social class IV on the basis of their most prestigious job.

Family structure

The majority of the families were headed by both natural parents: 104 (91%) in the normal control group and 207 (80%) in the study group. Of the mothers in the study group, 6 were unmarried, a further 15 were single following divorce or separation, 17 were in common law marriages while in 14 cases there were other domestic arrangements, including one long-term foster child.

Employment

Unemployment was a problem. In the study group 69 main breadwinners (27%) and in the screen negative control group 16 (14%) were unemployed throughout the year. This was a significant difference. Others in both groups had been unemployed for varying parts of the year up to interview, with only 56% of the study and 66% of the control group being fully employed through the year up to interview. In 30 of the study group (12%), the mother was the main breadwinner.

Education

Educational attainment of the mother was low, with 153 (59%) of the study group and 56 (49%) of the screen negative controls leaving school with no qualification at all. For the fathers, there were 100 (38%) in the study and 38 (33%) in the control group with no qualifications. However, 7 study mothers and 15 controls had education above A level standard, and this was true of 21 study fathers and 15 control fathers.

Housing

There were 16 study families and 9 screen negative controls living in overcrowded conditions of over 1.5 persons per room. In 36 study and 6 control families, physical conditions in the home were described as damp or crowded or no play space or above the fourth floor in flats. In 12 study families, housekeeping was described as dirty, smelly or chaotic.

Health

In general, health was good in these young families, but 22 study and 10 control fathers had had to visit or be in hospital in the year up to interview; this was also true of 21 study and 11 control mothers. There were 18 study fathers and 2 controls who were said to suffer from nerves, as were 50 study and 6 control mothers. There were 20 study and 3 control fathers who had drink problems; in 4 study fathers this was physical dependence.

In the previous year 54 of the study children and 17 controls had visited hospital; 10 study and 2 control children had had life-threatening illnesses. Furthermore, 69 (26%) of the study parents and 18 controls (16%) had sought advice from their GP about the index child's behaviour; 27 (10%) study parents and 12 (10%) controls had sought advice about a sibling's behaviour.

Marriage

Of the study group marriages, 68 (26%) were described as marked by important episodes of open disruption or by general indifference, dislike or avoidance; this was true of 7 (6%) control marriages.

Home environment (HOME interview)

The results of the HOME scales indicated a very high quality of environment, compared with the criterion groups on which the instrument was developed in the USA. Table 5.4 gives a comparison of the study families, in the treatment and screen negative control groups with the figures published by Caldwell and Bradley (1979). The data come from study of a mixed race group in Arkansas. It will be seen that our families achieved near the ceiling of the scales. This suggests strongly that our sample, despite the many economic problems of the area, may have been offering a much better environment for childrearing than were the families involved in, for example, the Headstart projects described in Chapter 4.

Table 5.4 Results of the HOME interview, compared with those of Caldwell and Bradley (1979) for a group of 24 month olds in Little Rock, Arkansas (standard deviation in brackets)

	Screen pos.	Screen neg.	Caldwell study
Responsivity	1.28	0.67	8.57
	(1.74)	(1.36)	(1.99)
Play material	1.12	0.72	6.36
	(1.54)	(1.23)	(2.03)
Avoid punish	1.99	1.61	5.24
	(1.40)	(1.14)	(1.64)
Organize	0.97	0.49	4.93
	(1.11)	(0.75)	(1.24)
Maternal involvement	2.36	1.79	3.54
	(1.75)	(1.71)	(1.79)
Variety	1.02	0.68	3.03
	(1.11)	(1.02)	(1.52)

Findings on the social adversity scale

There were significant differences in the level of social adversity, as defined above, between the screen positive and screen negative group. For the screen positives there were 101 below and 159 above the cut-off of 4 and above, while for the screen negative group reassessed at first follow up there were 41 below and 19 above ($F = 23.1$; $df = 1318$; $p < 0.00005$).

SUMMARY

In this chapter we have introduced our own project for mothers and toddlers. A main feature of it is that it was a secondary prevention project based in the community. The area which constituted the centre of the study is a traditional working-class area in the north-east of England with strong ties and loyalties but a high level of poverty and unemployment.

The hypotheses of the study were stated and concerned the effectiveness of psychological approaches to help with mother's depression, marriage, toddler behaviour and developmental problems, taking the social situation of the families into account. To test the hypotheses a clinical trial was carried out using random allocation to three treatment and to a control group. The treatments were special health visiting, family therapy, and mother and toddler groups. An extensive programme of testing was required to measure outcome, and we described the instruments used and their characteristics together with the construction of a social adversity index. Finally, using the findings at baseline on some of the measures made, a portrait of the social circumstances of the study families is given. Social adversity was much higher in the screen positive than in the screen negative group.

Chapter 6

The Intensive Health Visiting Approach

In this chapter we shall give details of the problems encountered in the 65 families who took part in the intensive health visiting programme and the way in which these were tackled. We also report the evaluation of outcome by the health visitors themselves. To start with, the reader may be interested in why we chose the health visitor for a key role in the project; indeed those readers not familiar with the British system may ask what a health visitor is.

WHAT IS HEALTH VISITING?

In the British health care system, the health visitor has a key role in the primary health care team as a preventive health professional. The profession of health visiting is a branch of nursing, and was a concept originated by Florence Nightingale. One of the strengths of using a specialized health visitor as an intervener in secondary prevention for mental health problems was that they are a familiar figure to all families with young children as they undertake health surveillance, check on immunization and undertake regular health and developmental checks in the preschool years. They are in a prime position, as someone who visits all mothers and children, to offer a non-stigmatizing service from a normative stance. With their intensive training in child development and the management of difficulties in small children, it was a small step to develop more specialist mental health skills and concepts. The fact that it was a familiar figure offering advice meant that the mother could accept day-to-day advice without feeling that she was seeing an "expert". It was hoped that this would raise the mother's confidence in her own handling skills.

The basic tasks of the health visitor role were set out in 1973 by the Council for the Education and Training of Health Visitors (Owen 1977) under five headings:

1. To prevent emotional and mental as well as physical ill health.
2. To undertake early detection of such ill health.
3. To be able to recognize the need and provide or facilitate the appropriate help and support.

4. To provide adequate care either to resolve or to alleviate the difficulty.
5. To aid and inform the client in an effort to enhance the mother's own strengths, trying to accentuate the positives in the situation.

It can be seen clearly that these five areas include, potentially at least, a major role for health visitors in mental health work with children, particularly in work with mothers and toddlers and their emotional and management problems.

The idea of a role for health visitors in this area of work has attracted widespread interest. In a survey of health service support for the under 5s conducted by the National Children's Bureau (Stevenson 1990), a question was included: are health visitors involved in any specially designed programmes concerned with assisting parents in the prevention and management of aspects of children's behaviour perceived by the parents as outside normal limits? In the responses, engagement with families whose children had sleep disturbances was often mentioned. There have also been a number of training initiatives (Hewitt and Crawford 1988; Douglas 1990), consultation programmes (Sanger, Weir and Churchill 1981) and publications (Douglas and Richman 1984). Clinical psychologists and sometimes child psychiatrists have offered training and consultation to health visitors to work with preschool children. To us, all these developments contributed to a powerful case for using health visitors in secondary prevention. If this was so, then the case for including a health visitor programme in our evaluation project was compelling.

The families in the health visitor programme

Returning to our project, about one-third of the children did not have any siblings. Nine mothers were pregnant at the time of the study which underlines the point that these were expanding families. In 11 families, at least the eldest sibling was over 5 years, and there were 17 families with three or more children.

For each mother and toddler, as described above, psychiatric assessment was made at an interview and data review by a child psychiatrist. It was found that 19 mothers showed significant depression; in addition, 6 mothers had significant symptoms but life adversities were so great that these seemed a natural response to events. A further 18 mothers were variously diagnosed as anxiety state, mixed anxiety and depression, premenstrual tension (as main symptom) and other neurotic symptoms. Toddlers were simply diagnosed as having a significant disorder, with no additional diagnostic statement. Table 6.1 shows estimates of the levels of disorder in the mothers and toddlers.

It will be seen that about one-third of both mothers and toddlers showed

Table 6.1   Severity of psychiatric disorder in study sample overall rating

		Severity of disorder		
	None	Minimal	Moderate (primary care level)	Severe (psychiatric referral)
Mother	24	20	17	4
Toddler	23	16	23	3

no disorder. While there was an overlap between mother and toddler problems, it was quite common for there to be difficulties with the toddler but for the mother to show no disorder and vice versa. Attempts were made to get data concerning the father's mental health. In the event the best estimate that could be made was mother's report of his "nerves". Eight fathers were reported as having problems with their nerves; two of them had consulted a psychiatrist.

There was quite a wide range of social class groups, but higher social class was under-represented. This was by design, since we were taking our cue from Brown and Harris' (1978) hypothesis concerning the vulnerability of working-class mothers.

The state of the labour market at the time of the study was appalling: 30% of the breadwinners of these young families had been continuously unemployed for the last year and a further 15% intermittently employed. Among the married couples, 45 marriages were rated generally satisfactory, ten were marked by severe quarrels and discord and four by significant coldness and indifference. There were six single mothers.

Family support was found to be extensive in this closely knit area. Two-thirds of mothers saw a relative several times per week. Whole families often lived within a few streets of each other. Another way of looking at this was to see who the mother turned to with a problem. The fact that only half turned first to their husbands may be an indication of family dysfunction or may support the common belief that working-class family life in north-east England is characterized by a segregation of roles and tasks between the spouses.

The health visitors

The two health visitors in the project had respectively four and seven years' experience; one had an additional seven years as a child psychiatric nurse while the other had run groups for mothers of young children extensively in the community as part of her health visitor role before the onset of the project. In addition, they took on clinic cases from the child and adolescent psychiatry department and had some experience in the adult psychiatry department with depressed women. They took part also in a special training programme with a clinical psychologist. Throughout the project, the health visitors had regular supervision of their work from a member of the child psychiatry clinic team. It is important to stress the extensive experience of and support available to the two health visitors in our project: they were already highly trained before the project started. Extensive and carefully thought out training programmes have been advocated for health visitors wanting to take up behavioural work (eg Douglas 1990). We support the need for this type of well-structured and broad-based training since the task is a sophisticated one and something of a new departure in health visitor training.

The analysis attempted by the therapist, in this case the health visitor herself, is to some extent subjective but we assert that only by an honest appraisal of one's own work can further understanding of its subtleties and complexities be reached. It was important that we employed professional appraisal to complement the more objective appraisal of the main study.

ASSESSMENT

The assessment phase is crucial to any intervention programme. It consists of three main components: establishment of rapport, identification of problem areas and evaluation of the problems.

Establishment of rapport

Initial impressions seemed to be very important. Obviously the approach varied slightly according to responses received but successful interaction seemed to include conveying the following:

1. warmth and friendliness
2. a confident but not coercive approach
3. simple, clear communication
4. enthusiasm and a positive attitude (showing positive interest in the family without prying)
5. politeness and respect.

It was useful to establish an early relationship with the child. Mothers seemed to notice the health visitor's attitude towards the child and his or her reactions. If the child responded well the mother seemed more interested in what was on offer. Finally, the use of first names helped to smooth the way.

Identification of problem areas

Discussion and observation were used. First, it was important to listen to what parents had to say, giving encouragement, asking questions and generally guiding conversation in the right direction. This discussion approach helped to develop an atmosphere where parents were able to confide. Problems would often emerge only gradually as trust was gained over several sessions.

Second, the home is an excellent place to make observations about the family. The experienced health visitor observes such things as the general atmosphere and emotional tone as well as specific observations about family members. Do the children seem happy or sad, anxious or relaxed and are their interactions generally positive or negative? These are useful questions to ask.

Appleton (1990) describes a similar process of problem identification under four headings: an open request for help, parent describes problem without request for help, multi-problem presentation where one or more problems may be amenable to help and health visitor detects problems while the family is unaware of them. These categories were very relevant to the experience in our programme.

Evaluation of the problems

It was important to assess the problem from the mother's point of view. To take an example, a mother might have a child who doesn't sleep at night or spends time in a parent's bed. It was only when this was a problem to the mother and she stated it as such that the health visitor defined it as a problem. Table 6.2 gives the frequency of some of the most common problems. Not only the type of problems that the family had but also the number of problems they were coping with were important: this was extremely variable, as shown in Figure 6.1.

DECISIONS ABOUT INTERVENTION

Developing the response

It will be seen that in our study we found that problems were rarely single or clear cut (when this occurred intervention decisions were easier). More commonly, toddler problems, mother's emotional state, and marital and environmental problems all seemed to be inextricably linked. Cause and effect were blurred. Similarly decisions regarding where, how, when and if to intervene were correspondingly difficult and influenced by a variety of factors. To give an example, a single mother living in a small upstairs flat

Table 6.2 Main problem areas encountered in the families (% of the 55 families engaged in treatment)

	No.	%
Target child		
Disruptive, negativistic behaviour and tempers	23	41
Sleep	23	41
Toilet training	16	29
Feeding	12	22
Overdependency	6	9
Language delay	5	9
Mother		
Low morale and depression	18	32
Premenstrual tension	7	13
Physical illness	7	13
Anxiety	5	9
Tiredness	3	5
Siblings		
Enuresis	4	7
Sleep	3	5
Non-compliance	3	5
Family		
Low income	15	27
Marital problems	11	20
Housing	10	18

is worried about money and feels unable to cope with the constant demands of her active toddler who can't get out to play. She "gives in" to keep him quiet, thus reinforcing his behaviour. Instead of understanding the root of her problem she may feel that she is a failure as a mother and blame herself. She may look to a "short cut" such as rehousing to solve her problems. We had to decide whether to direct our attention towards the housing problem, financial problems, toddler's behaviour or mother's feelings and morale. It was important to decide in advance where the main effort should be made. The following points influenced the decision that was made at this stage.

First, the mother's morale was of paramount importance to the well-being of the whole family. It seemed to be closely associated with her underlying self-esteem.

Second, parental motivation had to be encouraged. This was dependent on a reasonable level of morale and also on the health visitor being able to establish a good relationship. Developing motivation proved one of the most difficult tasks.

Third, parents may see one problem (such as housing) as overriding all others. The worker may lose credibility if she appears to disregard this

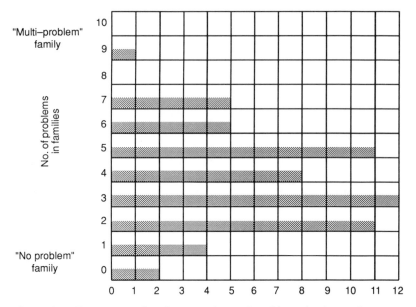

Figure 6.1   Frequency of various numbers of problems in the study group

major concern. Moreover, giving respect to parents' own evaluation of their difficulties and supporting or encouraging them in their efforts to bring about improvements can in itself be therapeutic. To use the housing example, the worker's task may involve liaison with the housing department to obtain full information about housing possibilities in relation to a particular family. This information can then be discussed with the parents and possible courses of action outlined.

Fourth, toddler problems can respond well to simple, properly conducted treatment programmes.

Finally, an improvement in one area can often lead to other improvements. Simply relieving pressure on a family with many problems can help enormously.

Rate of response

Not all the mothers were interested in the help offered by the project; however, most were, and a total of 82% of them engaged in treatment. Of the remainder, 9% were not seen as requiring any help by the health visitor after preliminary assessment, while 10.5% withdrew on their own accord, although the health visitor considered that they may have benefited from help. In two families no contact was ever made and in one family the problems were so severe that social services became involved; it was not felt that further visits were likely to be fruitful (we had an agreement that the project would hand over to statutory services if there was a major issue of child abuse or neglect).

THE RELATIONSHIP

In this section and the next principles will be presented. Specific examples with more detail of the most common problems are given below. The intervention had two components – first, the formation of a relationship, and second, more specific interventions.

As so much of our intervention hinged on the interpersonal relationship with the client, this warrants further analysis. Good relationships tend to make us feel more positive about ourselves, give pleasure, contain trust and honesty, mutual respect and some "give and take". In the professional context, a good relationship is a prerequisite to effective intervention (Goldstein and Simonson 1971). People who are having problems, especially with their children, often blame themselves. Helping parents to feel better about themselves often leads to the acceptance of ideas that would otherwise be blocked.

Some of the components which were considered to enhance relationships are as follows:

1. relating in a personal way, that is to the person behind the problems
2. remembering names and information previously given
3. fulfilling promises and commitments
4. sharing professional knowledge and "working with" parents rather than pretending to have all the answers
5. conveying respect.

Lastly, the importance of non-verbal communication must not be overlooked. Impatience or boredom will be noticed immediately.

TYPES OF SPECIFIC INTERVENTION TECHNIQUES

In our study we used nine specific intervention techniques:

1. raising parents' confidence/self-esteem
2. enhancing the mother–child relationship
3. behaviour modification (used in 32 families)
4. recording (used in 15 families)
5. the diary (used in 14 families)
6. scheduled specific activity (used in 13 families)
7. reinforcement by health visitor (used very generally, but specifically with 19 families)

8. referral (used in 21 families)
9. counselling (used in 50 families).

We shall now describe these in more detail.

Raising parents' confidence/self-esteem

This was an integral part of our intervention. Some techniques that were involved were looking for and commenting on positives, seeking opinions and ideas from the parents, working together with parents on a particular problem, recognizing achievements, praising "here and now" handling where appropriate, for example "I like the way you did that".

Enhancing the mother–child relationship

This is a question of encouraging mother's pleasure or pride in her child. A child who is developing well and liked by others is a compliment to the mother. Mothers who are having problems are sensitive to criticism – they often feel other children behave better; friends and relatives may criticize and this can lead to a negative attitude towards the child. We can help by emphasizing the child's positive qualities. If the mother is encouraged to look for these herself, perhaps by keeping a record of the child's behaviour, it is more effective.

Sometimes a specific play period, for special one-to-one interaction each day may help. The promotion of positive play seemed particularly useful to break into a pattern of toddler negative behaviour. This could be supplemented by discovering, with mother, things she enjoys with the child; not dismissing but rather exploring feelings of anger towards the child, asking appropriate questions, getting her to talk about her feelings and helping her to understand how the child may be feeling by putting herself in his place. These interventions were possible if the relationship was good.

Behaviour modification

This was employed in various forms with variable success. The type of problem and parental motivation were key factors. Problems which responded well were concerned with sleep and toilet training, perhaps because it was easy to identify the appropriate behaviour and reward it. General behaviour problems, such as non-compliance or excessive attention-seeking, responded badly to a formal programme due mainly to lack of parental motivation and the difficulty in isolating behaviours to be rewarded. With experience it was realized that with this type of problem it is vital to get the parents to talk about their own ideas on handling and get them to actually discover for themselves the appropriate responses, by guiding and nudging in the right direction. If we could get them to do any recording of behaviour so much the better, but this was difficult to achieve. An alternative was to make very frequent visits, sometimes daily so that behaviour changes could be noted while still fresh in mother's mind and her effort reinforced. The chapter in McAuley and McAuley (1977) on "Simple contingency management" was an excellent guide.

Recording

This was used to chart a child's behaviour, to give insight into the causative factors and to find the appropriate form of management. In this way we were able to see what exactly precipitated the child's behaviour and we often learned the reason why some incidents occurred. Recording also gave us a method of finding the appropriate form of management: the mother was able to find, sometimes by trial and error, what worked best with her child.

The diary

This is a technique used where the mother is feeling either despondent or anxious. Keeping a diary allows the mother to understand her own feelings and often changes her negative way of thinking.

Scheduled specific activity

This means structured time spent with the child, either playing or reading or even just talking with each other. This is done in an effort to encourage interaction and stimulation; it proved very useful for behaviour problems including tempers.

Reinforcement by health visitor

This is done in a positive way to enhance the mother's ability and encourage her efforts. If a mother should be having difficulty in any of the regimes it was important to stress the positives; for example, if she had a child who wasn't sleeping we would concentrate on one day or one episode where she had been successful, even if for the rest of the week she had been unsuccessful.

Referral

This was done mainly to housing departments or to nurseries after consultation with the family's regular health visitor. Any other referral was done through the family health visitor as the primary worker; these included referrals to social services or back to the family's general practitioner.

Counselling

This we found was a rather ambiguous term but could be summed up as careful listening to the mother, acting as a mirror or sounding board for the mother to clarify her own situation and giving advice or guidance where appropriate. In idealistic terms, it was designed to show the mother her own worth and the importance of her role as a mother and member of the community.

Conclusion

In this secondary preventive project the health visitor was ideally placed to provide help needed for these families in need. More complex and severe psychosocial or development problems that may be encountered by the health visitor in her work will still require appropriate assessment and referral. Throughout this project, the health visitors had ready access to consultation and back up support from a department of child and adolescent psychiatry.

DESCRIPTION OF INDIVIDUAL INTERVENTIONS

In this section some case reports are given to illustrate in more detail the management of sleep and toilet training problems, temper tantrums, and low morale in the mother and family, and social adversity.

Although intensive training in the various methods of treatment was given and rules for the management for each particular problem were developed, these rules in every case were tailored to the needs and particular situation of each mother and child. This approach was adopted to fit in with the general philosophy, that at all times one should attempt to raise the self-esteem of the mother and her own confidence in her handling skills. It is important for the health visitor to avoid being seen as "an expert" but rather as a facilitator or guide who works out a regime or pattern of management with the mother and helps her to undertake it. Greatest success was where, after the resolution of the problem, the mother could say that she had eradicated it herself with some help from the health visitor.

Sleep

Sleep was one of the most common of the problems found in the toddlers. It was essential at the outset to have a clear understanding of the context, including an estimate of the reinforcers that were maintaining the child's deviant behaviour. There were often reasons in the wider family for the difficulty, for example the child could be being used to act as a barrier in the marital bed. Before embarking on any kind of treatment regime but after obtaining a full understanding of the difficulty and how the parents perceived it, a description of what measures could be employed was given to the family. They were left to think over whether or not they felt they wanted to continue or indeed were able to continue. The family were always told that especially with a sleep problem there was usually a marked deterioration before any improvement was obtained. This gave the family insight and sometimes strength to carry on. The family were usually also told that monitoring would take place, daily if possible. After getting some idea of what the problem involved, the family were then asked to "think like the child"; to try to understand the child's motives and exactly why certain things were happening. Sometimes this involved a recording of how the parents handled each aspect.

The family were asked to find what would be a suitable bedtime for the child; this had to be reasonable for both the child and the family. A winding down routine was then suggested, that is doing the same thing each night prior to bedtime, for example, a bath, a hot drink and a story, so that the child knew that the time was getting near to go to bed. Inappropriate stimulation of the child was avoided. The child was then put to bed with much encouragement and kisses, etc. If the child got up from bed and came into the parents' room he was quietly taken back without any reinforcement at all. Often when children wake up and come downstairs they are cajoled back to bed, given biscuits or a drink, or allowed to watch TV. The family were encouraged to take the child directly back to bed, sometimes without even a look. This had to be done up to a dozen times on the first night. Should the child require comforting this was done in the child's bedroom or in the child's bed. If the child had stayed in his bed through the night he was congratulated and sometimes given a reward. Usually the pattern of sleep deteriorated over the few days from the start of treatment: the family were asked to record this if possible so that they could mark the improvement when it occurred. Daily monitoring at this stage was very important both to reassure the family and to encourage their efforts.

Case example: Johnson family

Sam had never slept in his own bed during his 2½ years. Mrs Johnson was now four months pregnant and was eager that a bedtime be established. The sleep regime was outlined and the parents were left to consider the possibilities. At the next visit both parents had agreed to undertake the regime. For the first two or three nights the situation was almost intolerable with the child getting out of bed up to 20 times on the second night of treatment. This gradually improved until by the end of a fortnight, he was going to bed without any difficulty and sleeping through the night. This progress is shown in Figure 6.2. The family were congratulated on their efforts. There was some regression after the birth of the new baby and again the regime was implemented. However, the problem took less time to respond on this occasion and the child continued to sleep through the night.

Toilet training

Again a full clear picture of the problem was obtained with an analysis of reinforcers; the most appropriate method of handling was then arranged for the family. With this kind of problem a means of positive reinforcement was used, for example if the child should use the potty or the lavatory a reward was given immediately. Any failure to use the potty or lavatory was ignored. The reward system was usually by means of a star chart which at this age could be adapted so that the child herself could stick a picture into her book. This is an adaptation of the standard star chart which is particularly successful with younger children; in this a picture is given to the family, usually either a farmyard scene or a country scene. Along with this various smaller pictures of animals are given. Each time the child uses the potty she is allowed to stick a small picture on the bigger picture. It was essential that the child and family understand that this chart be kept

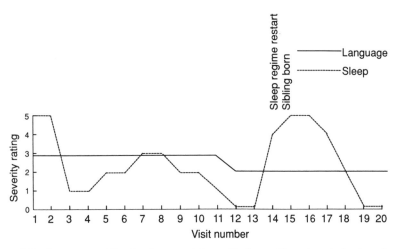

Figure 6.2   Progress of Sam's sleep problem. Each problem is rated at each visit on a five point scale of severity (5 is most severe and 0 is no detectable problem)

for one purpose only and not for general 'good behaviour'. It was quite useful to hang the picture actually in the lavatory to emphasize this point so that the child could connect the two. Again, very frequent monitoring was necessary to encourage and to reassure the family.

Case example: Anderson family

The Anderson family consisted of mother (36 years), father (37 years), Sharon (12 years) and Angela ($2\frac{1}{2}$ years). Father worked as a groundsman at the local race-course. He was not seen by the health visitor. Mother appeared quiet, conscientious and caring. The home (modernized terraced accommodation) was very well-ordered. The children appeared happy, intelligent and friendly. The main problems to emerge concerned Angela. She wouldn't settle properly at night, crying to come downstairs after her story. Mother usually gave in. The second, more pressing, problem concerned toilet training. She would use the toilet to pass urine but not to defecate; instead she went into the corner of the room and passed a motion into her pants. Mother admitted to scolding her and getting angry.

The mother was well-motivated and intelligent and very willing to listen to advice and suggestions. The bedtime problem responded quickly to a more consistent routine of bath, supper and story and a firmer attitude by mother. Angela was not allowed to come downstairs again and mother stayed with her in the bedroom for a while until she fell asleep. The toilet-training problem would have been more difficult but for several factors which seemed conducive to success: mother's high motivation and very loving relationship with Angela, Angela's intelligence, and the health visitor's relationship with Angela encouraged by play activities during the sessions. It was decided to use a star chart as a method of rewarding Angela for defecating into the toilet. Because of the groundwork in establishing an early relationship the health visitor was able to gain Angela's attention and interest. A detailed explanation was given to mother. During the first week she achieved success on two occasions and had two "accidents" in her pants. It was important for the health visitor (and mother) to give ample praise for these "stars" thus motivating Angela even more. The following week she was so enthusiastic that she earned 18 stars and had no soiled pants! Mother was advised that the novelty might wear off and encouraged to reinforce progress with an extra "treat" (eg outing or gift) at the weekends. After four weeks progress was being maintained. Mother was advised to continue with the chart, gradually transferring emphasis to social reinforcement but still allowing Angela to stick stars in if she wanted to. The graph in Figure 6.3 charts progress. It must be emphasized that this was an unusually straightforward and successful outcome but when

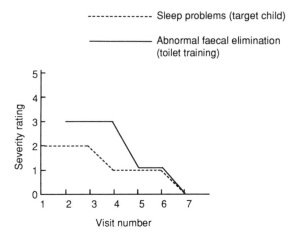

Figure 6.3   Progress of Angela's soiling problem. Each problem is rated at each visit on a five point scale of severity (5 is most severe and 0 is no detectable problem)

motivation is good and the problems are fairly clear-cut the use of this form of behaviour modification is very effective.

Temper tantrums

The concepts of positive reinforcement and positive mother–child interaction were both very important here. The problem was tackled at several levels. First, any negative behaviour, for example the temper tantrums, was ignored. In the case of temper tantrums this was extremely difficult as often the $2\frac{1}{2}$ year old can become quite violent and begin to actually destroy a room.

First, it was important to show the mother how to try to divert the child's attention. Usually she was encouraged to hold the child at the peak of the temper tantrum and point out things in the room or suggest different activities for the child, trying to ignore the behaviour. It was important to tell the mothers that at this age any attention is reinforcing and that there are problems if the child can get what he wants from the mother by being "naughty" more easily than he can by being "good".

Second, the mother was encouraged to recognize good behaviour and shown that sometimes when a child was being good, for example drawing in a book or looking at a book and being quiet, this behaviour could easily be ignored but if a child suddenly throws a temper tantrum he has his mother's attention completely. The mother was encouraged to congratulate the child on good behaviour and to actually interact with the child at these times.

Third, a treatment for the temper tantrums that was sometimes used was a very modified form of "time out". The child was removed from the room so that the behaviour could be ignored completely. It was stressed to the mother that this should be for no longer than about three minutes and that when the child was brought back into the room he was cuddled and reassured. This was really used only for the more extreme types of temper tantrums. Recording was another very useful technique with temper tantrums. By recording the child's good and bad behaviour the mother could see what preceded this behaviour and what causative factors there were. She was also made aware of good behaviour and how she could reward it.

Case example: Lennon family

Jim (aged $2\frac{3}{4}$) would have quite severe temper tantrums and would at these times completely gain the attention of his mother and father; usually this culminated in raised voices or a slap. Mr and Mrs Lennon were asked to record all Jim's behaviour – the good and the bad – and they could very quickly see that Jim would resort to bad behaviour if he was being ignored (see Figure 6.4). They could also see that a slap or raised voices didn't really work with him. It was also shown by the recording charts that Jim responded very well both to praise for his good behaviour and to interaction with his parents. Because Jim's temper tantrums were so severe at times a very modified form of "time out" was used. His mother would go into the kitchen and leave him in the living room and then come out after a few seconds. Usually Jim had calmed by this time. The family also

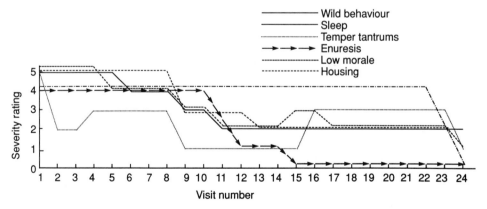

Figure 6.4   Progress of Jim's behaviour problems. Each problem is rated at each visit on a five point scale of severity (5 is most severe and 0 is no detectable problem)

made it a habit to bribe Jim into good behaviour. This was discouraged in favour of giving a reward for his good behaviour when the behaviour occurred. The reward could be a cuddle or conversation or some play with his parents. Jim responded slowly but very well and by the end of a few months was much calmer. The confidence of his mother was increased in that even when Jim had the temper tantrum she felt confident enough to control it and didn't feel the guilt and worry that she had felt in the past.

Low morale in the mother and family

This was a very common problem and ranged from a feeling of mild despondency in some mothers to quite severe depression in others. A technique that was used widely in this problem was that of the diary. The mother was asked to keep a day-to-day diary of her feelings and thoughts. She was asked to chart her anxieties: this was used in an effort both to clarify her feelings and to give her insight. She was encouraged to use the diary as a kind of sounding board or mirror where she would write down her feelings and then look back on them and try to make sense of what she was feeling or to use them in a more positive way. Her attention could be focused by asking her to make ratings of various activities during the day. For this, the method of Beck et al (1979) was used. This consists of two ratings: mastery and pleasure which record respectively how well the task was done and how much enjoyment the mother got out of it. In this way the mother could be shown in discussions that there were various parts of her life where she was competent and got pleasure out of her activities.

Case example: Green family

Jack and Julie Green had one child, Tom, aged $2\frac{1}{2}$. On the first visit to Julie she was very unhappy, crying for most of the time and feeling generally despondent about life. After a long counselling session Julie was left with the task of writing down exactly what she was worried and unhappy about and what she had to be glad about. The following day a list of both things was discussed and it was possible to use these quite well in showing Julie, without dismissing her feelings, that although there were bad points in her life there were also very good and satisfactory ones. Julie used the diary very well to chart her innermost feelings and to work out some of the confusion she felt about her life. She used the diaries almost religiously, keeping the entries up to date and over the days and weeks a marked improvement could be seen (see Figure 6.5). This type of technique again requires intensive monitoring to reassure the mother and to go back over the diaries with her and try to interpret them.

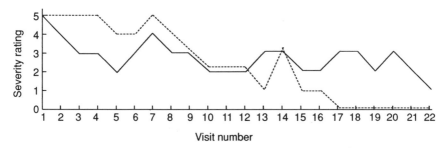

Figure 6.5   Progress of Julie's low morale. Each problem is rated at each visit on a five point scale of severity (5 is most severe and 0 is no detectable problem)

Social adversity

The effects of social adversity may eat into family morale – unemployment and poverty being common examples. The therapeutic effects of improvement in life opportunities often assisted the health visitor.

Case example: Smith family

The Smith family consisted of mother (24 years), father (24 years), David (2 years 11 months) and Amanda (1 year). The problems which gradually emerged were the parents' low morale connected with Mr Smith's long-term unemployment, the accompanying financial problems and the pressures from caring for two small children. Father, a skilled fitter, had been made redundant two and a half years previously and searched daily for work. The family had been buying their own home but the redundancy had forced them to move into a council house.

The other problem concerned David's behaviour: he was described as awkward, disobedient and defiant. Constructive work with the family was difficult. A total of nine, approximately fortnightly visits (one to one and a half hours) were made. After the fifth visit the health visitor recorded: "This couple strike me as being depressed due to long-term unemployment. They are both very caring, conscientious and determined to raise their children properly. The children are their main focus and receive plenty of attention, care and discipline. The component I observe to be lacking in all interactions, however, is *joy* or *fun*. Their prime concern is that David should be well-behaved and he is constantly cautioned/corrected even when all he obviously wants is a bit of fun or rough and tumble. The lightheartedness has gone from this family." Initially attempts were made to get mother to record some of David's behaviour but this was unsuccessful. She said that she kept forgetting and wasn't sure how to put it down on paper. This was possibly because it had been difficult to find a focus for observations or because of the high frequency of commands and corrections given to David throughout the day. (Recording behaviour should be kept very simple and easy for parents to understand: the objectives are to encourage observation and an understanding of precipitators and reinforcers of behaviour for use in discussion.) Later it was felt that focusing on the parents' own feelings, acknowledging the stresses of their situation and looking for ways of relieving these, such as an occasional night out together, was a more satisfactory approach which also had the effect of shifting the emphasis from David's behaviour. Discussions about handling techniques remained a feature of the visits but the parents' self-esteem was given major consideration in that it was important to highlight and work on their assets and achievements with the children. This was combined with actual demonstrations of a more playful attitude towards the children and father certainly appeared to be adopting this attitude more with David. Mother

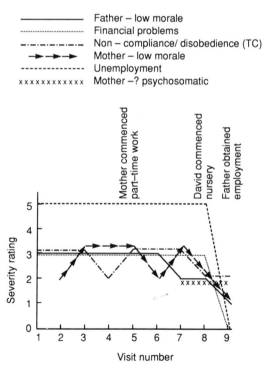

Figure 6.6   Progress of Smith family. Each problem is rated at each visit on a five
point scale of severity (5 is most severe and 0 is no detectable problem)

voiced some understanding of the concept of "nagging" and how this could have the effect of encouraging disobedience in David. She also discovered praising him was helpful: "it works to tell him he's a good boy". It will be noted from Figure 6.6 that definite improvements were observed during the concluding visits. Changes in family circumstances, with mother finding part-time work, David commencing nursery and father obtaining permanent employment, seem to have been important in the improvements in relationships.

SUMMARY

This chapter has given the approach and some illustrations of the techniques used in the special health visiting approach. These needed adaption to the individual circumstances of each family. The final case illustrates the important fact that changes in family circumstances in these families can be as effective as professional interventions in improving outcome. It may be that a combination of improved economic circumstances and professional support could be a powerful combination in improving parent–child relationships.

Chapter 7

Family Therapy in the Community

Of the three approaches to intervention used in the study, the family therapy was the one that stood out as being an innovation in the secondary preventive field. Our thinking started as we considered the importance of the family life cycle. The preschool phase seemed to us to be one of stress and change (see Chapter 1) yet one where, since the family was of comparatively recent origin, maladaptive transactional patterns might yet be open to change. The rationale seems quite sensible, yet a lot of thought was needed in fitting what started as a clinic-based set of techniques to a secondary preventive frame.

THE FAMILY AS A PROBLEM-SOLVING SYSTEM

There is a body of sociological theory which has sought to conceptualize the family as a problem-solving unit and a problem-solving framework has proved very useful in developing some therapy procedures (eg Epstein and Bishop 1981). First, however, there are a number of conceptual issues and findings that merit discussion.

There is general agreement that the process of problem-solving is complex. Much of the understanding of its various phases has come from small group research where a group of strangers meet for a circumscribed problem-solving task. Brim (1962), for example, identified the following stages: problem recognition, information collection, idea generation, decision implementation and finally evaluation. Similar categories have been used in therapy (Epstein and Bishop 1981). In moving from these laboratory categories to explore the nature of family problem-solving, one is moving into largely uncharted waters. However, an attempt to delineate the possible contrasts may help throw light on the special nature of family problem-solving.

First, there is the matter of problem recognition. Family life occurs in a rhythm of transactions which go largely unremarked and unreflected upon by family members. In order to become a problem, some issue has to "stick out" from the rest of experience and become an object of reflection and concern. We know very little systematically about how this happens in families. Westley and Epstein (1969), in an interview study of the families of college students, found that well-functioning families were better at defining problems. The families of emotionally troubled students were more likely to be living with unresolved problems which they attempted to cope with by repression and denial. The denial of the better-functioning families to define problems was associated with generally better communication, particularly of feelings. Two sorts of poor communication were identified: "masked" communication where the content of the communication was unclear, and "indirect" communication where the communication was directed to the wrong person. Families who showed poor problem-solving capacity tended to accumulate more and more secondary problems until in some cases they seemed overwhelmed by them.

Weick (1971) suggests several distinctions between laboratory problem-solving groups and the family as a problem-solving system. While put forward as a suggestion rather than the object of empirical observation at this stage, many of these distinctions make intuitive sense and clarify what may be important in family problem-solving transactions. With reference to how family problems are posed, Weick suggests that there are not the firm boundaries between one problem and another in the way that these are in more formal settings. Thus a problem may gather accretions of other and often past unresolved problems. This "problem hitch-hiking" is familiar to the family therapist and particularly likely to occur with emotionally charged problems: "She throws it all in your face". "He rakes up the whole past". It is a common experience in initial family interviews to be met with a conglomerate of family problems that have to be disentangled and clarified before any solution can become even a possibility. This is particularly the case if there is a habitual pattern of masked or indirect communication.

However good the family communication, family problems are not likely to be identified round a table in a balanced and rational atmosphere (except possibly in a family therapy session). As the family encounters problems it is simultaneously engaged in numerous other activities. While this may hamper the efficiency of problem identification and information collection, it may have advantages. Thus a problem may be first identified when chance circumstances throw a long-term predicament into sharp relief or provide an unexpected solution to an only half-acknowledged problem.

Another difference between problem identification in the family and the formal group is what Weick calls the "developmental confound" summed up by the common phrase "he'll grow out of it, it's just a phase". The family's capacity to take this course is no doubt highly adaptive on many occasions; the therapist tends to hear of the cases where such a course was a mistake.

Moving on to problem-solving patterns, the family again has many unique characteristics. The fact that the family has many other functions such as the maintenance of a power and affectional structure, the need to maintain resources such as shelter and nutrients, status and child socialization will radically affect its problem-solving. However, particularly in well-functioning families, as in other stable institutions, the resulting ready-made structure should assist problem-solving (Aldous 1978). It is likely that the family problem-solving group is less likely to seek novel solutions to problems and take risks. The family is an essentially conservative institution (Minuchin 1974). At a more superficial level, the fact that the family is solving problems in the context of numerous other activities may be an advantage, particularly where there are highly charged problems. In the ongoing stream of family life, opportunities may arise to tackle problems during some distracting activity or to engineer a solution to an otherwise intractable problem.

An unresolved problem may lie dormant for years to be re-evoked by new factors at a later stage, or short-term resolution of the problem may contribute to a new set of problems at a later stage. Good examples of these processes can be found in Lieberman's (1979) book on intergenerational family therapy.

These are some of the considerations that guided the development of our therapy programme. To summarize, we noted that families may not be very good at identifying their problems, especially major ones; they may be helped by objective delineation and clarification of the problems; problem solution is intricately bound up with other aspects of the family function; families may have difficulty deciding what is a problem requiring action rather than a "passing phase".

There were 59 families who took part in the family therapy programme; they shared the social disadvantages of the rest of the study population. Thus 59% of mothers and 66% of toddlers in the family therapy group were estimated to have a psychiatric disorder of at least minimal severity; 10% of the families had single parents; 31% of principal breadwinners in the families had non-manual and 69% manual occupations; 31% of the group had been unemployed for more than one year. The level of extended family support was high, with 66% of the sample seeing members of their extended family several times per week.

THE THERAPY REGIME

Choice of therapy model

The approach adopted was the system-based problem-solving McMaster model (Epstein and Bishop 1981; Goodyer et al 1982). This is based on an extended research programme that included not only research into ordinary families and, in particular, family problem-solving, but also the development of a procedure for use in clinical work (Westley and Epstein 1969). This was followed by a number of clinical studies (Epstein, Sigal and Rakoff 1962; Guttman et al 1971) which laid the groundwork for the development of a Family Categories Schema (Epstein, Sigal and Rakoff 1962). The next major advance was the McMaster Family Therapy Outcome Study. The study involved a total of 80 therapists ranging in expertise from trainees in family therapy to experienced family therapists. Participating in the study were 279 families, the criterion for inclusion being that a child between the ages of 6 and 16 had been identified by the family as the problem. This study was specifically designed to provide information concerning the variables that relate to successful and unsuccessful treatment outcomes. A large sample size and a broad range of outcome measures were chosen in order to make a contribution beyond that of earlier studies.

Families were followed up at six months and reassessed on all the pre-treatment prediction variables plus a client satisfaction questionnaire designed for the project. At the closure of treatment most (76%) families had demonstrated moderate to great improvement and treatment gains were maintained at six months follow up. An important finding was that a deterioration effect occurred in 3% of the families. The results of this project have been reported extensively in the literature (Sigal, Rakoff and Epstein 1967; Rakoff, Sigal and Epstein 1975; Santa Barbara et al 1977; 1978; Woodward et al 1978).

The conclusions of this study led to further discussion among the McMaster Group who reformulated their ideas concerning family function in order to try and satisfy the needs of practising clinicians and provide a model of family function that lent itself to research. This resulted in the development of the model used in our study and its treatment approach, the Problem-Centred Systems Therapy of the Family (Epstein and Bishop 1981).

The model consists of six dimensions of family function and while it does not claim to encompass all aspects of family life or consider itself 'the theory of family function', the McMaster Group thought that they had identified the essential areas that are necessary to understand the way in which a family works. The dimensions are problem-solving, communication, roles, affective responsiveness, affective involvement and behaviour control. Brief definitions of the dimensions follow.

Problem-solving

Problem-solving is a family's ability to resolve problems to a level that maintains effective family functioning. A family problem is seen as an issue that threatens the integrity and functional capacity of the family. Problems are divided into instrumental and affective types: these refer to the behavioural problems of everyday life and problems related to feelings respectively.

Communication

Communication is how families exchange information: this focuses on verbal exchange. Non-verbal aspects of communication can be important but are excluded because of their potential for misinterpretation and the methodological difficulties of collecting and measuring such information. Communication is also divided into instrumental and affective types and is assessed along two vectors: direct versus indirect; clear versus masked. With these distinctions, there are four styles of communication: clear and direct; masked and direct; clear and indirect; masked and indirect.

Roles

Roles are recurrent patterns of behaviour by which individuals fulfil family functions. Assessment of this dimension involves a detailed inquiry into seven areas: provision of resources, nurture and support in the family, adult sexual gratification, personal and life skills development, systems maintenance and management, and allocation and accountability of role behaviours.

Affective responsiveness

This refers to the experiencing of feelings by each family member. It is different from affective communication, which refers to how family members convey their emotions to each other. The focus of interest is in each individual family member's ability to respond to a range of stimuli with an appropriate quantity and quality of feelings. Can the individual experience the full range of emotions and does he or she experience them with appropriate intensity? The feelings assessed are both welfare feelings, such as affection and happiness, and emergency feelings, such as anger and sadness.

Affective involvement

This is the degree to which the family, as a whole, shows interest in and values the activities and interests of individual family members. The focus is on how much, and in what way, family members show an interest and invest themselves in each other. This is assessed along a continuum ranging from over-involvement to absence of involvement.

Behaviour control

This is the pattern that the family adopts for handling behaviour in physically dangerous situations, situations involving socializing behaviour, both inside and outside the family and in situations involving the meeting and expressing of psychobiological needs and drive. Families develop their own standards of acceptable behaviour. The nature of these standards and the amount of latitude allowed for acceptable behaviour determine the four styles of behaviour control: rigid, flexible, laissez-faire and chaotic.

Approaches to assessment

Each of these six dimensions and their respective component parts have been defined to allow the development of instruments capable of assessing family function. These include the Family Assessment Device, a self-report questionnaire for family members, and a Family Clinical Rating Scale, completed by the therapists. In the present study, a much simplified clinical rating scale was used (Nicol, Koziarski and Hodgson 1986).

The McMaster approach was adopted for five reasons.

1. The model is based on work both from clinic attenders and research with non-clinic families (Westley and Epstein 1969), thus it was well adapted to a non-clinic group.
2. It provides estimates of the adaptive function of families, not just dysfunction.
3. The therapy is carried out according to a clear set of principles.
4. It takes as its starting-point the definition of family problems; these could be defined phenomenologically and progress could be measured in terms of improved family solutions to these unique problems.
5. Since it is based on clear, explicit principles, the model is comparatively easy to teach.

Geneograms

As well as offering an essential framework to enable current understanding of the family, a systems approach has a historical dimension. Lieberman (1979) has led the way in developing a technique to understand how the systems of transactions, emotional bonds and relationships develop through time, in particular across the generations. In the context of a whole family interview, and with the collaboration of the whole family, a diagram is drawn which charts the members of the extended family over at least three generations, together with the main events in the development of the family. The inquiry should be structured and the completion of the diagram detailed: the more accurately the events of the past can be reconstructed, the more relevant affect-laden material can be brought into therapy in a manageable and useful way.

Geneograms are particularly helpful with single parents, as they help to bring to life adult relationships in this situation. They are helpful in families burdened by dysfunctional secrets and family myths. They also help where there are a complex of tangled relationships to elucidate, for example where the spouses have had previous marriages and there are stepchildren.

With practice, both the McMaster approach and geneograms offer a framework for the understanding of the family which is clarifying for both the therapist and the family.

The therapists

The therapy was carried out by two social workers. Both were graduates and had a certificate of social work. They had, respectively, seven and four years' fieldwork experience in local authority social services departments.

Training programme

To become proficient in family therapy, both therapists went into full-time training in a child psychiatry department. The programme of training was specially tailored for the project and consisted of taking on individual clinic cases, audio- and videotape as well as live supervision, a programme of reading and workshops, the attending of local and national conferences and of a sensitivity group. Both during the course of training and in the project itself, there was regular supervision and discussion. The intensive training phase took about six months. We can now turn to the experiences in the project itself.

SETTING THE SCENE

Pre-visits: convening the family

We quickly found that, despite the introduction of the project and its aims by the research staff, pre-visits were essential. Inattention to detail at this stage was shown to be catastrophic to subsequent work. The pre-visit was made to any family member who was prepared to see us and who was available. In practice, this was usually the mother. Appointments were made by letter, phone call or by simply turning up on the doorstep. The meeting place was, without exception, the family home. There were a number of reasons why the pre-visits were so essential.

Informed consent

Even though the total project had been explained, there were a few families who had had second thoughts and wished to rediscuss their involvement.

Beginning engagement

To this end, even at the pre-visit stage, the therapist was careful to interact with all those present and to begin to make a relationship, for example to play with the toddler, to make acknowledgement if there was a new baby or to converse with older children.

Who is in the family? Was the non-living-in partner a stable enough entity to be considered part of the family? Does one include the grandmother who gives daily or more frequent support? This was a common feature of the local, somewhat matriarchal culture. What about the father who, ostensibly divorced, visits the home frequently? In general we adopted the guideline of who actually lived in the house as the basis for inclusion; however, there were many cases where operational decisions had to be made.

Involving all family members

On some occasions, it was necessary to ask the mother to speak to her husband about the proposal and gain his consent. In some cases, the wife expressed reluctance to approach her husband, or, when she did so, she returned with a refusal. Under these circumstances, the therapist would try to meet the husband and elucidate what was being offered. We recognized that in dysfunctional families communication can be distorted, including messages from the therapist. There were also reality problems in this time of high unemployment, since many of the fathers were working abroad, in other parts of Britain or on the North Sea oil rigs.

Setting up the first family interview

Even at the pre-visit stage, the therapists were able to recognize some helpful reactions. The fact that the therapist asked to see the family as a family seemed enough in itself, in some cases, to enhance family identity. In particular, the idea that family members affect one another seemed new. The expectation of the family sessions often aroused considerable curiosity.

Timing of meetings

While families may be 24-hour, 7-days-a-week institutions, when they are able and prepared to meet as a family may depend on a number of factors. One rather obvious example are families where one or more members may work away for prolonged periods of time. In other cases objective closeness did exist but there were other problems.

Case example: Yeats family

Mr and Mrs Yeats ran a business and lived on the premises. The therapist discovered that although interested in being involved, the couple seldom interacted meaningfully because one or other of them was involved in the business. While there were reality problems, the work situation did also seem to be an effective distance regulator of the couple, who met only by organizing foreign holidays that they could ill afford. One outcome of the intervention was that the therapist brought the couple together, if only for limited periods for the family sessions. This modest goal took a lot of patience and willingness to negotiate on the therapist's part. A path had to be found between being too accommodating for the sake of co-operation and too demanding of rapid change which would have been frightening and unasked for by the family.

Not surprisingly, some families wanted practical help, such as the arranging of a move of house or a nursery place for the toddler. We tried to side-step such requests in the first instance until an assessment had been carried out. However, as social workers with families who had major reality problems, the therapists felt that it was part of their role to provide such support where indicated.

THE CONJOINT FAMILY MEETINGS

The fact that meetings were invariably held in the family homes carried special difficulties, in addition to the fact that the therapist was in a sense a self-invited guest. However, in order to function effectively the therapist had to generate a formality about the proceedings and impose structure in a low-key but authoritative way. For example the television had to be switched off, the furniture arranged appropriately (rather than all facing the television), and the children had to be properly settled, so that their attention could be engaged.

Families were often apprehensive about the process of family interviews and in some families the idea of sitting down and talking was quite unfamiliar. Sometimes background noise such as television had to be eliminated to allow communication to take place.

Sometimes, especially with single-parent families, a geneogram was a useful way of engaging and assessing the families.

Case example: Allan family

Mrs Allan was separated from her husband and lived alone with her son (aged 2). Her parents were very supportive and lived locally. She did not feel they should be included in the family assessment, however, and defined her family as herself and her son. Mrs Allan was only recently separated, rather fragile and lacking in confidence in her new single-parent status. By drawing up a geneogram we were able to discuss sensitive areas like her relationship with her ex-husband which might otherwise have been emotionally difficult. The geneogram also allowed her to talk about her feelings for members of her family of origin and enabled her to see them as potentially supportive. After doing the geneogram Mrs Allan wrote to her brother in London, with whom she hadn't had any contact since her marriage broke up. In this way she was able to move towards revitalizing older supportive networks.

THE FAMILY ASSESSMENT: PROCEDURE

A family assessment was completed by 46 of the 57 families. Of the remainder only one family was prepared to take part but it was never convenient, four families refused and a further six withdrew during assessment. These 11 families showed no consistent characteristics which marked them out from the 46 families which took part. We shall now describe the assessment phase for these 46 families.

Orientation

This is where the therapist fully explains the therapy procedure to all family members and answers any questions. This had to be carried out fully, despite the fact that information on the procedure had already been given at pre-visit. This was to set the scene and also to include all family members equally. There was usually an opportunity, early on, to establish expectations and if necessary ground rules about listening and giving others an opportunity to talk.

Within our approach, the importance of individual members understanding what is to happen is of paramount significance. One cannot assume, irrespective of certain factors, for example keenness to take part or compliance, that either information was being understood or being circulated in the family. The other important effect of good orientation was the respect it showed for each family member.

Problem identification

The pattern of problem identification was much influenced by the fact that the families had been identified by screen rather than through self-referral to a service. Some families did not see themselves as having any problems, despite the fact that they had been identified as at risk in the screen questionnaires. For example, the parents of one non-sleeping child actually enjoyed his company in the evenings. Having checked that this permissiveness did not have less desired side-effects the therapist agreed there was no problem. Other families complained of the children's sleep problems or of tempers or toilet-training difficulties. Apart from this, unemployment, money worries or difficulties with the housing department over accommodation were common. In many families, problems that had been denied for long periods of time were brought into focus during family assessment. This problem denial is common with dysfunctional families.

It became clear that it was especially important to establish the type of problem solution patterns that the family had used. This was because as relatively competent families, these solutions had often been successful. Such exploration could, therefore, throw light on family strengths. In other cases less adaptive problem solutions, such as denial, had been used. The family assessment meant that such issues could be looked at afresh. As might be expected, problems rather commonly came to light during the systematic assessment rather than in the problem identification phase.

The most frequently encountered problems were marital problems. Next most common were childhood behaviour problems such as sleep and toilet-training difficulties. All these could be seen as developmental problems but with the potential to set up long-standing vicious cycles of difficulties. Unemployment was commonly a problem reflecting the lamentable economic condition of the local area.

We also noted the family member who seemed to 'own' the problems. This is not equivalent to scapegoating since it does not necessarily mean that the individual is blamed but it is interesting that the toddler was most often seen as 'a problem'. Next come 'real' social problems and marriage and after this problems with the parents.

Systematic assessment

A full family assessment was then carried out where possible. This consisted of more direct exploration of areas of family function but with continued attention to the need to stimulate and reinforce family interaction and provide clarifying feedback. Assessment was done on 46 of the 57 cases. The results were analysed and will be reported separately (Nicol, Koziarski and Hodgson, unpublished). By the time the assessment was complete, the therapist and family had spent several hours together. Thus a relationship had formed which we called the therapist–family system. The next stage was to look at treatment options.

Table 7.1   Options chosen by the 46 families who completed the assessment

Families chose	No.	%
Not to proceed to negotiation stage	7	17
No change	10	24
To work on problems	10	24
To work with the therapist	19	35

Selection of options

The main options that were offered in the study were as follows:

1. *No change*   if there are problems, perhaps the family would prefer to leave them alone, and hope that they will get better by themselves.
2. *Self change*   the family say they will work on the problem by themselves.
3. *Treatment*   the family and therapist will work together on the problems.
4. *Referral to another agency*   conclusion that the family could be better helped elsewhere.

The choices made by the families are listed in Table 7.1. It should be emphasized that the therapist often concurred with the more conservative choices: not all these families needed treatment.

TREATMENT PHASE

In this section we describe our experience with the 19 families who chose the treatment option. Table 7.2 gives an overview of the sorts of problems the clients had. This list gives a static 'snapshot' of what were in fact parts

Table 7.2   Total number of problems experienced by the 19 families who chose treatment and those worked on

	Present	Worked on
Marital problems	11	10
Toddler sleep problems	8	7
Financial/low income	8	3
Non-compliance of index child	7	3
Sibling's difficulties		
behaviour control	2	
peer relationships	2	
health problems	2	
Housing	5	3
Mother's physical health	5	
Unemployment/unsatisfactory employment	4	

of subtly articulated systems problems, unique to each family. It will be more helpful therefore to describe some of the interventions used with the families at this stage.

Energizing the family and negotiating priorities

An essential prelude to any change in the family is an involvement of all family members in the therapy and a heightened state of awareness and expectation in the family. This is what we call energizing the family. If the changes needed and the resistance to them is high – as in severely dysfunctional families – then the amount that the family needs to be energized is greater. On the whole the families in the study were less severely dysfunctional than clinic families and energizing techniques could be correspondingly more gentle. One of the advantages of starting therapy with an assessment procedure was as part of the energizing process. An integral part of this was the stimulating of interaction between family members. As we have already mentioned, this was new to many families. Further, the therapist brings the expectation of debate about family function. The therapist is helped in this aim if he or she can take charge of the family session and so provide a safe area in which family members can speak openly. More forceful methods of confrontation to energize the family were seldom if ever used in this project.

The second form of energizing that was used was to centre the intervention on a problem of genuine concern to the family. Equally, this did not mean that the problem had to be dealt with in a narrow way. The art of therapy at this stage was to respect the family's concerns but attempt to widen the discussion to consider a range of priorities.

This brings us on to the next stage, the negotiation of priorities in what changes were wanted. Several techniques proved useful in this. First, in the assessment stage, a number of areas or dimensions of family function were discussed. This allowed the family and therapist to view any particular problem from a variety of vantage points, each of which constituted a different facet of family function. This process played a major part in freeing the family from problem-solving attempts which often seemed to have become progressively ossified as the family struggled over long periods of time to find a solution.

Another method that proved useful was to review previous attempts at problem-solving. Even if these had proved unsuccessful they often gave clues as to what might be successful approaches.

The process of negotiating priorities ended in an agreement between the therapist and family on what areas might be worked on.

An example of treatment

The full flavour of the treatment approach can be transmitted only by describing a case in detail. The main problems that were encountered in the project were marital problems and behaviour problems in the toddlers; we therefore give an example of where the treatment was focused on improving marital communication and toddler behaviour.

Case example: Jacobs family

By the therapist's fifth visit to the Jacobs family, the therapist and family had completed an assessment and had identified a number of problems which included Mrs Jacobs's depression and her behaviour control management of their son, Ian.

Family circumstances and appointments for the therapist were difficult because Mr Jacobs worked away during the week and the family met as a family only at weekends. In this fifth session the therapist intended to undertake three tasks: first, feedback of information and observations, and feedback of therapists' observations, second, negotiation of options, and third, negotiation of behaviour changes.

In the following sequence the family and therapist explore Mrs Jacobs's request for greater responsiveness from Mr Jacobs when she is feeling low – in particular on Wednesdays and Thursdays while he is away. The left hand side of the page is taken from an unedited tape recording of the session. On the right hand side the therapist activity is labelled using the terminology of Cleghorn and Levin (1973).

	Therapist's micro moves (Cleghorn and Levin 1973)
THERAPIST: Okay, just for the moment and coming back to these phone calls have you perhaps noted any pattern to the phone calls? If you are depressed is it likely to be a bad phone call on a Thursday night? You're quite happy with Monday, Tuesday and Wednesday?	Affect query and relating affect to transactional process
MOTHER: It's funny you should say that – I don't know if Willie [husband] has noticed but on a Monday I'm really nice to him on the phone, on Tuesday I'm okay . . .	
THERAPIST: Hang on, hang on. Is that true, Will?	Affect query to relevant other
FATHER: I haven't taken a great deal of notice, if it's been a bad time on the phone. I haven't really noticed.	
THERAPIST: But what about Monday. Do you feel that	

Linda is "really nice" to you on a Monday?

FATHER: Well, she's generally nice on the phone anyway.

MOTHER: Oh thank you very much!

FATHER: In general terms she's generally okay on the phone, it's just now and again, she'll say such and such.

THERAPIST: Okay, but can we come back to what you were saying. (*looking at mother*) — Refocusing

MOTHER: On Monday and Tuesday I'm nice to him. Mainly on a Monday I'm worried in case he doesn't get there, or if he has an accident – that's on a Monday morning when I get up; by dinner time I'm not so worried cause I know he'll be there now. I'm not anxious but I'm on edge till he phones etc. By about Wednesday I'm . . . he'll say I'll have to go cause I'm going out with Ronnie for a pint or something – right? and then I'll put the phone down and I'll be sitting – here we go again – me stuck in you know and by Thursday, by the time I've thought about it, what's happening on the Wednesday I might be a bit ratty on the phone but by Friday when he's ready to come home I'll say sorry love, it was just because I was a bit down in the dumps – as I was saying Monday and Tuesday I'm fine but by Wednesday I'm ready to get out on me own or whatever and I think I resent the fact that he's been out.

(*Everyone talks at once. Mother makes room for therapist.*)

THERAPIST: But – what . . . can I ask what out of all that, Will, does anything come out, which you think well? — Relates affect query/transactional process to relevant other

FATHER: Well, yes she's said this to me many times before. I say get a babysitter. I can't force her – she's got to think for herself and do something about it. I mean I said to her "you've got to think individually".

THERAPIST: (*Acknowledges points raised and comes in*) I am wondering if what Linda's saying though is that on Thursdays and Fridays the extra bit of attention during the phone call would make . . . — Refocuses affect query/transactional process to relevant other

MOTHER: All the difference.

In the remainder of this session the therapist fed back information gained in the assessment to the family. He then returned to the family and asked if there were any problems they would like to work on. While Mr Jacobs felt that more or less everything was all right, Mrs Jacobs wanted to work on her husband's responsiveness and on her control over her son.

It is worth pausing for a moment to comment on the interaction. It will be noticed that the therapist holds the focus of the conversation on the issue of the weekly phone calls. As well as this he stimulated interaction between the couple without becoming directly involved as a switchboard. The result is that the problems have now become somewhat redefined: mother's 'depression' has become redefined as a wish for more responsiveness from her husband.

We shall now follow this family through subsequent encounters with the therapist since their progress was rather typical of the therapy in this study.

By the end of the above session it was clear that Mr Jacobs wanted the family to work on the problems on their own. However, the therapist was able to propose two courses of action. First, he acknowledged Mr Jacobs's reticence and suggested that they discuss on their own whether to take up the therapist's suggestions, and second, that Mr Jacobs might like to help his wife compile a list of strategies of dealing with their son.

The family agreed and the therapist arranged a further meeting ten days later to check progress. During the next session Mrs Jacobs reported a dramatic change in Ian's behaviour including walking obediently with his mother from nursery, not running across the road and not answering back or being cheeky. He was also going to bed without crying, and sleeping through the night.

Although Mr Jacobs had compiled a list of strategies for dealing with Ian, these included nothing new and interestingly the parents had not discussed the list. Mrs Jacobs commented, however, on how she had had a good week and not felt depressed. By the end of this session, the therapist and family had agreed upon a task which took the form of a semi-structured activity between Ian and his mother. The therapist and family agreed to meet again.

Over the next few weeks the therapist endeavoured to make an appointment to see the family but was told that Mr Jacobs was feeling a bit 'fed up' and was busy. Contact was, however, maintained and the therapist and family eventually made an appointment four weeks later. In this session, the therapist confirmed that the improvements had been maintained. However, a new problem had surfaced in that Mr Jacobs had become depressed.

The root of his dysphoria seemed to be that he was missing the enhanced rewards of his family life. During a follow up visit the therapist learned that Mr Jacobs had managed to find local employment and both parents were feeling much closer to each other.

This family illustrates a common experience in the project. The family did not seem to work particularly hard and homework was only rather fitfully followed, yet important changes occurred which seemed to relate in time to sessions which facilitated communication and pinpointed and focused family problems. It should be added that in other families the level of commitment was very high so that it was possible to have very frequent sessions, sometimes daily, and to work on problems very intensively.

Having given a detailed example of the techniques used, we need now to give an indication of the variety of the therapy in the project.

THE VARIETIES OF TASKS AND TECHNIQUES

Supportive networks

Members of families were sometimes advised and agreed to form closer alliances/partnerships over particular issues to encourage and support each other. This proved to be very useful with families where relationship difficulties prevented common approaches to problems (for example bedtime routines).

Diaries

Members of families were sometimes asked to keep semistructured diaries or star charts. These were used as a means to heighten awareness of transactions and were particularly useful with families who, while motivated to change, found this difficult. There were a number of spin-offs from diary-keeping: it kept the family focused on important transactions; it kept the therapist focused in the same way, and it provided evidence of what had happened between sessions.

Geneograms

These ranged from asking family members to construct a family tree to family members representing their ideas of the 'family' through drawing or painting.

Use of tape recorders

Although visiting at home clearly reduces the 'technology' that is often associated with family therapy such as one-way screens or video-recorders, it is possible to use portable equipment imaginatively and to much the same purpose. In general we found using tape recorders useful for joining the family – they helped us to engage the family especially the children; they helped to add to the sense of occasion of the sessions, which was particularly important in home-based treatment; they were a means of feeding information back to families both during and in some cases between sessions, as the tape could be left with the family to listen to; and most important, they were used as a recording, supervision and rating tool.

Rehearsals and role play

Members of families were asked to enact behaviour to introduce new patterns of response. This could be done during or in between sessions. One couple were asked simply to listen and give total concentration to their partner, without responding for very limited periods of time (two minutes). (This particular exercise rehearsed a small part of the couple's earlier courtship when they "listened" to each other.) In other cases a more elaborate role play task was devised.

Referral to other agencies

While the family therapist can approach many problems and explore their dimensions with families, there are obviously limits to their expertise and occasions arose where it was necessary to refer to other agencies for appropriate advice or help. Aspects of the referral could be used as tasks in the therapy so it was not either a therapy or referral situation.

Material help

Social workers have traditionally been associated with attempts to alleviate poor material and physical conditions. This was not precluded, in these poor families, by our role as family therapists. It is most commonly carried out by representation and advocacy to a third party such as the social services, hospitals or housing department. By visiting at home the social worker or family therapist is often confronted by the realities or evidence of low or insufficient income.

Advantages of working in the home

While working with Mrs Cookson (a single parent) and her 2½-year-old son Stephen, the therapist, following the suggestion of his supervisor, conducted part of an interview about a soiling/management problem in the family bathroom. While adults can make the transfer from one setting to another in discussion the concrete stage of development of 2½ to 3 year olds may sometimes make real-life locations more potent. By asking Mrs Cookson to keep a diary of the events which surrounded her son's soiling, by calling this the 'poo-poo' file and re-establishing and supporting Mrs Cookson's previous attempts at behaviour control, the problem was resolved, although this meant Mrs Cookson having to say 'goodbye' to the toilet or talk to the toilet after successful episodes. Her son's delight at his newly learnt mastery was evident and this in turn encouraged Mrs Cookson.

Other potential advantages of working in the home included a greater sense of ease among family members and, most important, more regular attendance.

Length of involvement

Other action studies dealing with marital problems of more materially and emotionally deprived families conclude that time-limited work can lead to better results than intermittent long-term support, punctuated by hectic activity in terms of crisis, which rarely result in any change of behaviour or in personal growth (Mattinson and Sinclair 1979). In general we attempted to work within defined time limits and with this in mind the contractual nature of our involvement, referred to earlier, was beneficial.

General procedures of closure

In general there are four steps of the "closure" stage. These consist of orientation, summary of treatment, long-term goals and optional follow up by the therapist.

During the final interview with the family the therapist's task was to return to the original aims of the therapy and evaluate how these had been achieved. Emphasis at this stage was placed on how the family, rather than the "therapist–family system" might be able to bring about similar changes in the future if further problems should be encountered.

Finally the family are asked to anticipate any long-term goals or problems and how they might deal with these. This serves several purposes not least being another means for the therapist to check out the present problem-solving functioning of the family. Lastly it can positively convey to the family that while the future will undoubtedly hold problems, that they are in a good position to deal with these.

SUMMARY

In this chapter we have attempted to describe the basis of our approach to the introduction of family therapy and to record our experiences in the therapy process. There are many issues which merit discussion; two of these will be mentioned here.

The first issue is the implications of our experiences for research. The problems of psychotherapy research are immense and not the least of these is the need to describe exactly what treatment consists of. A common way to do this is to try to describe the processes of therapy and monitor the unfolding of the sessions to check that they remain within the prescribed guidelines (Waskow 1983). In the present study there was an additional problem in our project in that the application of the technique in the community is relatively untried. The present report presents an attempt to characterize and describe the process.

It was felt that, in the context of a community project, elaborate instrumentation and monitoring would erode co-operation and detract from the spontaneity of the occasion. However, we did adhere rigorously to the macromoves of therapy (Epstein and Bishop 1981). Thus the same sequence was followed with each family. Epstein and Bishop report that it is these macromoves which can be reliably measured in therapy whereas the detailed individual interaction is less easy to characterize. Since the intervention was experimental it seemed more appropriate to describe what happened rather than insist that the therapy fitted a preconceived mould.

Chapter 8

Mother and Toddler Groups

We have described the origin and contribution of playgroups to British preschool provision in Chapter 3. In our search for intervention programmes, we were greatly impressed by the potential of the playgroup movement. Crowe (1973) describes the way that playgroups can be fitted to different needs. Among families in areas of deprivation, there was a need to start by raising the parents from a state of low morale and passivity. Two ways are suggested to get playgroups off the ground under such circumstances. The first is for the local authority to start a playgroup, the second for a group to arise out of a mothers' club. The problem with the first approach is that as something that is provided for the mother, it plays into the passivity that is so much part of the problem. Mothers' clubs can work well, as the primary need of parents under stress is to feel that their own problems are going to be heard and understood. The playgroup is likely to develop out of this situation because the children will have to come as well. Crowe warns of the problems of an inexperienced playleader taking the children's group in order to give the mothers time to socialize. The mothers are likely to welcome such an opportunity for a break from domestic drudgery for a time. The problem is that the children's group will be under-controlled and tend to wind the children up or, in the smaller and weaker children, lead to heightened anxiety. At the end of the group the mothers are confronted with excited, wild children so that the restoration and encouragement of the group rapidly evaporates. The answer, of course, is to recognize that the toddlers' group is as important as the mothers' group and requires at least as much skill and careful planning. If the children have had an equally constructive afternoon, and indeed may have some work to show their mother, the relationship between mother and child can be enhanced. Under deprived circumstances, the playleader has to be aware that the children's level of play may be that of a younger child who had been brought up under more satisfactory circumstances.

For the most part, playgroups have grown up in answer to a general social need rather than for children with particular difficulties and needs. No doubt their potential has been used widely for special need children, but such efforts have largely gone unrecorded and unsung. The National

Society for the Prevention of Cruelty to Children (NSPCC) reported a study of ten therapeutic playgroups for preschool children (Rose 1972). The groups continued over a considerable period of time, so that the children were involved up to the age of school entry. The families involved were considerably more disadvantaged than in the present study, for example 20% of the fathers were in prison and nearly half the families had no employed member. Despite this, the functioning of the children in the groups was high in socialization and co-operation and low in aggressive and antisocial behaviour. Details of the regime are not given, but were probably various.

Within the mother and toddler project, we were seeking to provide more than a developmental or childminding experience for the mothers. Since we were concerned with families who were "at risk", we recognized that potential clients may be people who lacked the confidence to go to ordinary playgroups. However, a variation of the playgroup model seemed to us to have great advantages since it was a well-recognized institution, which any mother might attend, without feeling labelled as "needing special help". If the mothers did have special needs in the first instance, our hope was that with initial support, they might make the group their own and continue under their own momentum once the professional staff had withdrawn.

PREPARATION

Training

This was extensive. The project was undertaken by two fully qualified graduate social workers and two fully qualified health visitors. The social workers had had, respectively, four and seven years' experience and brought with them groupwork and casework skills. The health visitors had also had four and seven years' experience and brought considerable knowledge of developmental paediatrics, preventive medicine and health education. In addition one of the health visitors had had seven years as a fully trained child psychiatric nurse. The following additional training exercises were carried out before the groups started.

1. All the professionals concerned took part in a sensitivity group with other staff members from a neighbouring child psychiatric agency.
2. All four workers undertook a special training programme of ten sessions, organized and run by the social work staff of a neighbouring psychiatric agency.
3. The two health visitors in the project had some special training from a clinical child psychologist on behavioural management techniques for young children.

Equipment

The toys need to be many and varied, but not so many as to be overwhelming. The range of toys included toys for large muscle play such as tricycles, pedal cars and balls; quiet play with books, crayons and paper; messy play with Playdoh, sand and water; imaginative play with doll's houses, tea sets and construction toys such as Lego. Special structured sessions such as painting and collage sessions were a great success.

THE MOTHERS AND TODDLERS

Within the project, seven separate groups took place, and a total of 66 mothers and toddlers between the ages of 2 years 5 months and 2 years 10 months were invited. Of these 66, 38 of the mothers and 24 of the toddlers had a psychiatric disorder which had been judged in a psychiatric assessment to merit active intervention at primary care level; 50 of the mothers accepted the invitation. Of those who accepted, the highest overall attendance was at the first of the series of ten sessions. The average attendance at the first session taken over all the groups was 82%. The lowest attendance was at the ninth (penultimate) session, where the attendance was 66% over all the groups.

THE FORMAT OF THE GROUPS

The groups were carried in the local health clinics of the health authority. These were distributed in such a way that the groups were always held within walking distance from the homes of all the group members. Throughout, the health visitors were centrally responsible for the children's groups and the social workers for the mothers' groups. We were fortunate to have the help of student nursery nurses, who assisted greatly in the toddler groups. Each session ran for about 1 hour 40 minutes. This was divided between a preliminary period (between 20 and 30 minutes), a session in which the mothers and toddlers were taken in separate groups (between 39 and 57 minutes) and a final period (between 16 and 34 minutes) in which the mothers, toddlers and staff had the opportunity for a less structured winding down period. The staff found that the mothers were not in a hurry to resume charge of their children, and that considerable supervision was still needed at this time, the mothers collecting the children at the very end.

It is essential that certain ground rules were strictly kept to. These included having the same staff throughout the group, and sticking to consistent routines for the children such as a regular juice time and a similar layout of the group on each occasion.

Recording

Following the group session, both social worker and health visitor undertook a detailed write up of the session. They also completed a number of simple codings of events in the group. These codings will not be described in detail here, but will be mentioned in the context of the description of the groups which follows.

THE PRE-GROUP VISITS

Preparation of the families

Particular care was taken in preparing the mothers and toddlers for the groups. Each family was visited at home by the social worker and health visitor who were to run the group in order to begin to make an individual relationship. In these visits the role was carefully decided, with the social worker engaging the mother and the health visitor communicating with the child. The main emphasis was on conveying that the mothers would receive a warm welcome at the group. Some of the mothers were already prepared for the group by this time and were anxious for it to start. It was also necessary to ensure that husbands (or partners) were consulted about their wives coming. This concept for "seeking permission" was important because sometimes a father would come along to the group and bring the children when the mother was ill and unable to come. We successfully managed to sell our groups as beneficial to the whole family. The groups were presented in a positive way, rather than as for people with problems. It was emphasized that it was hoped that members could help each other with the common difficulties of having a $2\frac{1}{2}$ year old. Convenience of times for the group was checked. In some groups, this was followed up by a letter again stating the time and purpose of the group and welcoming the mother to it.

Preparation of the venue

Planning and preparation of the site was also essential: clinic staff had to be approached and convinced that their territory would be responsibly used. The premises also had to be inspected and decisions made about how the available space would be deployed.

THE TODDLERS' GROUPS

The first session was crucial to the whole course of the group. Being a new experience, the mothers were particularly watchful. It was clear that many were "giving it a try" and would decide very quickly whether it was for them. Particular care was therefore taken in planning. In this first session, the mothers and toddlers were welcomed when they first arrived at the group, this preliminary period being rather longer (average 30 minutes) than in any of the other sessions. A good start paved the way and made future sessions easier, more productive and more enjoyable (like igniting a vital spark).

The mothers and toddlers then separated into their respective groups.

Separation problems

It might be expected that these would be particularly marked in this first session but this was minimized by detailed preparatory work. The workers arrived early to arrange the toys tidily and attractively. When the time for separation came, the children were given time and space to settle, not pushed or forced, but gently invited to look at some of the toys. Gradually they all became involved in the play, at which time the mothers were invited to move into a separate room. The children were informed openly of the impending separation, at the risk of some disruption, since to do otherwise would have been to sow the seeds of mistrust. The door to the mothers' room was left open until the children felt completely safe.

The excellent records that were kept throughout this project allow us to see the rich variety of children's responses to the stress of short separations and a strange environment, and gain useful insights for management. A short period of hestiation was common. More prolonged separation difficulties were far less common but did occur. Other children seemed to cope with the stress being in the group "in body but not spirit". The majority of the children showed few if any separation problems; a small number showed problems of a different kind from the first group.

Case example: Shaun

Shaun, age 2 years 8 months, seemed a little hesitant initially, staying close to his mother outside the playroom. He was easily encouraged to join the others. He remained rather quiet and solitary throughout the course of the group.

Case example: Jill

Jill, age 2 years 8 months, was extremely hesitant on her arrival at the group and stayed very close to her mother, even sitting on her lap at one point. She was gently coaxed out to play, first by taking some stickle bricks to her where she was sitting and trying to get her to join in – she eventually did. She was gently taken to the sandpit and began playing, with a little reluctance, with two of the other children and an adult helper. She became so engrossed in play that she showed no distress at separation. She did ask where her mummy was at one point but was easily reassured. In subsequent sessions, Jill's difficulties continued in varying degrees. When she overcame her anxiety, which she always did by the end of the group, she became an active and enthusiastic group member with considerable social skill, both with adults and other children.

Case example: Kay

Kay, age 2 years 6 months, was very reluctant to leave her mother, venturing to play at times but returning to her mother's side. During the separation period she played alongside Carla under supervision, but, while showing no distress, she made it clear that she was only tolerating the session and was determined not to become too comfortable. She even refused juice, saying that she took it only from mammy. This little girl formed an attachment to a member of staff in the second session and after that gained confidence on her own.

Case example: Susan

Susan, age 2 years 4 months, was a bright demanding child. She easily became frustrated by the other children and readily resorted to tempers if thwarted. She needed to be controlled much of the time and watched for the safety of the other children. She did seem to respond to positive handling actually sharing the toys, if somewhat grudgingly, over the course of the group. Her aggression lessened considerably.

Variety of responses

Overall, serious separation problems occurred only in two groups, and even there in only two sessions of one of them and three of another. In one of these, it was one child, while in the other there were two children who had separation difficulties. In one session of this latter group, the distress of these two children reached epidemic proportions, with all the children (except one) having to be returned to their mothers part way through the group.

Problems of aggression were also unusual, with one session in two groups and two in one group where definite problems of physical aggression occurred. These seemed to represent, in some cases, difficulties in sharing and in others outright disruptiveness. Two children were frankly domineering and tried to lecture and coerce the other children. The therapists had to mediate and try to teach the arts of negotiation and compromise.

Compared with these rather few difficulties, there was a great deal of prosocial behaviour in the groups. Thus there were plentiful examples of co-operative play, and also of helping behaviour.

All groups were characterized by a lot of constructive play with the toys provided. The play was used, for the most part, to foster social interaction rather than for its fantasy, developmental or educational potential.

THE MOTHERS' GROUPS

The first session was also crucial to the success of the mothers' groups. Our ratings showed that in the first group, the leader imposed a relatively high level of structure. Thus most of the groups started off with structured exercises such as pairing off for introductions or throwing a ball to exchange names. The group leaders introduced the groups as offering the young women an opportunity to talk about anything they wanted to, but there was a deliberate policy of steering away from too early revelation of personal material.

In the first session of one of the groups, for example, the members were all initially shy, nervous and reserved. After a ball-throwing game to learn each other's names which broke the ice, the group leader sorted the members into pairs and to talk to each other. The leader specifically mentioned "safe topics" that could be discussed, and members became very animated, talking about mothers-in-law, sisters and what they did in their spare time.

The issue of confidentiality was specifically brought up in the first session. Group members were asked to be careful not to discuss members' personal business outside the group with non-group members.

Once trust was established the group leaders encouraged the members that they should think of the group as theirs and that, as a result, every group was unique, because of the people making it up, although the overall structure was the same for all the groups. Themes that emerged were quite varied. They included such topics as lack of confidence in social situations, how to deal with husbands' unrealistic expectations, difficulties because of husbands working away, and problems of poverty, illness and poor housing. There were also the more expected subjects: toddler problems such as sleep, temper tantrums and toilet training. Since the mothers had lived in the same neighbourhood for a long time, it was not surprising that many had seen one another before, and some knew each other. On the whole this seemed to be an advantage, especially in the early sessions of the groups.

In later sessions, considerably less leadership structure was necessary. Quite a wide range of topics were discussed. Among these, issues of child management and of the wider implications of being parents were taken up in nearly all the groups, although perhaps slightly less so towards the later sessions. Extended family came up as a topic, again mostly in the earlier sessions. Discussion of spouse and nuclear family was a feature of the middle sessions of the groups, perhaps when trust and intimacy were at their highest.

In the sixth session of one of the groups, for example, discussion of problems found in women's magazines provoked an interesting discussion of a real-life dilemma. One mother was having problems with her ex-boyfriend, who suddenly wanted access to his child, after non-involvement for two years. The group listened sympathetically and two other mothers told the group of their experiences of being unmarried mothers; this discussion was helpful to the first mother; who realized that her problem was not unique as she had feared.

Discussion of the groups themselves was a feature of the first and the last two groups; this seemed to be linked to reflection of the relationships between group members in general which, quite naturally, were most discussed in the beginning and ending sessions.

WORKER SUPPORT

Peer discussions

This was a major feature of the groups. Every problem, be it of difficulties over accommodation or concern over the emotional state of one of the mothers, was discussed in great detail. Time was set aside for a quite formal discussion period after each group. Areas of particular difficulty were identified which were then taken to the specific supervision session.

Issues were continually thrown up through the life of the groups, which needed to be talked through with colleagues. For example, in one mothers' group the members decided that they would bring in their knitting the following week. There was strong pressure on the group leader to bring her knitting too. In the de-briefing session at the end of the group session all the workers discussed this issue and concluded that the group leader should resist this pressure, since it was so clearly a group attempt to damp down anxieties, requiring understanding, not collusion.

In some early groups, quite specific objectives were set down before the group started. It was found that this was not a useful exercise and that it was more important to allow the mothers to develop the discussion themselves without a preconceived plan.

Supervision

Weekly supervision took place throughout the course of the groups. This was conducted by a principal clinical psychologist (TF) trained in psychotherapy and groupwork. It addressed the following considerations: discussing and clarifying the role of the group leaders/therapists in relation to the aims and objectives of the group meetings; discussing ways in which the therapists would encourage and facilitate the group to participate in the group tasks with a sense of trust and commitment; in the case of the children's groups, the therapists were given guidelines on how to facilitate prosocial behaviours; in the case of the mothers' groups, guidelines on promoting social skills and interpersonal interactions were given. Principles of social modelling and positive reinforcement were complemented by simple psychodynamic principles. Feedback by the therapists about their difficulties, anxieties and progress was actively encouraged by the supervisor, whose aim it was to provide the therapists with appropriate support and guidance towards enhancement of their understanding of group processes and of their therapeutic skills.

SUMMARY

Many mother and toddler groups are carried out throughout the country. The present programme merits reporting because we have unusual epidemiological data on the use of the group within one particular urban area, and because of the particular function of the groups with an "at risk" population. The staffing of the groups was generous and comparatively highly trained. We make no apology for this since the work is difficult and demands skill. The question that many professionals in the field may ask is whether the circumstances reported here can be reproduced in ordinary service conditions. We believe that with the better deployment of resources in any given area, such projects could be mounted more often than they are. From our experience in various agencies, we consider that expertise is often wasted due to unnecessary demarcation disputes and other interprofessional rivalries.

The ten-session duration of the groups was judged to be a reasonable length that would be long enough to allow group cohesion yet represent an economical use of staff time. A follow up questionnaire confirmed that the mothers had found the groups helpful, in understanding their children, and also their own reactions; they had appreciated the emotional support offered by the groups (see Chapter 9). Many mothers complained that the groups did not run long enough. The hope that the mothers would take the initiative and organize the continuation of their own groups was realized in four of the seven groups.

We questioned the wisdom of separating children from their parents, as was done in the groups, at such an early stage. There was little doubt that the mothers greatly appreciated the opportunity to have an adult conversation but a great deal of care was needed in managing the separation, and even then it caused obvious signs of stress in some children. Another solution might have been to conduct the two groups in the same room. To some extent, the format is also dictated by the facilities available.

Having described the three treatment regimes, we can now go on to consider the outcome of the study.

Chapter 9

Results of the Study: Parts 1 and 2

It is now time to pull the diverse parts of our study together and consider the outcomes of the treatments. This will be presented in four parts: parts 1 and 2 will be considered in this chapter and parts 3 and 4 in Chapter 10.

Part 1. The prevalence and associations of disturbance in the community
Part 2. The outcome of the intervention
Part 3. The consumer view of the help offered
Part 4. The outcome of disturbance and delay when no treatment is given.

In each case, we shall take the reader through the analysis step by step.

PART 1: THE PREVALENCE AND ASSOCIATIONS OF DISTURBANCE IN THE COMMUNITY

The analyses were concerned with two issues. The first issue was the prevalence of children's and mothers' disturbance in our sample. The literature is witness to a great weight of morbidity in the community (see Chapter 2); indeed, this is what persuaded us to undertake the present study in the first place. As far as our particular sample goes, we quickly found (as reported in Chapter 5), that a large number of mothers and children in our sample scored positive on simple screening questionnaires. This suggests that the rate of disorder was high, but does not give us accurate figures for prevalence. We now present the findings on prevalence in the study sample.

The second issue was the associations of mother and toddler disturbance with other social and biological stresses. In Chapter 2 we described many associations of disturbance that have been found in other studies. In particular, there are associations with the state of the parental marriage, with social class and with the state of development of the child. These associations have been found in numerous other studies: to what extent were they true of ours? We can now turn to this issue as well.

Description of the procedure

As described in Chapter 5, the study population was sampled according to a stratification based on three levels of score on the GHQ-30 questionnaire and the Child Behaviour Checklist, making a ninefold classification. These characteristics of the sampled screen had to be taken into account in determining the prevalence rates. It must be emphasized that the study was not primarily designed to assess prevalence rates. For this reason, rather complex statistical methods have had to be used.

The stratification used in the study design divided the population into nine samples (see Chapter 5, Figure 5.2). Each of these was likely to have a different proportion of cases or, put another way, a different sampling ratio. The prevalence rate in the population could be calculated from the nine small samples. The problem is that some of these samples were made up of very small numbers in a way that may have biased results. For this reason, prevalence rates were calculated using estimates of rates in each of the cells. The estimates were based on log-linear models, that is a statistical model was developed to fit the pattern of the data (see Appendix 1). This was then used to estimate the contribution of each cell to an overall prevalence rate.

In this way we were also able to estimate the association of disturbance to different social conditions and in different groups of the population. These included quality of marriage, social class and the Developmental Quotient of the child as well as, in the case of the mother, the child's disturbance, and in the case of the child, the mother's disturbance. Since the statistical details are rather complicated, we have reported a full analysis separately (Stretch et al 1992). The key results are, however, given here. Given the necessary complexity of the statistical technique, it was not possible to calculate significance levels. However, some of the associations were very strong, as we shall see, and others weaker.

The measures used

Further details on the measures used in the study are given in Chapter 5.

Mother and toddler disturbance

In Chapter 5 we described our categorization of severity of disorder into two strata: the level at which therapeutic concern would be raised at primary care level and the level that might trigger referral to a psychiatric clinic.

Quality of marriage

Marriage quality was derived from the Quinton, Rutter and Rowlands (1976) scale by dichotomizing the scale into two parts; scores 1, 2 and 3 were rated "good quality of marriage" while 4, 5 and 6 were rated "poor quality of marriage".

Social class

Social class was similarly dichotomized into non-manual and manual occupational classes, measured on the Registrar General's Office's classification of occupations (Registrar General's Office 1951).

Developmental Quotient

A quotient of 80 or less was contrasted with a quotient of more than 80.

Results

The prevalence of psychiatric disturbance in mothers and toddlers

It can be seen from Table 9.1 that the prevalence of psychiatric disorder in the mother was just under 21%. Within this, the prevalence of depression was 13.5%, the remainder being made up of much smaller proportions of anxiety state, obsessional disorder, psychosomatic symptoms and a range of incapacitating emotional problems which defied conventional classification. The rate in the mothers was somewhat lower than those of previous studies. For example, in the Brown and Harris study (1978) the rate of psychiatric disturbance in mothers with a child aged under 6 was 31% as against 20.7%, even for the mild level of disturbance in our study. Further, the Brown and Harris level was defined as a group who might merit hospital outpatient management, suggesting a higher level of severity than in our study. On this evidence, we had a much lower rate of problems. There are several reasons why this might be so. First, the community studied in the Brown and Harris (1978) research was in Inner London. It could be that this community lacked the close network of support that was present in the area of our study. Despite the economic stress on the families, there was a high degree of social cohesion in our community (see Chapter 5, pages 112–14). This could have offered protection against disturbance. A second possibility was that we under-diagnosed psychiatric disorder in our population. In a comparison with studies using similar methodologies, it did appear that this could be the case (see Stretch et al 1992). This could be due to the fact that in our study, the mother and toddler were usually seen together in order to assess interaction. Perhaps the mothers were less ready to confide their difficulties in front of their children, young as they were. A third possibility is that Brown and Harris's cut-off level for disturbance was more sensitive than they suspected, although more recent computer-aided diagnostic studies from this research group have yielded comparable levels of disturbance which makes this unlikely (Brown and Harris 1989). Turning to toddler problems, the levels were in fact comparable to those in previous studies. For example, in the Richman, Stevenson and Graham (1982) study (referred to extensively in Chapter 2), a very similar methodology was used and the results were very similar.

Associations of mother disturbance

Table 9.2 shows the associations of both a mild level and a severe level of disorder in the mother with four other factors: the quality of the marriage, social class, Developmental Quotient and disturbance in the toddler. It can be seen that marriage quality, not surprisingly, has a strong relationship with a nearly ninefold difference in rate of severe disturbance between those mothers unfortunate enough to have a bad marriage, compared with those who have a good marriage, and a fourfold difference in the case of mild disorder. There is also a strong association with disturbance in the toddler, with a fourfold difference in rate of disturbance for severe and mild level disorder. Turning to social class and the Developmental Quotient of the toddler, the associations with adverse scores are present but less marked.

Associations of toddler disturbance

These associations are shown in Table 9.3. It can be seen that in the case of toddlers as well, the rate of disturbance is very much raised in the

Table 9.1 The prevalence of mother and toddler disturbance

	Severe level (psychiatric outpatient)* (%)			Mild level (primary care level)* (%)		
	boys	girls	total	boys	girls	total
Toddler's disturbance	2.9	1.7	2.3	27.9	18.8	24.0
Mother's disturbance			3.4			20.7

* The severe level refers to an assessed severity level where referral to a psychiatric clinic was judged appropriate, whereas the mild level refers to an assessed level of severity that should have aroused concern at primary care level.

Table 9.2 Associations of psychiatric disorder in the mother (the percentages in the table indicate the levels of disturbance in the families with the qualities indicated)

Background variable	Level	Severe level* (%)	Mild level* (%)
Marriage quality	Good	1.2	13.8
	Poor	10.5	48.6
Disturbance in toddler (mild and severe level)	No disturbance	1.9	11.6
	Disturbance	8.5	49.4
Social class	Non-manual	2.4	14.6
	Manual	3.7	22.6
Developmental Quotient of toddler	Not delayed	3.4	19.2
	Delayed	2.9	37.8

* The severe level refers to an assessed severity level where referral to a psychiatric clinic was judged appropriate, whereas the mild level refers to an assessed severity level that should have aroused concern at primary care level.

presence of a poor parental marriage. Equally, psychiatric disorder in the mother was associated with toddler disturbance. In both cases, the differences are particularly marked where the level of disturbance in the toddler is severe. The rates are also raised in families from manual occupations and where there is a developmental delay, although the contrasts here are not as great.

Table 9.3 Associations of disturbance in the toddlers (the percentages in the table indicate the levels of disturbance in the families with the qualities indicated)

Background variable	Level	Severe level* (%)	Mild level* (%)
Parental marriage quality	Good	0.6	18.0
	Poor	10.6	42.9
Disturbance in mother (mild and severe level)	No disturbance	0.8	15.3
	Disturbance	7.7	54.0
Social class	Non-manual	0.0	14.0
	Manual	3.0	27.3
Developmental Quotient	Not delayed	1.8	22.1
	Delayed	8.0	46.8

* The severe level refers to an assessed severity level where referral to a psychiatric clinic was judged appropriate, whereas the mild level refers to an assessed severity level that should have aroused concern at primary care level.

Conclusion

To summarize, the prevalence of mother's disturbance is rather lower than in many comparable studies, whereas that for toddlers is comparable to other studies. Disturbance in mothers and toddlers is associated with high levels of marital discord. In the case of mothers there is an association also with disturbance in toddlers and vice versa. There are weaker associations with social class and a low Developmental Quotient in the toddler.

PART 2: THE OUTCOME OF THE INTERVENTION

We have already stated the four hypotheses of the study in Chapter 5 (page 99). It is now time to present the results of the analyses and to consider how well our hypotheses were supported.

Description of How the Analyses Were Done

It is necessary first to introduce the reader to some of the problems of analysing these types of data. A more technical presentation is given in Appendices 1 and 2.

There are two ways of assessing the effectiveness of treatment; a simple example will help to clarify the difference between them. Take two children who are having temper tantrums. The first is having them once a week and the second is having them twenty times a week. We treat the first child with family therapy and the second with a behaviour modification programme. The tantrums of the first child stop altogether, while in the case of the second child the tantrums reduce to ten times a week instead of twenty. Which treatment is best? This may seem an impossible question but it is one we face every day if we try to assess the results of therapy. There are basically two ways of tackling the problem. First, we can look at the final outcome. Here the first child got on very well, and ended up completely cured of tantrums. Second, we can look at how much change there was. Here the second child did extremely well. Even though the end result was far from satisfactory, this child changed his behaviour not only more than the first child did but also, as it happens, more than the first child could possibly have done, given the starting-point. In choosing an approach to the analysis, we have a stark choice and the most important point is to think of which method is the most clinically meaningful. Here we had no doubt that it was most important to look at the end result: the state of health of the children and families at the end of the study.

If our problems ended at this point, life would be quite simple, but unfortunately this is not so. Despite the fact that cases were allocated to the three treatments and the control group on a random basis, there are inevitably differences in the baseline measures when one treatment group is compared with another. In other words, for each analysis that is carried out, the levels of severity of problems will be different at the outset.

For this reason a simple comparison of the levels of problems at the end of the study is likely to be highly misleading unless the baseline levels have been taken into account. The simple way to do this would be to subtract the original score from the final score and thus correct for the fact that the baseline scores differed between the treatment groups (in fact, for reasons to do with statistical regression effects, a fraction of the initial score should be subtracted).

Even if this adjustment is made, there is a further problem which must be addressed. It is an issue that applies particularly to young children who are developing rapidly and in ways that may make them qualitatively different at a later age if this is compared with an earlier age, as was the case in our follow up. As we have seen in Chapter 1, the child moves through many stages in development in the first few years of life and in many cases develops new competences that simply were not there at an earlier stage. Further, in our present state of knowledge, we have only a partial understanding of what qualities at an earlier stage might be precursors of those at a later stage. A simple example may help to illustrate this point. Two approaches are compared in the treatment of language delays in 3 year olds. The results favour one of the approaches but the result is not very clear cut. We want to test whether there are background factors, detectable at an earlier age, that influence outcome. Measurement of language function would not have been possible a year earlier since language would not have developed yet. However, there may have been precursors that were measurable reliably, elements of imaginative play for example. Such qualities could serve as a useful baseline in trying to balance up the effects of differences at baseline. In theory there could be many such factors. They can be distinguished in that they contribute to prediction of outcome, and different measures may do so to different extents. A statistical technique that will allow this to be quantified is the Conditional Approach (Goldstein 1979). This is the approach that we used in assessing the outcome of mother's mental state, child disorder and developmental level. For the state of the marriage, we used a log-linear modelling technique (Bishop, Fienberg and Holland 1975) because the type of data was rather different (categorical rather than continuous variables), but the principle was the same. Plewis (1985) describes how log-linear modelling can be used for measuring change. This technique was used in the present study.

There is yet one further issue that should be mentioned before going on to present the results. With four treatment groups one should not assume that there were reliable differences between groups simply because the outcomes were significantly different. Pair-wise comparisons had to be made. These are indicated in the tables that demonstrate the outcome (Tables 9.4 to 9.8). A horizontal bar over the comparisons in question indicates that there are no significant differences on pair-wise comparisons.

A major feature of our results was that for any given outcome measure (eg child behaviour or marital state) the results were different for those who had mild problems at the outset, as compared with those who had severe problems. Our approach to the analysis allowed us to establish whether the results for mild cases were different from those for severe cases. In fact, as will be seen, they often were. To present the results clearly, we have chosen two levels of severity of disturbance: the first is for cases which lie around the fiftieth centile at baseline. These cases were more severe than 50% of the cases within each treatment group. On the whole, it can be taken that in clinical terms this represents pretty mild disorder, since (as we have seen in Chapter 5) for any given scale, a proportion of the high-risk sample were not identified as disturbed in any particular area. To get a picture of more severe disorder, we present the case at the ninetieth centile. At this level, only 10% of the total sample will have more severe disorders than the case considered. At this stage, we are getting into clearly clinically significant disturbance, of a level that will commonly come to their family doctor, be referred to a child or adult psychiatry outpatient department, be judged as having special educational need or a family with severe marital problems as the case may be.

In short, we consider the fiftieth centile results to reflect the findings of a secondary prevention programme, while at the ninetieth centile we consider the findings to reflect those that might be found in a study of established cases of disorder. The one exception is in the developmental results where we consider the fiftieth centile in the same way but take the tenth centile (ie the most developmentally retarded end of the scale) as indicating a significant level of developmental delay. In the event, this level of delay was rather higher than that which might indicate that there were special educational needs on this criterion alone.

Significance level

We took a probability level of 5% as evidence of statistical significance throughout the analysis.

Conclusion

We took the level of disturbance or delay after treatment as our main outcome measure. In comparing different treatments in this way, an allowance has to be made for the level of disturbance or delay at baseline.

This has to take into account the fact that, particularly in young children, test scores may not mean the same thing at different ages. Statistical techniques (the conditional approach and log-linear modelling) were used to give the best estimate of the level of disturbance or delay at baseline. In assessing significant differences between the outcomes, a correction had to be made to allow for the fact that many comparisons had to be made. This is called pair-wise comparisons. Separate assessments of outcome were made for those who had moderate disturbance or delay and those who had severe disturbance or delay.

Results

The outcome measures

To recap from Chapter 5, there were four sets of outcome measures that we were interested in:

1. The mother's mental state: main measure was depression as measured by the Leeds scale.
2. The child's behaviour: main measure was overall child's behaviour as measured by the Behaviour Screening Questionnaire.
3. The quality of the marriage: main measure was overall rating of marriage on the Marriage Interview of Quinton, Rutter and Rowlands (1976).
4. The child's developmental level: main measure was the overall Developmental Quotient developed for the study (see Chapter 5).

There was to be a fifth set of outcome measures, those based on the Home Observation for Measurement of the Environment (the HOME Inventory of Caldwell and Bradley 1979). As reported in Chapter 5, however, the families in the study scored very high on this scale, leaving little variance in which to show differential changes such as might have resulted from treatment. Under these circumstances, null findings might be expected and indeed this is what was found. Because of the high initial scores, we do not regard these results as a fair test of the hypothesis. For this reason, the results of the HOME inventory will not be presented in detail here.

Within the remaining four sets of outcome measures a number of subscale measures were made in addition to the main measure. These were listed in Chapter 5 and we shall refer to them again as we go through the results.

Scores on social adversity

There were 142 cases below the cut-off of 4 on the social adversity scale and 178 above. The overall mean score for the group was 4.4, standard error 0.16. The composition of this scale is described in Chapter 5 and Table 5.3.

The hypotheses

The results will be presented according to the four main study hypotheses.

1. The three interventions differ from each other and from the control in reducing disturbance and delay.
2. There are other social and biological predictors of outcome. We chose to look for the influence of social adversity (as measured by the overall index of adversity that was described in Chapter 5 and summarized in Table 5.3) and for differences in the progress of boys and girls.
3. These other predictors (social adversity and sex differences) influence the effects of the various treatments on the various types of disturbance. This hypothesis is the most important one from the clinical point of view since it concerns the effect of treatment, taking the influences of social adversity and sex differences into account.
4. Independent of treatment, "high-risk" families have a poorer outcome than "low-risk" families. This hypothesis is about the natural history of untreated disorder. The findings will be reported in Chapter 10.

ONE YEAR FOLLOW UP

Hypothesis 1   Comparison of Treatments

See also the tables in Appendix 2, A2.1 to A2.4.

Overview of main findings

Of the four main measures, there were significant differences in outcome in mother's depression and in Developmental Quotient.

Depression

At both the secondary prevention and the clinical level of depression, there were significant differences between the treatment groups and the control. These results can be viewed only as trends, however, since none of the groups was distinguished by pair-wise comparisons. The ranking of these minor differences is shown in Table 9.4 (see however the picture when we come to consider Hypothesis 3, which takes social adversity into account).

Developmental quotients

As can be seen from Table 9.4, the developmental outcome of the family therapy group was lower than for the other three groups, particularly for those children who started out with a lower level of development, shown here at the tenth centile on initial score. This is a puzzling and worrying result, since family therapy stood alone at the tenth centile in pair-wise comparisons, indicating that family therapy actually had an adverse effect on developmental outcome as measured by a broad developmental quotient.

Findings on the Minor Scales

Mother's mental state

Inward directed irritability

There were significant differences between the treatment groups and the controls at both the secondary level severity of disorder and the clinical level. At the clinical level, mothers' groups stood out on pair-wise comparisons as having a worse outcome than the other two interventions and the control. Although, as we shall see in Chapter 10, mothers' groups were very popular, they seem to have done little for the mother's sense of inward directed irritability.

There were no differences between the treatment groups for anxiety and internal irritability.

Child behaviour

The total child behaviour showed no differences in outcome between the treatment groups. However, there were differences for two of the subscores: eating problems and bowel and bladder problems.

Eating problems

For mild cases, the health visiting stood out as being associated with a rather better outcome than the other treatments or the control. For the clinically significant (ninetieth centile level) problems, the family therapy and mothers' groups both seemed to be beneficial, showing differences from controls when pair-wise comparisons were considered.

Bowel and bladder problems

This is a case par excellence, where the results are influenced by developmental changes, since a large number of children had become clean

Table 9.4 First follow up at one year*

Results for Hypothesis 1: "The three interventions differ from each other and from the control in reducing disturbance and delay"

Measure of disturbance	Mild initial level of disturbance (50th centile)	Severe initial level of disturbance (90th centile)
Mother's mental state		
Depression		
Anxiety	Control > HV > FT & Gp	FT > HV > Control > Gp
Inward directed irritability		
Outward directed irritability	HV & FT > Control > Gp	FT > Control > HV > Gp
Cognitive failures		
Child behaviour		
Total score		
Eating problems		
Sleep problems	HV > Control & FT & G	Gps > FT > Control & HV
Bowel and bladder problems		
Attention problems	Control & FT > HV > Gps	Gps > FT > Control > HV
Relationship and temper problems		
Anxiety problems		
Marriage		
Overall marriage quality		
Irritability wife to husband		
Irritability husband to wife	FT > HV & Gps & Control	
Quarrels		
Nagging husband to wife		
Nagging wife to husband		
Child development	Average development (50th centile)	Delayed development (10th centile)
Developmental Quotient		
Mean sentence length	HV > Gps & Control > FT	Gps > Control & HV > FT
Identify shapes and objects		
Direct observations		

* The lines drawn over each set of findings indicate that there are no significant pair-wise differences between the results under the line. The treatment to the left of any symbol ">" showed better outcome than that to the right.

and dry through the year spanned by this follow up. At baseline, nearly all the children at the fiftieth centile were toilet trained, whereas at the ninetieth centile, hardly any were. By the time of the follow up, nearly all the ninetieth centile children had become toilet trained, whichever treatment group they were in. The differences shown in Table 9.4 reflect, therefore, rather small differences between groups against which there were massive differences due to simple maturational factors in the children. It can be seen that there were no pair-wise differences.

Marriage

Here five subscores were available, but in four subscores as well as in the overall score, there were no significant differences among the treatment groups.

Nagging of husband by wife

This was the only area where there was a significant difference. Again, the family therapy group showed a better outcome than the other three groups, including the control (see, however, the results from Hypothesis 3).

Developmental assessment of the child

The only differences between groups were in the overall Developmental Quotient, which is reported on page 176.

Summary of findings for Hypothesis 1

Of the main findings, there were significant differences between groups for depression; however, there were no pair-wise differences. Family therapy seemed to affect child development adversely. Of the minor scales, the group programme seemed to have an adverse effect on inwardly directed irritability. Health visiting had a good effect on secondary prevention level eating problems and groups and family therapy had a good effect on clinically significant children's eating problems. Family therapy had a good effect on nagging husbands.

Hypothesis 2 The Effects of Other Social and Biological Predictors of Outcome

Description of the procedure

This hypothesis was not a test of the treatments, but rather a consideration of how two other factors in the lives of the children and their families influenced the outcome. The first factor was the overall score of social adversity. In Chapter 5 we described how this scale was constructed. We decided to take a score of four or more of the qualities shown in Table 5.3 as high adversity. The second factor was sex differences. For the two child-centred measures of behaviour and developmental level, we assessed the progress of the boys and girls separately. (See also the tables in Appendix 2, A2.5 to A2.8.)

Social Adversity

Overview of main findings

High social adversity was associated with poorer outcome in three of the four main outcome measures: depression in the mother, total behavioural score of the child and Developmental Quotient of the child. This was true for both the more severe and for the milder initial disturbance. Curiously, there was no correlation with poor outcome of the marriage, but each of the subscores did show a poorer outcome of marriage under conditions of social adversity (see Table 9.5).

Mother's depression

High levels of adversity were associated with much higher levels of initial depression when compared with mothers living under more favourable circumstances. Allowing for this difference in levels by using the statistical adjustments described above, the outcome at both the fiftieth and ninetieth centiles on initial scores, the mothers with depression, whether mild or severe, did worse if they lived under high levels of adversity compared with those living under low levels of adversity. Not only did the high adversity families have a poor starting-point at baseline, but also their problems continued to get worse compared with the low adversity families over the year to the first follow up.

Child disturbance

Those living under conditions of high adversity showed more disturbance at baseline. They also showed worse outcome than those being brought up under low adversity. This was true despite the fact that, as described above, the initially higher scores had been corrected in the statistical procedure.

Developmental Quotient

This measure showed that adversity was again associated with poor scores at the outset, but that even allowing for this in the analysis, the developmental delay was more persistent in the children living under conditions of high adversity. This was particularly true of those children who started off with more severe developmental delays.

Table 9.5 First follow up at one year
Results for Hypothesis 2: "There are other social and biological predictors of outcome" – index of adversity as Low Adversity and High Adversity

Measure of disturbance	Mild initial level of disturbance (50th centile)	Severe initial level of disturbance (90th centile)
Mother's mental state		
Depression	Low > High	Low > High
Anxiety	Low > High	Low > High
Inward directed irritability		
Outward directed irritability		
Cognitive failures		
Child behaviour		
Total score	Low > High	Low > High
Eating problems		
Sleep problems		
Bowel and bladder problems	High > Low	Low > High
Attention problems	Low > High	Low > High
Relationship and temper problems	Low > High	Low > High
Anxiety problems	Low > High	Low > High
Marriage		
Overall marriage quality		
Irritability wife to husband		
Irritability husband to wife	Low > High	Low > High
Quarrels	Low > High	Low > High
Nagging husband to wife	Low > High	Low > High
Nagging wife to husband	Low > High	Low > High
Child development	**Average development (50th centile)**	**Delayed development (10th centile)**
Developmental Quotient	Low > High	Low > High
Mean sentence length		
Identify shapes and objects	Low > High	Low > High
Direct observations		

Findings on Minor Scales

Adversity and mother's mental state

The anxiety measure showed a poorer outcome under conditions of high adversity in the same way as depression. This was not true of indices of internal and external irritability and of cognitive failures. In these cases there were no differences associated with different levels of adversity.

Adversity and child behaviour

Here we found the same situation as in the mother's mental state: the children living under adversity had higher initial scores. After making adjustments for these initial levels, the children living under adversity still showed poorer outcome on a number of the scales.

Bowel and bladder problems

The same principle holds as was shown in our consideration of Hypothesis 1. At the fiftieth centile, nearly all the children were trained at the initial assessment. At the ninetieth centile nearly all had trained in the year between baseline at 2½ and follow up at 3½ years of age. The high adversity families had, however, still done rather worse in toilet training.

Attention problems

Here again, the picture is of worse outcome in the high adversity group. This was true both of those children who had mild problems and of those who had severe problems at the outset.

Relationship and temper problems

The children who were being brought up under high adversity showed much worse outcome on these behaviour problems. The scores were particularly high as compared with low adversity children where the initial level of tempers and relationship problems was at the ninetieth centile.

Anxiety problems

Again the children who were being reared under conditions of high social adversity had a higher proportion of severe disorders. However, as we have seen in previous symptom groups, anxiety difficulties were also more persistent, even after allowing for these baseline differences.

Adversity and marriage ratings

The effects of adversity on marriage were predictably detrimental, with differences between the advantaged and disadvantaged groups on all the subscale measures. The marriage component to the adversity score was removed in these analyses. We can be sure, therefore, that the results reflect the detrimental effects of poor circumstances, not simply an artifact.

Adversity and developmental assessment of the child

Identifying shapes and objects

This showed enormous change between the initial and one year follow up. However, the children in high adversity circumstances lagged behind their more advantaged peers.

Differences in Developmental Progress of Boys and Girls

Overview of main findings for sex differences

It is widely accepted that there are differences between boys and girls in developmental progress. These differences were found in the present study, as shown in Table 9.6. (See also the tables in Appendix 2, A2.9 and A2.10.)

Table 9.6   First follow up at one year
Results for Hypothesis 2: "There are other social and biological predictors of outcome" – sex differences

Measures of disturbance	Mild initial level of disturbance (50th centile)	Severe initial level of disturbance (90th centile)
Child behaviour		
Total score		
Eating problems		
Sleep problems		
Bowel and bladder problems		
Attention problems	Girls > Boys	
Relationship and temper problems		Girls > Boys
Anxiety problems		Girls > Boys
Child development	**Average development (50th centile)**	**Delayed development (10th centile)**
Developmental Quotient		Girls > Boys
Mean sentence length		
Identify shapes and objects	Girls > Boys	Girls > Boys
Direct observations	Girls > Boys	Girls > Boys

There were no sex differences in the progress on overall child behaviour. Among the children who were somewhat developmentally retarded at the outset (tenth centile), there were sex differences in developmental progress, with girls progressing faster than boys. The girls were generally more developmentally advanced at baseline, but even allowing for this, the delay in boys was more persistent among the children who had low scores at the outset. This was not true of the children who had average scores.

Findings on the Minor Scales

Sex differences in child behaviour

Relationship and temper problems

In children with high initial scores, the boys initially scored more highly on temper tantrums. Even after allowing for this difference, this disturbance was more persistent in boys than in girls.

Anxiety problems

Similarly, in the children with high initial scores, the boys improved less over time than the girls.

Sex differences in developmental assessment of the child

Apart from the differences in overall score, there were the following findings.

Identifying shapes and objects

The dominant picture was of enormous progress over the follow up year on this developmental ability. However, the girls got the hang of identifying shapes and objects rather more than the boys did, for each level of initial score.

Direct observations

The girls showed better progress than the boys at both the fiftieth centile and the ninetieth centile.

Summary of findings for Hypothesis 2

A large number of measures of the mother's mental state, child behaviour, marriage and children's development showed worse outcome when the family was living in conditions of social adversity. There was evidence that development in boys was somewhat slower overall than in girls among those whose development had been delayed at baseline. There was also some evidence that boys did worse on some behavioural subscores.

Hypothesis 3   The Influence of Social Adversity and Sex Differences on the Effects of Treatment

Description of the procedure

The demonstration that level of social adversity made such major differences in the children's and families' progress shows how essential it is to be able to examine the effects of treatment under different conditions of adversity. This set of analyses is similar to those used to explore Hypothesis 1, but the families living under high and low adversity are distinguished from each other in the analysis (high adversity indicates 4 or more of the adverse factors listed in Table 5.3).

A similar set of analyses was carried out which allowed us to examine the separate responses of boys and girls to treatment. Many of the results in these analyses showed that treatment and adversity summated in a simple way to influence outcome. Where the influence of treatment had been significant in Hypothesis 1, it tended to continue to be so when different levels of adversity were considered. The same was true of adversity. Where this had a significant effect on its own (which it so often did), the effect persisted when the effect of the different treatments was added to the analysis.

For clarity, in the overall picture of the results for Hypothesis 3 presented in Table 9.7, only those results where there was a difference among the treatment groups are shown. There were, not surprisingly, many other areas where the effects of high and low adversity came through, unaffected by treatment and this was also true in some cases with sex differences. The results in these cases were identical to those described in the section on Hypothesis 2.

The Influence of Adversity on the Effects of Treatment

Overview of main findings

There were significant findings for level of child disturbance and level of developmental quotient. The weak treatment effect of maternal depression found in Hypothesis 1 disappears (see Table 9.7 and also the tables in Appendix 2, A2.11 to A2.15).

Table 9.7 First follow up at one year*

Results for Hypothesis 3: "These other predictors influence the effects of the various treatments on the various types of disturbance" (results of treatments once level of adversity has been taken into account)

Measures of disturbance	Mild initial level of disturbance (50th centile)	Severe initial level of disturbance (90th centile)
Mother's mental state		
Depression		
Anxiety		
Inward directed irritability	HV & FT > Control > Gp	FT > Control > HV > Gp
Outward directed irritability		
Cognitive failures		
Child behaviour		
Total score	{ Low > High / Control & FT > HV & Gp	{ Low > High / Gp > HV > FT > Control
Eating problems	HV > Control & FT & Gp	FT & Gps > HV & Control
Sleep problems	FT & Control > HV > Gp	Gp > FT > Control > HV
Bowel and bladder problems		
Attention problems		
Relationship and temper problems		
Anxiety problems		
Marriage		
Overall marriage quality		
Irritability wife to husband		
Irritability husband to wife		
Quarrels		
Nagging husband by wife		
Nagging wife by husband		
Child development	**Average development (50th centile)**	**Delayed development (10th centile)**
Developmental Quotient		HV > Control & Gp > FT
Mean sentence length		
Identify shapes and objects		
Direct observations		

* The lines drawn over each set of findings indicate that there are no significant pair-wise differences between the results under the line. The treatment to the left of any symbol ">" showed better outcome than that to the right.

Depression

Although, as we have seen, both treatment and adversity had an influence, the adversity effect was the only one that was evident when the two were considered together. Thus the apparent weak effect of the treatment seen in Hypothesis 1 was due to the confounding of different levels of adversity in the treatment groups rather than to the treatments themselves. Any concerns we may have had about adverse effects of the treatments on maternal depression were unfounded. None of the treatments made an impact on depression.

Child disturbance

The total outcome score on child behaviour was affected by the treatments as well as adversity. The situation is set out in Figure 9.1. Adversity continued to have an effect on outcome, but for clinically significant disorder (ninetieth centile), the treatments were associated with better outcome than the control group. This was particularly true of the mothers' groups, which stood out as significantly better than the controls in pair-wise comparisons. Health visiting and family therapy showed lesser effects. For secondary prevention level disorder, however, the picture was different. Mothers' groups and health visiting were associated with a worse outcome than leaving the families alone and there were again pair-wise differences. The results are shown schematically in Figure 9.1. We can get some idea of the clinical significance of the findings from Figure 9.1. It can be seen that for secondary prevention level disorder, the adjusted scores at follow up ranged over about one unit of score and that they hovered around the score of 8 for low adversity and 9 for high adversity. This was just above our lower level screening cut-off for selection for the study. For the clinically significant disorder (ninetieth centile), the control group score remained at around 13 for both low and high adversity, well above the screen cut-off of 10 recommended by Richman, Stevenson and Graham (1982). This showed that these children still had significant problems. In the low adversity group, the children who had been in the mothers' groups (the most effective treatment) had a one year adjusted outcome 3 points lower. This suggests a useful treatment effect, although the children were far from "cured". While still significant, the results for the clinically disturbed group under high adversity were less impressive, with only a one and a half unit difference between the most effective treatment (mothers' groups) and the control. It does appear that mothers' groups were associated consistently with the best outcome for clinically significant disorder.

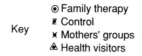

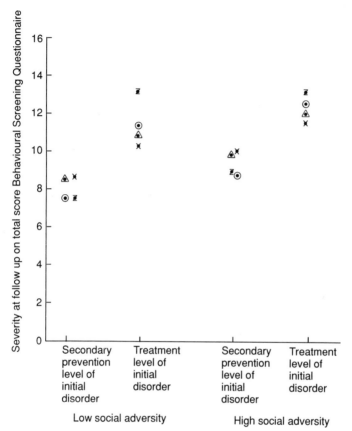

Figure 9.1   Differences in level of child behaviour at one year follow up measured on the Behaviour Screening Questionnaire. The baseline is adjusted to be equal for the four treatments (including the control). The follow up scores associated with two levels of severity of initial disorder are shown: that where secondary prevention would be appropriate (50th centile of sample) and that where treatment would be appropriate (90th centile of sample)

Developmental Quotient

Only the treatment comparisons come through as having an effect when treatment and adversity are considered together. Again, the family therapy unfortunately remains associated with the poorest outcome, particularly for those children with low initial scores around the tenth centile.

Findings on the Minor Scales

Mother's mental state: treatment effects taking background adversity into account

Anxiety

This showed a similar picture to depression. When the effect of adversity is taken into account, there were no treatment differences.

Inward directed irritability

The treatment effects that were presented under Hypothesis 1 persist when adversity is taken into account. For low initial scores, mothers' groups show the best outcome and family therapy is slightly better than the control group. For high initial scores, the mothers' groups and, to some extent, the health visiting appear to show a worse outcome than the positive control group, although it should be noted that the differences do not now hold up on pair-wise comparisons. Family therapy was associated with modest advantages compared with mothers' groups.

Child behaviour: treatment effects taking background factors of adversity and sex into account

Eating problems

The treatment effects were very similar to those presented under Hypothesis 1. This means that the outcome of therapy was the same for families living in high and low adversity. Health visiting seemed to do well with secondary prevention level disorder while for clinically significant disorder, none of the treatments came out as superior on pair-wise comparisons.

Bowel and bladder problems

In the same way, adversity did not modify the effects of the treatments on bowel and bladder problems. Small as these were, they were in fact statistically significant, but not strongly enough to come out on pair-wise comparisons.

Attention problems, relationship and temper problems and anxiety problems

All were unaffected by the treatment regimes; when treatment and adversity were considered together, they continued to show the same changes as with adversity alone.

Marriage

Three of the six measures – quarrelling and bickering, nagging of husband by wife and nagging of wife by husband – continued to show the effect of adversity once the effect of treatment was taken into account. The treatment effect on nagging of husband to wife disappeared.

Developmental assessment of the child

In the analyses of developmental progress, the results closely reflect those in Hypotheses 1 and 2.

Identifying shapes and objects

The pattern follows that described for Hypothesis 2. There are adversity but no treatment effects.

Differences in Treatment Effects for Boys and Girls

Description of the procedure

The procedure used in this analysis was the same as for the analysis comparing the effects of adversity on the effectiveness of treatment except that boys and girls were compared in place of families living under conditions of high and low adversity. (See also the tables in Appendix 2, A2.16 and A2.17.)

Overview of the main findings

Child behaviour

There was evidence of a treatment effect. For clinically significant disorder, the mothers' groups showing better outcome than the controls on pair-wise comparisons, with the health visiting not far behind and the family therapy group progressing somewhat better than the control group. This progress was the same for boys and girls: there were no sex differences.

Developmental Quotient

The pattern of treatment effects remained the same as in Hypothesis 1, with the outcome for family therapy being particularly poor. In addition, however, boys showed a worse outcome than girls in every group. This was particularly the case for boys who started with severe delay: these boys showed the worst outcome. These findings, for boys and girls separately, are shown in Figure 9.2. It can be seen that in both boys and girls, the health visiting programme is associated with the best outcome, scoring over two points higher than the controls for severe initial delay while family therapy is associated with a poor outcome in both sexes, especially boys.

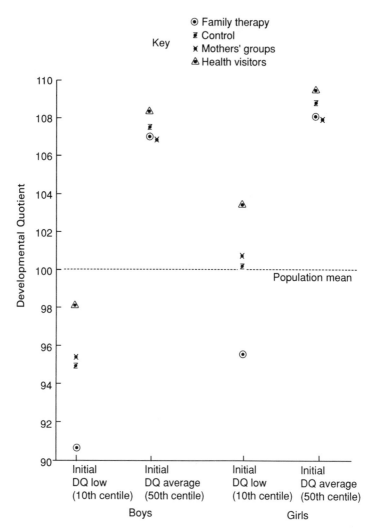

Figure 9.2 Differences in level of child development at one year follow up as measured by the total Developmental Quotient. The baseline is adjusted to be equal for the four treatments (including the control). The follow up scores associated with two levels of initial developmental level are shown: average (50th centile) and retarded (10th centile). The results are shown for boys and girls separately

Findings on the Minor Scales

Behaviour problems

Eating problems

The treatment effects were the same for boys and girls when these were examined separately.

Bowel and bladder problems

Similarly, considering boys and girls separately did not alter the picture, boys and girls seemed to respond in the same way to the treatment effects on bowel and bladder problems.

Relationship and temper problems and anxiety problems

The same was true when the effects of the treatments were considered separately on these problems for boys and girls. The treatments were not effective in these areas of disturbance in either sex.

Developmental assessment of the child

Identifying shapes and objects

As in the results of Hypothesis 2, the girls again had the better outcome, and there were no treatment effects.

Summary of findings for Hypothesis 3

The most striking finding when adversity was considered in the outcome of treatment was that mothers' groups were found to have a positive effect with clinically significant disturbance. Special health visiting also showed some good effects, not enough to stand on its own in reducing the overall measure of disturbance, but it did help with sleep problems. The curious but worrying adverse effect of family therapy on child development in retarded children was still present, and in both boys and girls, but more seriously so in boys. The weak treatment effect on mothers' depression disappeared altogether but the apparent adverse effect of groups on internal irritability persisted, although in a weaker form. There were no effects on marital problems.

THREE YEAR FOLLOW UP

Description of the procedure

The procedure used here was the same as that used in the exploration of Hypothesis 3 at the one year follow up with one important exception. At the one year follow up it was appropriate to use all the same measures that had been used at baseline. At three years, in these rapidly developing children, this was no longer so. Several tests were used that were not used at the baseline or earlier follow up. For child behaviour, the Behaviour Interview for Infant School Children (Kolvin et al 1975) was used and for developmental assessment, the Wechsler Preschool and Primary Scale of Intelligence (Anastasi 1982) was used.

Overview of main findings

See the tables in Appendix 2, A2.18 to A2.21. At the three year follow up, none of the major outcome measures showed a treatment effect but there were a large number of differences associated with social adversity. We confine our presentation here to the exploration of Hypothesis 3 and look at the treatment effects in the presence of differences in social adversity and in boys and girls separately.

Minor effects of treatment

Child behaviour

The only differences found at three year follow up were in the area of child behaviour. These differences were rather difficult to interpret for two reasons. The interview used at this follow up, when the children were now $5\frac{1}{2}$ years old, was rather different in character than at the earlier follow up (Kolvin et al 1975). Adjustments were made for baseline score but over three years at such an early age, there were marked qualitative changes in both normal and disturbed behaviour from the baseline measures. The differences in outcome concerned only the subscores of eating, sleep and anxiety problems; however, they were present among children from high and from low adversity backgrounds. Allowing for these reservations, it remains true that the health visiting regime did seem to do particularly badly, with these children showing a worse outcome than the control in eight of the twelve analyses that showed differences in treatment outcome. The picture is set out in Table 9.8.

Table 9.8 Second follow up at three years*

Results for Hypothesis 3: "The other predictors influence the effects of the various treatments on the various types of disturbance" (results of treatments once level of adversity has been taken into account)
No differences in mother's mental state, marriage or child development

Measure of disturbance	Mild initial level of disturbance (50th centile)	Severe initial level of disturbance (90th centile)
Child behaviour with low adversity		
Total score		
Eating problems	$\overline{\text{FT \& Control \& Gp}}$ > HV	$\overline{\text{Gps > FT > Control}}$ > HV
Sleep problems	$\overline{\text{FT \& Control > Gps}}$ > HV	$\overline{\text{FT \& Control > Gps}}$ > HV
Aches and pains		
Sleep problems		
Temper problems		
Anxiety problems	$\overline{\text{FT > HV > Gps > Control}}$	$\overline{\text{Control > FT > Gps > HV}}$
Child behaviour with high adversity		
Total score		
Eating problems	$\overline{\text{FT > HV > Control > Gps}}$	$\overline{\text{FT > HV > Control > Gps}}$
Sleep problems	$\overline{\text{FT \& Control > Gps HV}}$	$\overline{\text{FT \& Control > Gps}}$ > HV
Aches and pains		
Speech problems		
Temper problems		
Anxiety problems	$\overline{\text{FT > HV > Gps > Control}}$	$\overline{\text{Control > FT > Gps > HV}}$

* The lines drawn over each set of findings indicate that there are no significant pair-wise differences between the results under the line. The treatment to the left of the symbol ">" showed better outcome than that to the right.

The Effects of Social Adversity at Three Year Follow Up

Mother's mental state

All the measures – depression, anxiety, inward and outward directed irritability and cognitive failures – showed a worse outcome in those families living under conditions of social adversity.

Child behaviour

Here there were effects of adversity as well as the treatment effects that we have already described.

Child behaviour total score

There was an effect of adversity: the children brought up in adversity were more disturbed. Also the more disturbed they had been at baseline, the worse they had become in the intervening three years.

Eating problems

Overall, the high adversity group had a worse outcome.

Temper problems

There was an effect of adversity in such a way that the more severe the baseline score, the more deterioration there was over the three year follow up.

Marriage

There were no treatment effects on any of the measures. There was a background effect of adversity, with the families who experienced more adverse circumstances having, not surprisingly, more problems of irritability and nagging in their marriages.

Developmental assessment of the child

At the three year follow up, the WPPSI test (described in Chapter 5) was used. Change was estimated for each scale using the Developmental Quotient at $2\frac{1}{2}$ as the baseline variable against which the change was measured. Neither the full-scale IQ nor its subscores were affected by the treatment but the children from high adversity backgrounds showed slower progress on these measures. Equally there was no effect due to treatment or background adversity on measures of language skills, number skills or direct observations.

The Effects of Sex Differences at Three Year Follow Up

Temper problems

There were marked sex differences, with boys showing worse outcome than girls.

Developmental assessment of the child

There were no sex differences in the developmental measures.

School behaviour

At the three year follow up, teachers were asked to complete the Conners Scale and the Prosocial Behaviour Scale (see Chapter 5 for details). These results were analysed and there were no differences between treatment groups on the main scales or any of the subscales.

SUMMARY

This chapter was concerned with the outcome of the study. In the first part the prevalence and associations of mother and toddler disturbance are reported. It was shown that prevalence of mother's disturbance was somewhat lower than comparable studies in other inner cities, whereas the toddler rate of disturbance was comparable to similar studies. There were strong associations of mother and toddler disturbance with each other and with marital problems. There were weaker associations with social class and development of the child.

The second theme of the chapter was the outcome of the treatments. We first described how the analysis was carried out to overcome potential artifacts due to unequal scores in different groups (despite randomization) and changes due to the development of the rapidly growing children between baseline and follow up measures. A significance level of 5% was adopted.

The findings at one year follow up

There was no significant benefit for mother's depression with any of the treatments, although an important subscale, inward directed irritability, showed a poor outcome associated with mother and toddler groups.

The mother and toddler groups were beneficial for toddlers with clinically significant disorder. This was not true of toddlers with mild disturbance; here the controls and family therapy showed slightly but significantly better than health visiting and mothers' groups. Some of the more specific problems also showed differences from the control at one year follow up. In particular, mild eating problems showed consistent improvement with health visiting.

A worrying finding was that those toddlers who were developmentally retarded at baseline, particularly the boys, seemed to get more retarded if they were in the family therapy regime.

The findings at three year follow up

The effects on the major measures had washed out, although the long-term effects of health visiting seemed rather poor.

There were widespread differences in outcome with the socially deprived families getting on worse than those living under better circumstances. This was true of all four areas tapped in the outcome measures: mother's mental state, toddler disturbance, marriage, and toddler development. These differences were present at one year but more marked at three years.

The boys showed rather slower development and more persistent behaviour problems than the girls at one year, but the differences had disappeared at three years.

Chapter 10

Results of the Study: Parts 3 and 4

In Chapter 9 we discussed parts 1 and 2 of the results of our study. In this chapter, we cover parts 3 and 4:

Part 3. The consumer view of the help offered (and the use of other services by the study families during the project)

Part 4. The outcome of disturbance and delay when no treatment is given (this relates to Hypothesis 4 of the study).

PART 3: THE CONSUMER VIEW OF THE HELP OFFERED

Acceptability of the help offered is of prime importance in any intervention. Not only are clients free to bring the therapy to a premature halt by opting out, but also, even if they do continue but with less than full commitment, the effectiveness of the result is likely to be diminished. The consumer view of therapy may be influenced by the following factors.

First, there are differences in the therapist. In the mid-1960s it was found that effective therapists had particular qualities of warmth and empathy (Truax and Carkhuff 1967). These effects were found in a number of different settings. In children, in a therapy project in ordinary schools for example, the quality of openness was found to be most important (Kolvin et al 1981).

Second, there are differences in the clientele. Any client can decide that the therapy is not the thing for him or her but there do seem to be tendencies for some types of client to view therapy negatively. For example, Furey and Basili (1988) studied the relationship of satisfaction and continuation in therapy to characteristics of the clientele in a study of parent effectiveness training with young children. They found that mothers who dropped out of therapy were more depressed, were of lower social class and issued commands to their children that were less clear than mothers who continued in treatment. This illustrates a common and unwelcome finding, that those most in need are often the most difficult to engage in therapy. We shall return to this in relation to our own results below.

Third, some types of therapy may be more acceptable and popular than others. For example, Calvert and McMahon (1987) sought parents' view on the acceptability of different therapeutic manoeuvres within a parent effectiveness training programme for non-referred children. Introducing a new skill to a child was found to be a more popular procedure than using techniques such as "time out" or ignoring undesirable behaviours. It is this third question that we shall explore in relation to our own results. We were anxious to know whether the programmes we introduced into the community were found acceptable by those we were hoping to help and whether there were differences in the popularity and perception of the three programmes. This was a particularly sensitive issue since the help was unsolicited. A consumer view should give us a clear picture as to whether the concern of the workers involved in the project was welcomed or not.

There are two ways of looking at this matter. First, what was the uptake of the services? A high fall-out rate might indicate that the service was not welcome, not found useful, or both. Even if a kinder interpretation is appropriate, the service is not much use if the prospective clientele are not using it.

Second, how were the three programmes viewed by the mothers? The fact that there were three programmes allowed for comparison between them as well as evaluation of each in its own right. We assessed this in two ways: we developed an anonymous consumer response questionnaire and we asked the interviewers at one year follow up to note any comment made about the intervention they had received.

Service Uptake

Table 10.1 shows the way that the mothers used the three services. It can be seen that both the health visiting programme and the mothers' groups were well used. The high uptake of mothers' groups is more impressive as the mothers had to travel to the clinic, whereas the health visitor programme was brought to them.

Table 10.1   Service uptake

Health visiting	55 out of 67
Family therapy	46 out of 59 assessment
	21 treatment
Mother and toddler group	47 out of 66

A consumer response questionnaire

A 26 item questionnaire was developed based on a previous instrument that was developed to assess the response to a parent–teacher consultation programme (Kolvin et al 1981). The full questionnaire together with a scoring key is set out in Appendix 3. The questionnaire was given anonymously to the mothers at the time of the first follow up (one year after the start of the assessment and intervention programme). We estimated that the anonymity might enable mothers to answer without feeling that they might upset their helper, or to mistakenly feel that they might be prejudicing their chance of getting help from the health service in the future. On the whole, the responses to the questionnaire items were favourable, but in the absence of comparative data, the significance of this was not clear: it was quite possible that it represented a courteous response of little significance. Much more interesting was the way that the different programmes compared with each other.

Differences in total scores

First, the total scores were considered. Using the Kruskall Wallis test, the scores for the positive items and the negative items were considered separately. Overall differences were then looked for, using the algebraic sum of the positive and negative items (each positive item was given a score of +1 and each negative a score of −1 and the scores were then added and subtracted accordingly). The results comparing the three treatments are shown in Table 10.2. It can be seen that the mother and

Table 10.2 Comparison of popularity of the three treatments on the consumer response questionnaire (Kruskall Wallis ANOVA with Mann–Whitney post hoc comparisons)

Groups		Health visiting	Mothers
Family therapy	+ve	ns	M Gp > FT*
	−ve	HV > FT*	M Gp > FT**
	Total	ns	M Gp > FT*
Health visiting	+ve	M Gp > HV*	
	−ve	ns	
	Total	M Gp > HV*	

Notes   The treatment to the left of the symbol ">" is more popular (or less unpopular) than the treatment to the right
*   Significant at 5% level or less
**   Significant at 1% level or less

toddler groups were the most popular and the family therapy least popular; the health visiting occupied an intermediate position.

In Table 10.3 we present the significant differences between the three programmes for each item of the consumer response questionnaire that showed significant individual differences between the three treatments. It can be seen that the most favourable responses were for the mother and toddler groups and the health visiting programme. The mothers were much less certain about the family therapy programme. Several of the item-by-item results seemed to suggest that the mothers would like to have avoided the family therapy meetings, and that, compared with the other treatments, this programme gave rise to feelings of anxiety.

Individual Comments on the Programme

Although 183 spontaneous comments on the project were gathered at the one year follow up interview. It is not possible or desirable to reproduce all these here and it would not be appropriate in a scientific report to mention those responses which were particularly vivid or interesting. Instead, a random sample of five from each programme will give the reader a flavour of the responses that were received.

Comments on special health visiting

1. Enjoyed health visitor's visits: "nice to have someone to talk to".
2. Mother absolutely delighted with the help she got. Couldn't find enough praise for help and said HV always seemed to have the right answer to any of her problems. Mother used to look forward to the visits and misses them. Thought the whole idea of individual help splendid.
3. Couldn't remember health visitor's visits.
4. Mother enjoyed HV's visits. Good to have someone to talk to. It helped a lot.
5. Quite pleased with the help she got from the project and grateful for the help and advice.

Comments on family therapy

1. Mother said someone was pestering her on the 'phone, but her husband didn't like things like that.
2. Felt it was an intrusion. They would have liked some sound constructive advice on how to get the child to bed earlier. All they got was questions and repetition of the previous interview. Father was tired after a hard day's work and couldn't be bothered with evening interviews.

Table 10.3   Comparison of responses of mothers on the consumer response questionnaire for the three different programmes, item by item

---

Items where health visiting scored higher than family therapy

It helped to have someone to talk to.**
Other family members should have had a chance to join in the discussions.***
The meetings were useful to me in seeing that other people may have similar difficulties to me.**
I found it helpful on the whole.*

Items where family therapy scored higher than health visiting

Fewer visits would have been better.*
It was difficult to see the point of some of the things that were brought up.***
Discussions like that are just a waste of time.***
I sometimes felt upset after the discussions.***
I worried over what had been discussed.***

Items where mother and toddler groups scored higher than family therapy

It helped me to understand my child more.***
It helped me to think of ways to cope with my child's sleep and eating problems.*
It helped to have someone to talk to.**
It helped me to understand things about the whole family.*
It helped me to think of ways to cope with behaviour difficulties in my child.***
Other family members should have an opportunity to join in the discussions.**
It helped me to understand my child better.**
The meetings were useful to me in helping me to see other people may have similar difficulties to me.***
It helped me to understand my own reactions to things better.***
I found it helpful on the whole.***

Items where family therapy scored higher than mothers' groups

Too many questions were asked.*
Fewer visit would have been better.***
It was difficult to see the point of some of the things that were brought up.***
Discussions like this are just a waste of time.*

Items where mother and toddler groups scored higher than health visiting

It helped me to think of ways to cope with my child's sleep and eating problems.*
It helped me to understand my child better.*

---

*   Significant difference at 5% level
**   Significant difference at 2% level
*** Significant difference at 1% level

3. Couldn't see the point as they felt they were ordinary folk.
4. Not very impressed by the family discussions. Thought the worker was nice and friendly but didn't see the point of it all.
5. Mother thought the therapy was an excellent idea and made them discuss their plans for the future after the worker had talked over the options.

Comments on mothers' groups

1. Mother thought treatment helpful. Was particularly glad to have someone to talk to while her husband was away.
2. Like the mothers' group but didn't continue, as a place was already booked at a nursery for Sharon.
3. Full of praise for mothers' groups. Still has contact with other mothers and toddlers she met at the group. One of the best things she has ever participated in and it has given her more confidence and understanding of managing Colin.
4. Mother really enjoyed the groups and still meets four of the other mothers every week even though all their children are now at nursery.
5. Only attended mothers' group on one occasion. Didn't go back because "I can't talk when other people are there".

Possible explanations for differences in popularity

The random choice of examples may have fallen a little unfairly on family therapy, but in general this seems to be a reasonable spectrum of responses.

In looking for explanations for the difference in popularity of the different interventions there are various possibilities. First, the complexity and intrusiveness of the family therapy regime may have been simply an over-response to relatively mild problems in the community, especially as the families had not come forward for help.

A second possibility is that the families may have had severe problems of family function which they were not prepared to face, beneficial as it might have been for them to do so.

Third, we have seen in Chapter 3 that therapist interpersonal skill is a crucial ingredient for successful outcome of therapy. Perhaps the therapists assigned to family therapy did not have the same skill and sensitivity as those in the other treatment programmes. The third possibility can be discarded straight away since the family therapy was undertaken by the same therapists as the highly popular mothers' groups. The second possibility is based on the rather arrogant assumption that somehow we know better than the families what is good for them. The first possibility, that the intervention was unnecessarily elaborate and intrusive for a community programme, seems to have some truth, and is confirmed by several of the mothers' comments (eg see comment 2 on family therapy, page 200).

Use of Regular Services

Another simple way to assess whether the interventions were meeting needs was to see if they had any impact on the use of regular services by the study families. Accordingly, at the first follow up (ie at one year after intervention) questions were asked about various types of consultation by different family members. The consultation patterns of mother, father, index child and siblings were asked concerning visits to the family general practitioner, their regular health visitor and the doctor at the local health clinic. The positive results are set out in Table 10.4. It can be seen that there were some general differences, but when each intervention was compared with the at risk control, it was only in the area of sibling consultations that the differences held up. The picture here was that for those families in the mother and toddler groups, there did seem to be fewer consultations by the children's siblings than was the case in the at risk control group. This is a curious and indirect benefit of the treatment and its significance is not immediately obvious. Satisfaction with the service offered by the regular services was higher in the screen negative controls. This was presumably because they had a lower burden of need and thus less cause for dissatisfaction resulting from unfulfilled hope and demands

Table 10.4   Use of local services by study families

	Kruskal Wallis ANOVA	N.control	Gps	HV	FT
Amount of use of service					
Mother to GP					
Emotional problems	*				
Sibling to GP					
Total consultations	*		ARC > Gps*		
Physical problems	*		ARC > Gps*		
Satisfaction with service					
With GP service	*				
With HV service	*	NC > ARC*			
With clinic doctor		NC > ARC*			

Notes   The pair-wise comparisons are with the at risk control
The regime to the left of the symbol ">" showed more use of services and more satisfaction respectively than that on the right
* Significant at 5% level

of the services. The only pair-wise distinction was with at risk controls, which might in a tenuous way indicate that the three treatments had gone some way to improving relationships between the families and the services and reducing alienation.

SUMMARY

The evidence from collaboration in the project, from a consumer response questionnaire and from the spontaneous remarks from the parents involved were consistent in showing that the mother and toddler groups and the special health visiting regime were more popular than the family therapy.

Turning to the effect of the project on the use of normal health services, the only significant difference between the families who received treatment and the at risk controls was that the mothers who were in the special health visiting regime took the siblings of the toddlers in the study to the doctor less often.

PART 4: THE OUTCOME OF DISTURBANCE AND DELAY WHEN NO TREATMENT IS OFFERED

In Chapter 5 we described how, in addition to the four comparison groups that we have described so far in this chapter, we followed a screen negative group of 115 families. The reason for this was to have some way of comparing how the screen positives were getting on compared with the rest of the population of children and their families at the two follow up points at one and three years after the screen.

Ideally, it would have been helpful to be able to compare the number of screen positives and negatives in terms of the numbers of each group who had major disability in the areas of mother's mental health, children's behaviour, marital problems and developmental delay at the two follow up points. A helpful way of doing this would have been to have information on which to make a decision as to which of the mothers and children had clinically significant disturbance or delay. This would have meant interviewing the families again but unfortunately our resources were not sufficient.

Since we lacked resources, we adopted a different approach. In this, the screen negatives were compared with the screen positive controls using the same techniques to adjust for baseline as were used in Hypotheses 1 and 2. The interpretation of these results needs a bit of explanation. Results could indicate any one of three tendencies.

First, the screen positives and screen negatives might converge, suggesting that there was either a deterioration in the cases that originally had no problems or that the screen positives were improving.

Second, the groups might diverge in level of severity, with the screen positives showing a worse outcome despite the adjustment for initial score. This would indicate that there was further deterioration among the cases over the years between baseline and the two follow ups.

Third, there was the possibility that there may be no change in the relative positions of screen positives and screen negatives, indicating that each group was continuing along a path of disturbance or delay that had been predicted by the baseline measures, with the negatives having much lower levels on both.

Table 10.5 gives a summary of the results for the main outcome measures of the study, together with the main tendency in each case: to converge, stay the same or diverge. The main measures that we reported here do reflect the much larger number of minor measures and subscores that were also analysed.

Overview of Main Findings

Mother's mental state

See Appendix 2, Tables A2.22 and A2.23.

Table 10.5 Comparison of progress of screen positive control group with screen negative group at one year follow up and at three year follow up (Hypothesis 4)

	One year follow up	Three year follow up
Mother's mental state		
Depression	W	W
Child behaviour		
Total score (one year follow up)	S	N/A
Total score (three year follow up)	N/A	S
Marriage		
Overall quality of marriage	S	S
Child development		
Developmental Quotient	S	N/A
Full-scale IQ	N/A	W

Key
W =   Worse: the screen positives show an increase in severity, even after allowing for baseline differences

S =   Same: the screen positives and negatives follow a parallel course; the positives do not seem to be improving, but are not deteriorating compared with the screen negatives

B =   Better: the screen positives show better progress than the screen negatives after allowing for baseline differences

One year follow up

There was a worse outcome for depression among the screen positives than among the screen negatives, even when allowance was made for the state of affairs at baseline. This indicates that the mother's mental state was far from a passing problem that we would have done better to ignore. The situation merited clinical concern.

Three year follow up

The deterioration effect for depression continued.

Child behaviour

See Appendix 2, Tables A2.24 and A2.25.

One year follow up

There were no differences between screen positive controls and screen negatives after correction for initial scores. This coincides with the third possibility cited above. The message is not a comforting one: the disturbed children are not getting worse compared with the controls, but they are not getting better either.

Three year follow up

Some of the variables had changed, thus complicating interpretation. As far as could be estimated, the disturbance remained unchanged.

Marriage

There were no differences after the initial correction. Here again the two groups, screen positives and screen negatives, are running along parallel paths of severity, not a converging one as one might expect if there was a significant degree of natural improvement in the marriages. The same picture emerged at three year follow up.

Developmental assessment of the child

See Appendix 2, Tables A2.26 and A2.27.

One year follow up

There were no differences between screen positives and screen negatives in overall developmental level after correction for baseline level.

Three year follow up

The WPPSI was used, so the scores were rather different. For the full-scale IQ, screen positives showed deterioration after correcting for baseline differences in Developmental Quotient. Looking at performance and verbal IQ separately there were no differences for performance IQ. On the verbal scale, there was a greater deterioration for the children in the high adversity group.

Sex differences in outcome among screen positives and screen negatives

There is a lot of evidence, some of which we reviewed in Chapter 2, that the developmental paths of boys and girls are somewhat different. We therefore carried out the analyses for the children's measures for Hypothesis 4 again but separating boys and girls. There were no differences in overall scores, but the details of subscales are reported since they might be of general interest.

Child behaviour

Eating problems

The boys who were screen positive, that is the disturbed group, got on comparatively worse than the controls, whereas the girls got on better. It seems that on this measure the disturbance in the boys is more persistent, following a deteriorating course compared with controls. For the girls, however, there is a convergence with the screen positive group, moving towards the control in severity of eating problems.

Relationship and temper problems

Here the screen positives and negatives were comparable within boys' and within girls' groups. There were, however, differences between boys and girls, with the boys getting on worse. This was equally true of the mild disorders as with the severe.

Developmental assessment of the child

One year follow up

There were marked differences in the outcome of the two sexes. In the girls, there was a marked convergence, indicating that the screen positive group were tending to catch up with the screen negatives. For the boys, the reverse was the case, with the screen positives lagging further behind with the passage of time. These are quite dramatic sex differences and are in keeping with other studies.

Identifying shapes and objects

The same situation is found in this subscore.

Three year follow up

On the full-scale IQ, the same tendency was again found, with boys doing worse than girls and the boys with lower initial scores doing worst of all.

SUMMARY

Comparison of screen positive and screen negative controls

Hypothesis 4 was concerned with untreated progress in each of the areas of disorder: mother's mental state, child behaviour, marriage and child development. For each area the outcome for the untreated screen positive controls was compared with a group of screen negative families. In the vast majority of the comparisons made, outcome showed parallel progress of the screen positive and screen negative groups. This means that the disturbed families tended to remain disturbed.

Chapter 11

Discussion and Conclusions

Can one effectively help families with young children in the community using simple techniques that could be used on a wide basis? This was the question that fired our interest and curiosity in setting up the project that has been presented in this book. In this chapter we need to consider what the answer was, and how the results we got were determined by how and where we looked.

The basic question heading this chapter quickly breaks in two. The first is about whether it is in fact possible to reach the families, whether they want to be engaged in the interventions on offer in the context of fully informed consent and whether, having accepted the offer, they go through with the programme. The second question is whether the resulting intervention actually does any good. To tackle these questions separately would be both long winded and costly. To attempt to answer both at once (as well as all the subsidiary questions that they entail) has the advantage of answering the overarching question intact, but the research strategy needed to tackle this question is a very harsh test for the treatments that were employed, since if any one of the questions proved substantially negative, the others fall down as well. For example, if the parents did not want to be involved in the study, we would never have known about the effectiveness of the mothers' groups, the special health visiting or the family therapy since the study would have stumbled at this first hurdle. Under these circumstances we could have decided that the whole enterprise should be abandoned or that some modification might be the way forward. In the event, most families did take part in what was on offer. What drop outs there were occurred at two levels.

The first was that our results showed that many of those who were in the greatest difficulties as parents were the ones who refused to take part at the early stage. This was shown when we compared the community health visitors' reports for the non-responders and the responders (Nicol et al 1987). In this analysis we found that the non-responders scored higher than the responders on three items of the health visitor questionnaire:

Mother seems unaware of what correct supervision of the child ought to be

There is an atmosphere of rejection towards the child in the home
The children seem passive

All these areas are ones that should give rise to the greatest concern and indicate that we were only partially successful in reaching some of the families in the community in greatest need. The results must throw doubt on those many well-meaning projects which hope to tackle the problems of child deprivation by asking families to come forward voluntarily. However, if families are avoiding involvement at even the most simple level, what hope is there that psychological interventions will have any effect?

On a more optimistic note, 85% of those approached at the screen level did co-operate; of those judged to be in need, 81% came into the programme. At one year, we achieved 100% follow up of those who took part. The intervention was quite brief with some families, sometimes because they did not feel that they wanted further help (10.5% of the mothers in the health visiting regime, for example, withdrew of their own accord, although the professional thought that they did need help; 20% of the family therapy families did not complete the assessment stage); sometimes there was agreement that no more than minimal help was needed: 9% in the case of health visiting, and all but 19 of the family therapy group. We never aimed to solve all the families' problems, merely offer some useful advice and support.

In the families who did take part, we had the task, first mentioned in the Preface, of developing a holistic picture of the impact of the therapy. When we consider the wide variety of problems that were encountered, as shown for example in the health visiting regime (Table 6.2), our measures suddenly look inadequate to this ambitious task. Given limited resources, a tight timetable and, most important, the need not to overload the families with long interviews and other psychological investigations, the best compromise was to select markers of function in different areas of family life. This broad sweep might give a better idea of child and family adaption in the whole, than would a very narrowly based group of measures, even if these might, by a concentration of effort, be more sensitive. Furthermore, a broad spread of measures might offer pointers and detect possibly unexpected effects of the interventions.

INTEGRATION OF THE FINDINGS

Mother's mental state

Although the community was poor and unemployment widespread, there was a relatively well-preserved network of family relationships. This might have explained why the prevalence of maternal psychiatric disorder was relatively low. Our interventions were not helpful in alleviating this problem, indeed rather the reverse: the only result with any consistency was that mothers' internal irritability seemed to get worse within the mother and toddler group regime. While this is only a subscore, the result cannot be ignored. This short scale had the following items:

I feel like harming myself
I get angry with myself and call myself names
The thought of hurting myself occurs to me
Lately I have been getting annoyed with myself.

We return to the problem of negative outcome below. In the meantime, it should be noted that the mother and toddler groups were, in fact, both popular and associated with improvement in the children's behaviour. This seems an odd result, but a recent report by Fleming, Klein and Corter (1992) is rather similar. These workers offered a support group to mothers in the puerperium. There was a no-treatment control group and a group of mothers who were not depressed. All the depressed women in both treatment and control conditions improved over the five months of the follow up, but the treated mothers improved significantly less. At the same time, it was the depressed mothers who increased most in approach behaviours and it was their children who cried less at the five month follow up. It seems unlikely that this would be so if they were actually making the mothers feel worse. We shall return to this issue of negative effects.

Toddler disorder

Here there was a volte-face for mother and toddler groups, with evidence on pair-wise comparisons that they were effective, with more severe clinically significant disturbance, but not with mild disturbance. The other finding that stands out is that health visiting was beneficial for mild eating problems. These are the most hopeful positive findings of the study. They fit with the popularity of special health visiting and mother and toddler groups.

Marital problems

Little seemed to move the problems of this area but it should be noted that family therapy did have a significant impact on the subscore nagging of wife by husband. This finding was an isolated and rather unstable one. It would need replication before any weight could be put on it.

Child development

Here we have to confront the strange but apparently consistent adverse effect of family therapy on child development. One might not expect the results of such short-term intervention to persist over long periods of time, although the evidence from school-based studies is that such interventions can have very persistent effects (Kolvin et al 1981). In the current work, most of the effects, and indeed all the major negative outcomes, had washed out by the three year follow up. The only changes that persisted were on behavioural subscores: here there were poor outcomes for health visiting and mother and toddler groups in families living under low and high adversity and a good outcome for eating problems in family therapy for high adversity families. After three years, these are remarkable and unexpected findings.

Social adversity

In the analysis of this study we have adopted the concept of social adversity as a simple question of adding together a wide range of areas of adversity to make up a total index. As we have seen in Chapter 2, the separate components of the index each have their own element of risk and characteristics. For the effective therapies which are influenced by adversity, there will be a need to unpack the total index and look at the power of its components individually.

EVIDENCE THAT THE FINDINGS OF THE STUDY WERE VALID

Before coming to conclusions about the findings of the study, it is important to look for any internal checks that might reassure us that the picture is a consistent one. In particular, it is very easy, when some of the findings are negative, to adopt an approach that uncritically emphasizes the finding of effectiveness of intervention while looking for methodological weaknesses that can explain away findings of ineffectiveness, let alone evidence that therapy actually makes things worse.

In this section, we shall look for evidence of internal consistency in the results and also for whether the study supports well-known findings from other studies in a way that might be expected.

On the question of consumer response, it does indeed look as if the findings of treatment uptake and the results of the consumer response questionnaire are consistent. If one takes into account the fact that the mothers' groups were held away from home while the other two interventions were brought to the families, the drop out is somewhat higher for family therapy, which was also less popular. In the gathering of spontaneous comments at one year follow up, these were distinctly less kind in the case of family therapy.

Turning to the results of the main analysis, the outcome for levels of adversity show an all too familiar consistency, with the families living under high adversity showing poorer outcome in all four of the areas of outcome. This was true of mother's depression and anxiety. The children themselves also showed a strong association between high adversity and more severe disturbance and delay. Marital problems, apart from the overall score, showed a similar picture.

When we consider sex differences, among those with severe symptoms at the outset, not only temper and relationship difficulties but also anxiety were initially more severe and more persistent in boys, as were developmental difficulties. All these findings, with the possible exception of anxiety, are consistent with those of other studies.

All this evidence demonstrates that, in a general way, some reliance can be placed on the findings of the study. A further issue to mention at this stage is the importance of using methods that will detect negative outcome as sensitively as positive outcome.

Turning to the measures of therapeutic outcome, the findings are far less consistent.

NEGATIVE OUTCOME: POSSIBLE EXPLANATIONS

It has to be said that had we not adopted an approach which included a broad range of measures and had instead concentrated on an in-depth assessment of the child's functioning, we would have missed important, if uncomfortable, findings of the study. There are a number of levels at which one might look for an explanation of why some of the results were unpromising.

Factors in the measurement instruments

In Chapter 1 we reviewed ways of studying psychopathology in the individual and also the quality of relationships. The selection of instruments in the study has been determined in large part by its size and situation; however, we have been able to mix partially direct observational techniques such as the HOME Inventory (which in the event was not helpful), estimates of relationships, such as the marriage ratings, and direct test situations for the child, such as the developmental tests. A great deal of reliance (albeit not exclusively) has been placed on the mother as an informant. The evidence of negative outcome at one year comes from the Leeds scales and developmental tests. The Leeds scales were chosen as scales that could discriminate well between different levels of severity of depression (Kearns et al 1982). The problem cannot be that we used an unvalidated test.

There are other possible interpretations for the internal irritability findings. The first possibility is particularly pertinent in a secondary prevention study. All the regimes might be seen as introducing a new set of concepts and a new psychological language to the mothers. It could be that the apparent negative effects are due to the fact that, post treatment, the mothers answered the questionnaires in a more psychologically sophisticated way. This would thus be similar to a "practice effect" in the context of cognitive testing. The lack of negative effects on mother's depression in the family therapy group could then be seen as an index of the relative lack of engagement of the families in this treatment modality. This would help to explain why the mothers seemed to get more depressed, yet their children simultaneously improved. Perhaps if we had been able to avoid these practice effects, there would have been even more positive results in the area of child behaviour.

The same effect could be operative in the totally inconsistent finding of negative outcome at three years in the case of health visiting. The areas which showed the poor outcome were the very areas that had been targeted for treatment, further, the immediate treatment had been successful. It seems possible that these mothers were more aware of sleep and eating difficulties in their children.

It is difficult to see how practice effects could have had any bearing on the poor results of family therapy in development; however, it could be that in these families there was a degree of apathy and disillusion with the project which affected the children's motivation to perform well on the tests.

Factors in the therapeutic relationship

The fact that the help was unsolicited could be important. There is little direct evidence on this matter, but it should be noted that in the preschool programmes such as project CARE (Ramey et al 1985; Wasik et al 1990), the home component of the intervention was markedly less effective than the centre based component. The results of home based education programmes in general have been modest and mixed (Farren 1990). Since no measures of maternal distress were made in these programmes, there are no bases for comparison. It does seem possible that, however well intentioned, the offer of help gives the message to the mothers, "you are not OK", when in fact they thought they were managing quite well under difficult circumstances.

Another area that requires examination is the therapeutic relationship. Variation in the effectiveness of different therapists has for a long time been a source of interest. In Chapter 3 we outlined some of the evidence that some therapists offer a more helpful quality of interaction to their clients than do others.

Recent research evidence has taken the story further. In meta-analytic studies of adult psychotherapy, some 9% to 11% of results have shown treatment outcome worse than control (Lambert, Shapiro and Bergin 1986) and attention has been focused on therapists who may be actually harmful. Techniques that confront in the absence of support and caring and therapists who are impatient and authoritarian have, for example, been found to lead to deterioration in more seriously disturbed young adults in encounter groups. Following another theme, Sachs (1983) applied a scale to therapy interaction with the help of blind independent raters. Negative effects were found to be associated with a therapist who failed to find a focus or to organize the material that came up in the session.

The relevance of this research to the present study is not obvious. In all the treatment regimes, high priority was given to finding a focus, and there was no evidence in tape recordings made for supervision that the therapists were pushy and authoritarian. The most persuasive evidence that the negative outcome was not due to the therapists, however, is the fact that the same therapist played a major part in both the mothers' groups and in the family therapy, yet the two regimes came out with such divergent results. This finding makes it extremely unlikely that the quality of the therapist was the cause of the puzzling differences between the regimes.

As a further check, we compared the exposure in this regime with outcome. Had the regime itself been the cause of the negative findings, one might expect a correlation between amount of contact and amount of negative outcome. In fact, there was no correlation.

The brevity of the therapy

In the general literature on psychotherapy, there is agreement that brief therapy is as helpful as more long-term therapy (Lambert, Shapiro and Bergin 1986). Nevertheless, it could be that what was needed with these families was a more long-term supportive role: this was certainly the essence of many of the spontaneous comments that were recorded in feedback at one year follow up. It could be that at this time the mothers were feeling the effects of the withdrawal of therapy. On the whole, this seems unlikely since, in the group regime at least, the formal groups had ceased many months earlier.

Mismatching of diagnosis and therapy

A lack of match of diagnosis to therapy could have been an issue; here our project varied importantly from ordinary professional practice because of our need to have comparable groups for the different treatments. The negative outcome of maternal depression consisted of only one subscale but an important one. Hollon and Emerson (1985) found little evidence of negative effects of psychotherapies. They note, however, that there is no established knowledge on the effects of relatively unstructured therapies in depression. In developing their structured cognitive therapy approach, Beck et al (1979) assert that unstructured therapies tend to exacerbate the difficulties of the depressed patient. In the present therapy, care was taken to establish a structured approach so there is little evidence that the wrong therapy was to blame for the mother's depression results. The most frequently quoted agent of positive changes in group interventions is group cohesiveness or the attractiveness of the group for its members. There can be little doubt that the groups in the present study were highly attractive to the members, so this seems an unlikely cause of negative effects.

Community factors

Factors in the community might be another source of negative influence. Our adversity index identified a high degree of disadvantage, deprivation and powerlessness existing in the community. It could be cogently argued that instead of professional help, what was needed were jobs, hope and enfranchisement. In our fieldwork, there were dramatic examples of families where problems ceased as soon as father got a job (see the last case example in Chapter 6, pages 133–5: this was one of several). The poor progress of the high adversity groups compared with the low is no doubt related to this and related factors. To offer psychological intervention in these circumstances could be seen as inappropriate and indeed insulting. Several attempts have been made to offer intervention programmes which offer empowerment by giving choice and instilling self-confidence. Such efforts seem a bit illogical unless power is actually given to the people. While confidence and skill-building can make a contribution, empowerment is primarily a political matter, involving a reordering of social priorities in favour of the poor and away from the rich. Recent trends in the United Kingdom have, unfortunately, been in the opposite direction.

Conclusion

Of all the explanations considered, the ones most likely to account for the negative outcome in the areas of inwardly directed irritability seem to be the fact that the help was unsolicited, and the fact that the mothers might have become more psychologically minded as a result of the intervention. As far as the developmental effect on the children in the family therapy group goes, it could have been lack of motivation at the follow up interview to get the child to perform well on the tests, due to loss of faith in the programme. There was no other evidence, however, to support this conclusion, and the cause of the finding remains a worrying mystery. The measures that are used in evaluation studies in child mental health would benefit from urgent review.

ETHICAL CONSIDERATIONS

We were particularly interested in families that are difficult to reach. Had we been setting out to help adults alone, we would feel little obligation, and even less right to offer help to families unsolicited. Where children are involved, however, society at large feels a greater obligation to intervene to promote development. The principle of compulsory schooling is one example of state intervention in childrearing which is both intrusive and almost universally accepted. The intensity and character of other state interventions have varied from time to time in keeping with variations in public and professional opinion. At the time of writing, in the United Kingdom, the Children Act 1989 is beginning to show its effect (White, Carr and Lowe 1990). Local government authorities are charged with wide duties to support children in need by supporting voluntary organizations and providing day care. There is a broad and pervasive emphasis in the Act towards the support of parenting and the encouragement of parental responsibility. Our project falls plumb in the middle of this philosophy of supportive intervention, with the decision left with the parents as to whether to partake in what is on offer. Our offer of help was, in many cases, to those who seemed to be in the early phases of having difficulties, earlier, no doubt, than was envisaged by the designers of the Act.

There is a second ethical point of wider importance. Most psychological interventions which, in the broad interpretation we have used, include much of day care and early education, carry little in the way of evidence of effectiveness. It is not in the nature of legal documents to question effectiveness, but the broad recommendations of the Children Act 1989 and similar legislation in many countries does raise this question. The ethics of introducing interventions on a wide scale without providing adequate resources for research and development must be questioned. The fact that such provision has hardly ever been made and that most innovations in education, health and the social services are led by ideology, not research evidence, is no excuse. In the present project we have taken a small step in the right direction.

The third ethical point concerns how to act when there is some knowledge of effectiveness, and we return to this in our final comment.

SCREENING

There has been much debate over many years about the status of screening in child health. Before getting on to the question of whether screening is practical, there are a number of considerations about whether it is even desirable. Wilson and Yunger (quoted in Hall 1989) offered the following criteria, among others.

1. The health problem must be an important one.
2. There must be an effective and acceptable treatment that will result.
3. The natural history must be adequately understood.
4. Facilities must be available for treatment and management.

The results of our project argue against the widespread introduction of screening and treatment programmes for mother and toddler problems of the type studied here, largely because our findings were least impressive in the milder cases. More severe disorder is likely to be picked up in the usual referral procedure. A more helpful approach might be to alert general practitioners and health visitors to the fact that effective intervention is possible for preschool children with behaviour problems. This should eventually feed through to parents who can then use the help available. Community mother and toddler groups are already common: some of these could be encouraged to adopt a more therapeutic role.

RECOMMENDATIONS

A number of practical and research recommendations arise out of this study.

Practical recommendations

The health visiting and mothers' groups regimes tested in the study are ones commonly used in practice. If they are to continue to be used, and there is evidence that they have benefits for children's behaviour, they should be carefully audited for effects on the mother's mental state as well as the child's behaviour.

They should be used only where clinically significant toddler disturbance is present.

Family therapy has a place in management of family problems, but again, should be offered as a result of clinic referral for clinically significant problems in motivated patients. There is a need for clinical trials to test its effectiveness in this setting.

From our findings, there is very little justification for the widespread screening for emotional and behaviour problems in young children. A better idea would be to alert primary care professionals to the fact that, with good training, mothers' groups and health visiting can be helpful.

Attention placebo control groups

A lot of attention is paid in the psychotherapy outcome literature to the need for attention placebo control groups. The concept is similar to the use of placebo in controlled clinical trials of drugs. We have mentioned it several times in our discussion of programme evaluation in Chapter 4. In the present study, three approaches were used as active treatments, and these had widely different effects. While it is not clear that any of these were due to simple "attention", this leads on to the question of what is attention anyway. Useful information has come out of the present study despite the fact that there was no treatment group specifically labelled an attention control group.

Description of the individual treatment regimes

A great deal could have been learned if, instead of relying on therapist reports, we had been able to develop independent measures of the content of the individual treatments. This was done in the important collaborative treatment project for the psychotherapy of depression (Elkin et al 1989). It is an extremely expensive undertaking, even in a clinic-based project with motivated adult depressives. Sadly we have to be content with the more obvious contrasts between our treatments, such as whether the whole family was present, as in the family therapy regime. As mentioned above, it seems unlikely that the therapeutic qualities of the therapists were a major factor since the same therapists were involved in treatments with markedly different outcomes.

Research recommendations

All child therapy research should be designed in a way such that negative as well as positive effects can be detected.

Investment should be made in developing a series of standard measures to be used in child psychotherapy research. These should be sensitive to change and, because of this, will need extensive piloting to establish validity. Such a package of measures should not stifle innovation, but will help to establish a means of comparing one study with another.

The measurement of outcome in psychological intervention should be designed with an awareness of the possible widespread systemic changes that may occur, that is, on an interpersonal and family level as well as in the individual. Kniskern and Gurman (1985), in their discussion of family therapy outcome, advocate individual, marital and family measures. If this advice is to be followed, the measures will have to be developed.

Measures in children need to take account of development, as we have done with the conditional and log-linear approaches.

FINAL COMMENTS

Throughout the developed world, important questions are being asked about the effectiveness of medical interventions. The need for audit and quality control is rising to the top of the agenda and clinicians are being asked to justify their pattern of work. These very reasonable questions can be answered only in two stages.

1. There must be investment in adequate clinical trials which can be carried out with the necessary rigour to establish conclusive results.
2. The treatments that are found to be effective must be introduced into clinical practice in a rigorous and professional way.

There is a belief that both these tasks can be covered at the same time and that busy clinicians can prove effectiveness within their own practice. This is a futile and unfair requirement. There must be investment in proper evaluation.

Appendix 1

Detailed Account of Specimen Sets of Analyses

INTRODUCTION

In this appendix, we describe in more depth the reasons that we considered in deciding upon the analyses reported in Chapters 9 and 10. Furthermore, we then explain the two techniques of analysis used to evaluate the interventions – one where the technique was based on multiple regression, and the other where the technique was based on log-linear modelling.

The first section deals with the conceptual issues in the measurement of change that were used to help us determine the methods of analysis we used. The second section introduces the basic ideas of statistical modelling. This is a comparatively brief exposition, intended to provide sufficient information to understand the following sections and, hence, the analyses and results presented in this book.

The third section explains the details of the multiple regression types of analysis; the fourth section explains the details of the log-linear types of analysis. The statistical techniques described in this section have been available for many years, but it is likely that many readers will not have come across them before when they are cast directly in terms of statistical modelling.

Throughout, we have used a significance level of 0.05, which is a typical value used very widely.

1 CONCEPTUAL ISSUES IN THE MEASUREMENT OF CHANGE

This study is concerned with measuring change and, more specifically, measuring differential change among a number of interventions. The measurement of change is fraught with difficulties, many of which are discussed in Bereiter (1963), Harris (1963), Goldstein (1979), Levy (1981), Plewis (1981a) and Plewis (1985). We now briefly discuss the main issues relevant to the research described here.

A "simple" way of measuring change involves looking at difference scores. Because this is still the most frequently chosen method of measuring change, it is worth considering the technique here.

1.1 The "simple" way of measuring change

If we want to measure change over merely two occasions, one way of doing this is to carry out a matched-pairs t-test, where a significant result indicates that there is a difference between the two occasions in terms of their mean scores on the measured variables. If there are one or more groups of people (perhaps falling into different treatment groups), or if there are more than two occasions on which measures from each person were obtained, then the matched-pairs t-test is not easily carried out, and so a more usual method of analysis is to use a Repeated Measures Analysis of Variance (ANOVA), where the measures taken on the different occasions together are the within-subjects factor, and the different treatment groups of people and any background variables are the between-subjects factors.

1.2 Some problems that the "simple" approach has

While these basic analyses can be further complicated (by converting them into Analyses of Covariance, for example), these "simple" approaches all possess the following three features:

1. They implicitly or explicitly look at difference scores on what is assumed to be the same psychological factor.
2. They do not build into the statistical model any notion of time-precedence, and hence, possible causal influences that may exist between the scores on successive occasions.
3. It is difficult to see how the "simple" approach can be modified so that outcome measures that are categorical or ordinal in nature can be handled without making other assumptions that may not be sustainable and which could have an undesirable effect on the statistical conclusions.

The first point is an important one that needs to be considered carefully given that we are interested in looking at measures of child development and other psychological variables. When we are measuring psychological variables, it may be that scores from the same apparent measuring instrument administered on different occasions are not, in fact, measuring the same things. If they are measuring different things, then taking simple difference scores to look at changes in the scores from occasion to occasion cannot be justified. This point has been made very well by Plewis (1981a), and an example can be used to illustrate the point.

Consider a simple arithmetic test, testing addition and subtraction. It is administered to 5 year old children on one occasion, and the same test is administered to the same children when they are aged 16. The question is, can we assess the changes in performance of the children from the first to the second occasion by merely looking at the difference in the scores between the two occasions? Plewis would argue, and we would agree, that you cannot. On the first occasion, the test will measure the extent to which the children have acquired the concepts of addition and subtraction, etc. On the second occasion, the test will almost certainly measure the efficiency with which the children can apply already acquired concepts of addition and subtraction. Some extreme behaviourists may be happy with looking at these difference scores, but any attempt to assess cognitive development, or any theoretical approach that hopes to investigate the psychological processes that underlie behaviour, would not be happy with such an approach. This objection can apply to any situation in which psychological measures are taken on a number of occasions, where there is the possibility that developmental changes or other internal restructuring of psychological constructs or variables can take place between the different occasions. In an intervention study, such as this one, developmental changes obviously do happen in the children, and it is quite possible that some psychological restructuring can have happened in the mother. Since an alternative method of analysing change is available that does not look at simple difference scores, it seems prudent to use this method of analysis, thus side-stepping any possible objections based on the above points.

The second point has also been made by Plewis (1981a), though Goldstein (1979) and Levy (1981) also touch on this issue. Simple difference scores do not take any account of possible causal influences that may exist from occasion to occasion. For example, consider a psychological variable x, measured on two occasions. At time one its value is x_1, and at time two its value is x_2. Both the matched-pairs t-test and the ANOVA approach essentially look at the mean difference scores, thus

$$d = (x_2 - x_1)$$

where d represents the difference score. (The ANOVA approach does not model this difference so that it appears clearly in the usual mathematical description of the model, though.) This does not build time into the analysis in any substantive way, as, apart from a change in the sign of the difference measure, we could subtract x_2 from x_1 and end up with the same statistical results.

The advantages that would accrue if time-precedence was built into the analysis would be that much more specific and sensitive hypotheses about possible causal influences could be tested, and these would clearly have a greater impact on the evaluation of the different interventions. Kenny (1979) and Goldstein (1979) both talk about a general method of causal analysis that can be adapted for use in such situations known as *path analysis*, though Goldstein (1979) refers to this as the *conditional approach to measuring change* when it is used in the more restricted context of assessing changes using the basic statistical technique of *multiple regression*. This will be discussed in more detail below.

For the third point, it is obvious that if one's outcome measures are ordinal in nature, then, even though we may assign consecutive integer scores (eg 0, 1, 2, 3, . . .) to consecutive levels of the ordinal variable, this is an assumption that need not necessarily be true. For example, if we consider the nagging subscores of the marriage ratings, this has four ordinal levels, "Less than once per month", "Occasionally", "Frequently, but not constant", and "Daily". Although it is customary to assign consecutive integer scores to these four levels so that, in this case, "Less than once a month" is given a score of 0, "Occasionally", a score of 1, "Frequently, but not constant", a score of 2, and so on, we cannot really justify adopting the "simple" approach of looking at difference scores, as this necessarily assumes that the difference between "Less than once a month" and "Occasionally" $(1 - 0 = 1)$ is the same as the difference between "Frequently, but not constant" and "Daily" $(4 - 3 = 1)$. Although this topic (axiomatic measurement theory) is receiving a great deal of research attention within mathematical psychology with Krantz et al (1971), Suppes et al (1989), and Luce et al (1990) being the main references, the work is highly technical and not useful at the moment for our purposes here. Instead, there is a statistical analysis technique that can easily handle such data, although its breadth and capability is less than the techniques being developed within axiomatic measurement theory. This statistical technique makes use of log-linear modelling. Thus, Plewis (1981b) describes how log-linear modelling is an appropriate statistical technique to use to assess outcome measures when they are ordinal and categorical in nature rather than interval or continuous. The technique is comparable in overall form to the conditional approach, but modified to handle ordinal and categorical data. For the marriage ratings (which were ordinal measures), we have adopted this form of analysis, which is explained in more detail, below.

1.3 Statistical solutions to the problems of the "simple" approach

As has already been stated, there are two statistical techniques that can be used to side-step the problems that have been raised above. One is the conditional approach to measuring change, which uses multiple regression, and can be used for the continuous data (Goldstein 1979; Kenny 1979; Draper and Smith 1981; Plewis 1981a; Plewis 1985; Fleiss 1986); the other technique is known more generally as log-linear modelling (Bishop, Fienberg and Holland 1975; Fienberg 1977; Plewis 1981b; Upton 1978). These will be explained in more detail in later sections.

1.4 Summary of conceptual issues

First, there are potential problems with assessing changes over time in outcome measures if one uses a "simple" approach based on difference scores or Repeated Measures Analysis of Variance (ANOVA). The main problems are as follows.

1. The assumption that the outcome measures on separate occasions are directly comparable, even though developmental and psychological changes may mean that the same instruments are measuring different things on each occasion.
2. The failure of this approach to build into the statistical analysis any idea of time-precedence, and hence, the direction of any causal influence among the outcome measures from occasion to occasion.
3. The difficulty of modifying this approach in a manner that can be easily justified so that ordinal or categorical data can be analysed.

Second, there is an overall approach that does not rely on difference scores, that builds time-precedence into the analysis, and can easily be modified to handle ordinal or categorical data.

1. For continuous or interval data, this is known as the conditional approach, and it makes use of multiple regression.
2. For ordinal or categorical data, the comparable technique has not been given any special name, but it makes use of log-linear modelling.

2 STATISTICAL MODELLING

2.1 How frequently are statistical models used in research?

Draper and Smith (1981) write: "the question 'What model are you considering?' is often met with 'I am not considering one – I am using analysis of variance'."

This is humorous to many people with expertise in statistics: every statistical test that people perform, be it ANOVA, Wilcoxon Rank-Sum Test, multiple regression, or log-linear modelling, involves the application of a statistical model. It is easy to see how the idea encapsulated in the above quotation could come about.

Although in the psychological sciences, theories and models are often mentioned and discussed – often inaccurately, as there is a difference between theories and models, as Coombs (1983; 1984) points out – when statistical tests are performed, outside psychometrics, mathematical psychology, and similar areas, statistical models are rarely mentioned. Thus, if the person quoted by Draper and Smith (1981) was carrying out an exploratory study, with no specific theory or hypothesis under examination, then the reply is quite understandable. Furthermore, it is still usual that there is a large emphasis on significance testing solely as a statistical end in itself within the psychological sciences, rather than seeing its potential as a means of explicitly aiding statistical modelling.

In fact, in psychological research, there are three overall types of model that are always used: the psychological model (derived from an underlying psychological theory), one or more measurement models, and a statistical model. Proper research design relies on ensuring that every instance of these three kinds of model used in a piece of research fit together rather like the pieces of a jigsaw puzzle. This point is discussed further in Coombs (1983; 1984) and Stretch and Stoker (in preparation). In the subsections that follow, a variety of sources are used, but especially Coombs (1983; 1984) and McCullagh and Nelder (1983).

2.2   What exactly is a statistical model?

For the purposes of the research contained in this book, the two major kinds of statistical model that are used are the Linear Model, used in the multiple regression that constitute the conditional approach to measuring change, and, as its name suggests, the Log-Linear Model, a generalization of familiar χ^2 tests, used to assess the changes in ordinal and categorical data. In fact, both of these are special cases of a still more general model known as the General Linear Model (McCullagh and Nelder 1983).

However, this still begs the question that heads this subsection. When a research project is carried out, a set of observations and data are collected within the context of predefined hypotheses that determine what one observes, and under what conditions these observations are made. There is then the need to interpret these data, and to do this, we look for patterns in the data. Here are examples of the kinds of patterns we may look for, together with the statistical test or procedure that we might normally carry out to investigate them.

1. Whether the scores obtained from the Behaviour Checklist are generally higher in children who have a lot of siblings rather than one or two (a test for difference between two typical scores).
2. Whether there is a positive association between the depression score that a mother obtains and the degree to which she lives in conditions of social disadvantage (a test of correlation).
3. Whether the quality of a marriage ("good" or "poor") tends to remain "good" or "poor", after an interval of one year (a χ^2 test for association, for example).
4. Whether responses to the items on a proposed "neighbourliness scale" indicate that they have the same, unmeasured factor underlying them (factor analysis or latent class analysis, for example).

The above examples of patterns will often be difficult to detect, just as a blurred photograph can make identification of its subject difficult. In the case of data from intervention studies, it is the presence of all sorts of uncontrolled variation that affect the people we are observing that makes the patterns "blurred" or "smeared". We need a formal and structured method of pattern recognition to help us detect any underlying patterns and regularities that might exist in the "blurred" set of data. In statistical terms, the patterns we want to detect are often referred to as *systematic effects*, whereas the uncontrolled variations are often called *random effects*, but sometimes alternatively (and somewhat misleadingly to non-statisticians) they are known as *random error*, or even just *error*. The statistical models that we use encompass both the systematic effects and the random effects. And they do this so that the systematic effects summarize the data. As McCullagh and Nelder (1983) write:

> Statistical models contain both . . . systematic and random effects, and their value lies in allowing us to replace the individual data values by a summary that describes their general characteristics in terms of a limited number of quantities. . . . [The] problem of looking intelligently at numerical data demands the formulation of patterns which can in some way represent the data and allow their important characteristics to be described in terms of a limited number of quantities that the mind can encompass relatively easily.

So, a statistical model summarizes a set of data in such a way that we can identify possible systematic effects (patterns) in the data that are blurred or made difficult to detect by the presence of random effects (uncontrolled variation).

2.3 What are "degrees of freedom"?

We can measure the number of systematic effects a model includes. It is useful to think of this measure as being a count of the number of *parameters* a model includes, and this count is referred to as the *degrees of freedom* of the *model*. There are also *residual degrees of freedom* that are sometimes known just as degrees of freedom too; although this may be confusing, context usually shows in which sense this term is used. We shall explicitly use "degrees of freedom" and "residual degrees of freedom" to make clear which we mean. Residual degrees of freedom refers to the number of extra parameters (or the number of systematic effects) we need to add to a specified model so that all aspects of the data are included in its systematic effects. We refer to this again when we talk about what makes a "good" model.

The term "degrees of freedom" is probably the greatest source of confusion among people who come to statistical modelling from just using significance tests, and so it is important that the above paragraph is fully understood.

2.4 How do we "fit" a statistical model to our data?

In order to detect the patterns that a model describes, we need a way of determining, in absolute terms, the discrepancy between a model's systematic effects and the actual data. Because a model consists of a mixture of systematic effects and random effects, the discrepancy, mentioned above, must consist entirely of the random effects. Thus we can state a simple equation to be used as an *aide-mémoire* for this:

$$\text{Data} = \text{Systematic effects} + \text{Random effects}$$

This is really a more general form of the rule that is often stated within psychometrics:

$$\text{Observed score} = \text{True score} + \text{Error}$$

There are many statistical criteria that can be used to determine the discrepancy between the model and the data, and the fine details are not, at this level of explanation, important. Furthermore, for the statistical techniques we employed for the analyses used in this book, statisticians have derived criteria that are sensible and can be easily translated into the statistical tests and computer programs often used by researchers. These tests and programs have undergone extensive testing over long periods of time. Consequently, it is not necessary for us to fully understand the mechanics of *how* the discrepancy is measured. Instead, it suffices for us to know *that* the discrepancy is measured. The general term which is used to describe this process is *model fitting*, and the aim of model fitting is to determine how closely a model's systematic effects summarize the data.

Finally, because the next subsection depends on it, the following sentence restates a fact given above: *The discrepancy between a model's systematic effects and the data consists entirely of random effects.*

2.5   What makes a "good" statistical model?

A naive view might be that a "good" model is a model that shows hardly any discrepancy between its systematic effects and the data. This would necessarily mean that the uncontrolled variation, random effects, or random error in this "good" model would be almost non-existent. This view would be a mistake, though, because if we took this view to its logical extreme, the "best" model would include *all* aspects of the data in its systematic effects, leaving no random effects at all. In this case, no simplification would be involved. This state of affairs may be thought of as a good thing at first sight, but it would mean that this "best" model would have features that are not desirable, especially in the research considered here. Among the undesirable features would be, first, that the model would merely be a complete and exhaustive (re-)description of the data, involving no simplification, and therefore it would be impossible for us to make sense of or interpret. Second, the systematic effects of the model would be so specific to the set of data to which the model was fitted that it would be incapable of being generalized to situations or people who were not studied (McCullagh and Nelder 1983: 6 refer to this as lack of "scope").

In a slightly different context, Coombs (1983) writes about having a choice of saying "more about less, or less about more" – in this situation, the choice being between having more systematic effects in a model which has less scope (or is less generalizable), or having fewer systematic effects in a model which has more scope (or is more generalizable).

In practical terms, when we fit a specific model (denoted, say, by M), to data, we determine, for each data point, a *fitted* or *predicted* value that has been derived from the systematic effects included in M. This means that we can measure the discrepancy between the data points and the fitted or predicted values of M. So, using a relationship mentioned in the previous subsection, by measuring the discrepancy between the data points and the fitted values of M, we are measuring the random effects. Furthermore, if we assume that the random effects are a result of a particular underlying probability distribution, then we can calculate the *likelihood* of obtaining a discrepancy between the data and the fitted values of M which is at least of the size we observe.

The measures of discrepancy are also known as measures of *goodness of fit*; for specific kinds of models, these can take on different forms. For example, for the multiple regression models used, the measures of goodness of fit used are F Ratios, whereas for the log-linear models, they are χ^2 values. In both cases, the residual degrees of freedom play a key role. In the log-linear analyses, the residual degrees of freedom are used with the χ^2 goodness of fit measures to determine the likelihood of obtaining at least the observed discrepancy between the data and the fitted values of the specific model. In the multiple regressions, the residual degrees of freedom are the degrees of freedom in the denominator of the F Ratio, while the degrees of freedom of the model are the degrees of freedom in the numerator of the F Ratio.

There are two special models that lie at either extreme of a "goodness of fit" scale. One, called the *null model*, contains no systematic effects, and hence contains the maximum amount of random effects. The other is called the *full model* by McCullagh and Nelder (1983), or the *fully-saturated model* by Bishop, Fienberg and Holland (1975) in the context of log-linear models. This other model contains the maximum amount of systematic effects and no random effects. All other models lie in between these two limits, and the scale provides a baseline against which intermediate models can be assessed. This assessment is usually in terms of the likelihood (mentioned above).

Now, within the limits of this scale of goodness of fit there will be a region within which all models are judged to be "good". What this means is that all the models included in this region are models which do not have significant discrepancies between their fitted values and the data. So, as long as a significance level, α is specified, we can state that all models within this region are, in a sense "good" models, because there is no evidence to suggest that these models contain statistically significant random effects or random variation.

If the analysis uses log-linear modelling, the χ^2 values are direct measures of whether significant discrepancies exist between a model's fitted values and the data. Correspondingly, *non-significant* values of χ^2 are taken to be good indicators for models.

If the analysis uses multiple regression modelling, the F Ratio values are measures of whether a model's fitted values account for a significant amount of the total variation in the data. Correspondingly, *significant* values of the F Ratios are taken to be good indicators for models.

2.6   How can we decide between two or more "good" models?

The problem with the region of the goodness of fit scale that contains all models judged to be "good" is that there will often be more than two models included in this region, and so we have to formulate a method of choosing one of these models as "best".

The basic method of doing this is essentially the same for multiple regression and log-linear modelling. However, beyond a given point the explanation is easier for log-linear modelling than it is for multiple regression. The sources cited earlier for each type of analysis can be referred to if more detail is needed about these methods.

To begin with, in the region on the goodness of fit scale where all models have non-significant discrepancies between their fitted values and the data, it is still possible to have one model showing a significant improvement in its (goodness of) fit over another. In other words, although all models are "good", some can be assessed as being statistically "better" than others.

If one has two models, A and B, such that one (A) contains all the systematic effects that the other (B) contains, as well as some additional systematic effects, then the two models are said to be *nested*. In particular, the simpler model, B, is said to be nested in the more complicated model, A. If this condition is satisfied, it is possible to evaluate whether the more complicated model, A, shows a significantly improved fit to the data when comparing it to B. If we are carrying out log-linear modelling, B will be a log-linear model nested within A. Under these circumstances, to determine whether A shows a significant improvement in fit over

B, one substracts the χ^2 value for model A from the χ^2 for model B. As long as the two models both lie within the region of "good" models (that is that region where all models have non-significant measures of goodness of fit), then the resulting difference is also a χ^2 value. Furthermore, the associated degrees of freedom of this χ^2 value are calculated by subtracting the residual degrees of freedom of model A from the residual degrees of freedom of model B.

So, if model A has the following: $\chi^2 = 1.42$, $df = 2$, $p > 0.05$, and model B has $\chi^2 = 6.84$, $df = 3$, $p > 0.05$, in order to determine whether model A shows a significant improvement in fit over model B, we work out the difference between the two χ^2 values and the two residual degrees of freedom, and treat the resultant pair of numbers as being a χ^2 value with associated degrees of freedom. In the example, the difference between the two χ^2 values is $(6.84 - 1.42) = 5.42$, and the difference between the two degrees of freedom is $(3 - 2) = 1$. A χ^2 value of 5.42 with degrees of freedom 1 is statistically significant at the 0.025 level. Consequently, we can conclude that model A shows a significantly better goodness of fit over model B. The argument can also be turned around, and we can state that model B shows a significantly worse goodness of fit over model A. So, dependent on whether one believes it important to complicate simpler models, or simplify more complicated models, one or other of the two strategies can be adopted. Since the research described in this book investigated very complex social, psychological and developmental phenomena it was decided that the modelling should strive to simplify more complicated models.

A similar procedure can be, and was followed in the case of multiple regression, though it is rather more difficult to explain. More information on the strategies described above can be found in the sources already cited, above, for each specific kind of model.

3   MULTIPLE REGRESSION MODELLING (THE CONDITIONAL APPROACH)

In this section, the techniques being described will use examples taken from Hypothesis 1 of the research, as this will not unnecessarily obscure the description. The analyses for Hypotheses 2 and 4 will not differ too much from the description offered here. However, the analyses for Hypothesis 3 require a slight complication of the described approach because of the addition of both the background variable of adversity or sex of index child, together with the "bundle of contrasts" (see page 231) that described the differences between the four treatment groups. In essence, the analysis and interpretation will follow the same general course as that described below, but they will be more involved as there are a greater number of model parameters that can be fitted to the data.

3.1   Overview of what the conditional approach does

The conditional approach is so named because it looks at the end-points or follow up measures of interest, conditional or fixed values of (possibly different) variables taken at an earlier time. In this research, the initial baseline measures were taken to be the fixed values, and the one year and three year follow up assessments provided the variables for the end-points.

It can therefore be seen that this approach does not look at differences between the initial assessments and the end-points or follow up assessments at all. The reason for us doing this is that we are not convinced that the repeated administration of some of the same assessments over time, particularly in the children, are measuring the same underlying psychological, developmental or sociological constructs. Rather than leave the research open to criticism on this count, we took the advice of Goldstein (1979), and used this conditional approach, which does not take difference scores between initial and follow up assessments, and consequently, is not obliged to assume that the measures on the different occasions are identical in what they measure. We also considered that to look at adjusted end-points rather than change would be of greater clinical value.

Furthermore, the fact that it is a conditional approach means that we can attempt to answer the following question. What would the difference in scores be among the four treatment groups at the one year follow up assessment using *this* variable if we assumed that the four groups started off with the *same* score as each other on this *possibly other* variable at baseline?

So, in a related manner, we could find out what would happen if we took two people who scored the same on an initial assessment variable, exposed them to different interventions, and then saw if they differed at all on a follow up assessment that may not use exactly the same variable.

Clearly, this is a method that allows us to assess the relative efficacy of the four treatment groups, and it also has the potential for being predictive in a way in which the "simple" difference score approach would find difficult (Plewis 1981a).

3.2   Describing the multiple regression model

A multiple regression model consists of an equation that describes how the dependent variable can be predicted from a weighted sum of the predictors. Using terminology better suited to the research included in this book, we can recast this thus: a multiple regression model consists of an equation that describes how the outcome measure can be predicted from a weighted sum of the baseline measure and the contrasts that describe the differences between the four treatment groups. In mathematical terms, we can specify the regression equation for the *full model* as follows:

$$
\begin{aligned}
F = \quad & \beta_0 \\
+\ & \beta_1 I \\
+\ & (\beta_2 t_1 + \beta_3 t_2 + \beta_4 t_3) \\
+\ & (\beta_5 (It_1) + \beta_6 (It_2) + \beta_7 (It_3)) \\
+\ & \epsilon
\end{aligned}
$$

The regression equation consists of the weighted sum of five kinds of components, and to make these clear, they have been placed on separate lines. Noting the line of the equation by a number in the explanation below, this equation can be interpreted as meaning:

1. the follow up measure, F, is predicted by a constant, β_0 (also known as the intercept)
2. PLUS a weighted contribution of the initial baseline score, I
3. PLUS a weighted sum of a *bundle of contrasts* (t_1, t_2, t_3) that describe the difference among the four treatment groups
4. PLUS a weighted sum of the *interaction* between the initial baseline score and the bundle of contrasts (It_1, It_2, It_3)
5. PLUS a component that corresponds to all the random effects (ϵ).

The β's in the equation are known as the *regression weights*, and it is whether these are zero or not that determines whether a particular component modifies the predicted value of F or not. The individual components of the contrast bundle have their values fixed according to one of a number of coding schemes (see Kenny 1979: ch. 10) and we chose a form of deviation coding because Kenny advises this form if interactions are to be examined, which in our research, they were. For each of the four treatment groups, the exact values of the individual components of the contrast bundle were varied in a systematic way, as advised in all books dealing with *dummy variable regression* (Kenny 1979; Myers 1979; Fleiss 1986) so that for each model that contained the bundle of contrasts, *four* separate regression lines could be produced, one per treatment group.

For statistical reasons, given in the sources listed above, the entire bundle of contrasts had to be either included together on a line in the model (line 3 or line 4), or else all excluded together on a line. Furthermore, if the interaction bundle was included, then it was advised that both the initial score component and the contrast bundle component on lines 2 and 3 were included in the model. This corresponds to what is known as the "hierarchy principle" in modelling (Bishop, Fienberg and Holland 1975): it is very seldom that one can be justified in violating it. A serious problem that arises if one considers *non-hierarchical* models is that systematic effects become mixed up with each other so that one cannot see which systematic effects have the greatest contribution to the underlying patterns in the data.

Finally, as the analyses we wish to consider all look at end-point differences between the four treatment groups conditional on the baseline (initial) measure, all models that were considered necessarily contained the initial baseline score. This means that there were for Hypothesis 1, only three multiple regression models that could be chosen as the best model.

1. a model which contains only the intercept and the initial baseline score:

$$
\begin{aligned}
F = \quad & \beta_0 \\
+ \ & \beta_1 I \\
+ \ & \epsilon
\end{aligned}
$$

2. a model which contains the intercept, the initial baseline score, and the bundle of contrasts on their own:

$$
\begin{aligned}
F = \quad & \beta_0 \\
+ \ & \beta_1 I \\
+ \ & (\beta_2 t_1 + \beta_3 t_2 + \beta_4 t_3) \\
+ \ & \epsilon
\end{aligned}
$$

3. and the full model, given above.

3.3   A simplified notation for depiction of the multiple regression model

It can be seen that having to write out the full multiple regression model each time could result in readers becoming confused about what is or is not included in a model. It would also mean that tables giving results would be very difficult to construct and follow because of the space limitations. Consequently, a simplified notation has been devised which one of us (DDS) modified from a standard method of depicting log-linear models (Fienberg 1977).

In this notation, the full model under consideration here would be written as:

$$[I] + [T] + [TI],$$

the model containing just the initial baseline score would be

$$[I]$$

and the model containing just the initial baseline score and the bundle of contrasts would be

$$[I] + [T].$$

As can be seen, since the ϵ term (the random effects) and the intercept (β_0) will always be present in every model, we can omit them. Then, if we are merely trying to specify a particular model by the components it contains all the β's can be omitted. Finally, each bundle of components that must be included or excluded from a model together are surrounded by square brackets ([and]), thus emphasizing the fact that they function as inseparable components in the model.

3.4 Interpreting the results tables

We are now ready to begin interpreting the tables that display fitted multiple regression models. We shall deal with Table A2.1 in particular, it being easy to apply the rules for this table to the others. Even more specifically, we shall spend most time talking about mother's depression on this table as a means of illustrating how to understand and interpret the results table for multiple regressions.

The first column merely lists the follow up variables being predicted. In most cases, the variable represented by I in the next column will be a similar (but perhaps not an identical) variable measured at the baseline or initial assessment. The second column gives the chosen model for each particular outcome measure. So for depression, the chosen model contained the initial score $[I]$, the bundle of contrast components $[T]$, and the interaction between the initial score and the bundle of contrast components ($[TI]$). This means that the follow up measure of mothers' depression was best modelled by a weighted sum of the initial mothers' depression score $[I]$, the bundle of contrast components $[T]$, and an interaction between the initial mothers' depression score and the bundle of contrast components $[TI]$.

The next column is labelled R^2. This is the square of the *multiple correlation coefficient* between, in this case, the follow up measure and the weighted sum of the best model's systematic effects (which are the fitted values). So, in the case of mother's depression, the square of the multiple correlation coefficient is 0.372 and this is the square of the (multiple) correlation between the follow up measures of mother's depression and what the chosen model predicts or fits these values to be. The value of R^2 gives the proportion of total variability in the follow up measure of mother's depression that is contained, or explained by the chosen model's systematic effects. Ideally this should be high, but Kenny (1979) remarks that the number of unmodelled "random" effects in any kind of applied psychological research means that seemingly small values are often obtained.

The last column gives the statistical test for the adequacy of the chosen model. Remember that for multiple regression, a good model is one in which the F Ratio is significant.

3.5   Interpreting the model

Continuing with the model for mother's depression, the chosen model can be verbally interpreted thus: After controlling for the initial mother's depression score ($[I]$), the four treatment groups differ on the follow up measure of mother's depression ($[T]$), and that, furthermore, this difference at follow up among the four treatment groups itself differs systematically, dependent upon the initial mother's depression score ($[TI]$). These results can also be shown in a graph (Figure A1.1). In this graph, note that the initial, baseline score goes along the horizontal axis, and the follow up score goes up the vertical axis. In the body of the graph are four regression lines, one per treatment group. The conditional approach interprets the vertical separation of the four regression lines at given places along the horizontal axis. So, if the four groups all had initial mother's depression scores of approximately 4.3, at the one year follow up, they would have separated such that the mothers' groups scored higher than the other three groups, which remained very nearly equal

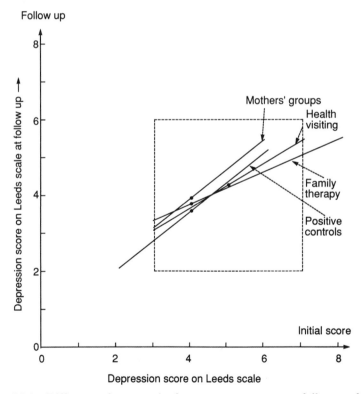

Figure A1.1   Differences between the four treatment groups at follow up dependent on initial score for depression. The dotted square represents the interquartile ranges on the horizontal and vertical scales

to each other. Note that at this given or fixed initial score, the follow up score of the mothers' groups is actually higher than the positive control group. So, if mothers who initially score the same on the depression scale were either offered no extra help, or were offered and attended mothers' groups, then the regression lines seem to indicate that the mothers who attended mothers' groups would be *more* depressed at one year than those mothers who did not take advantage of the extra "help". To investigate this more completely, it becomes necessary to perform *pair-wise* comparisons between the regression lines (Fleiss 1986); and this was done and reported in Chapters 9 and 10.

If the chosen multiple regression model did not include the interaction term between the initial, baseline score and the bundle of contrast components, then the four regression lines would be parallel, and the results would be easier to interpret, but potentially less interesting.

4 LOG-LINEAR MODELLING

4.1 Overview of what log-linear modelling does

Log-linear modelling is the general form of the kind of analysis carried out when a standard χ^2 test for association in two-way tables is carried out. It is flexible in so much as it can handle tables of counts that have more than the two dimensions of the standard χ^2 test. Additionally it can analyse various kinds of "incomplete tables", in which specified cells in a table of counts are fixed to have zero fitted or expected values (Bishop, Fienberg and Holland 1975: ch. 5). Additional sources of information about log-linear modelling can be found in Fienberg (1977), McCullagh and Nelder (1983) and Upton (1978).

As already mentioned, it works on tables of counts, and it uses the χ^2 statistic to assess a model's goodness of fit. The χ^2 value measures the extent to which the systematic effects of the model show significant discrepancy from the data, and consequently "good" models have non-significant χ^2 values associated with them.

4.2 Describing the log-linear model's notation

The systematic effects or components of a log-linear model are not added together to give the fitted data, as they are multiple regression. Instead they are multiplied together. Given that the data that a log-linear model fits are cell proportions (though it is usual to work with cell counts, which can easily be found from the proportions), this makes good sense from the point of view of statistical theory. The implication of multiplying the components together to yield the fitted, predicted or expected data is that if we take logarithms of the components of the models, we add these together to give the predicted logarithms of the cell counts or data. This is referred to as a linear combination of the logarithms, and explains the name "log-linear modelling".

The notation that can be used to depict a fitted log-linear model reflects the primary role of multiplication when we compare it with the notation that we designed to summarize a multiple regression model. Instead of using an explicit addition operator to link together the separate components of the model (which is what we have done in the multiple regression), we implicitly multiply them together in a manner described in more detail by Fienberg (1977).

Furthermore, because of the multiplicative nature of log-linear models, we do not have anything that is obviously an equation in the same manner as the multiple regression models. In log-linear models, the dependent variable or outcome variable is included in the notation of the model without an equation being explicitly given at all.

So, let us consider the quality of marriage score. If we denote the initial, baseline score with the symbol I, the one year follow up assessment with the symbol F, and the factor that encompasses the four treatment groups with the symbol T, the *full model* (McCullagh and Nelder 1983) would be denoted by $[FTI]$. It is important to keep firmly in mind the fact that the variable F has a different relationship with the other two variables compared with the relationship that the other two variables have with each other. The reason for this is that the variable F is the dependent variable or outcome variable in the model, whereas the other two variables I and T are explanatory variables or independent variables. This will affect the interpretation we place on the separate components of a log-linear model quite considerably.

Applying the hierarchy principle (Bishop, Fienberg and Holland 1975), we can "unpack" this model into eight separate components:

$$[FTI] = F.T.I \quad F.T \quad F.I \quad T.I \quad F \quad T \quad I \quad 1$$

Taking the broken down components on the left hand side in turn

1. The $F.T.I$ component refers just to the three-way interaction involving F, T, and I. Because F is the dependent variable in these analyses, it is helpful to view this interaction as being that variable T and I interact together so that, together, they affect the variable F.
2. The $F.T$ component refers to a two-way interaction between F and T. Again, because F is the dependent variable, we view this as an influence that T on its own has on F. This interaction is of the same form, regardless of what the value of the variable I is.
3. The $F.I$ component is similar to the $F.T$ interaction, except that it can be viewed as an influence that I on its own has on F. Also, this interaction is of the same form, regardless of what the value of the variable T is.
4. The $T.I$ component can be seen to reflect an interaction that T and I have together. This interaction is of the same form, regardless of the value of the dependent variable F.
5. The F component implies that there are differences in the counts between the different levels of the variable F, regardless of what values are taken for T or I.
6. The T component implies that there are differences in the counts between the different levels of the variable T, regardless of what values are taken for F or I.
7. The I component implies that there are differences in the counts between the different levels of the variable I, regardless of what values are taken for F or T.
8. The 1 component is a little different, and it can be viewed as a log-linear model's equivalent to a multiple regression's intercept.

Another log-linear model is the following, again unpacked into its separate components, of which there are six:

$$[FT][FI] = F.T \quad F.I \quad F \quad T \quad I \quad 1$$

And another one would be:

$$[F][T] = F \quad T \quad 1$$

Finally, a rather unusual one, but still possible, would be:

$$[\ ] = 1$$

Now, of the possible components that can be included in a model, some of them will not be interesting at all as they will reflect aspects of the data that were fixed by the research design. For example, we allocated fixed numbers of people to each of the four treatment groups, therefore any "legal" model ought to reflect this. The implication of this is that any legal model we consider here ought at least to include a component that describes or models the different numbers of people in the four treatment groups. Thus any legal model ought to include the T component. This means that the last example, given above, does not constitute a legal model in terms of the research design we adopted, and would therefore never be seriously contemplated.

Further interpretations of these kinds of models can be found in the sources already cited, and any particular issues will be dealt with as they arise in the data.

4.3 Interpreting the results tables

In the tables of results of the log-linear modelling, the first column specifies which outcome measure was being fitted by the initial baseline scores, and the factor that describes differences among the four treatment groups. The next column specifies the actual "best" model that was chosen. The third column specifies the χ^2 goodness of fit measure. Note that this is a measure of the extent to which the fitted scores (systematic effects, or *expected values*, to use a term more often used with χ^2 test on tables of counts) show discrepancy from the data. The next column gives the residual degrees of freedom – that is the number of extra parameters (or the number of systematic effects) we need to add to the chosen model so that all aspects of the data are included in its systematic effects. The last column uses the two immediately preceding columns in order to determine the significance level. For χ^2 tests, used in this way, non-significant results indicate "good" models.

4.4 Interpreting the model

Let us consider "overall quality of marriage" for Hypothesis 1 (Table A2.3) as an example. The best model is $[IF][T]$. The $[T]$ component is merely a reflection of the research design because we allocated fixed numbers of people to each of the four treatment groups, and the $[IF]$ component merely reflects the fact that the initial baseline score influences the final score. There is no differential effect of treatment on outcome, which would be indicated by an $[FT]$ interaction component in the model.

Complete Set of Statistical Tables for the Research

See Appendix 1 for guidance.

Table A2.1   Results of analyses of the mother's mental state variables for Hypothesis 1

Follow up measure	Model components	R^2	F Ratio
Depression	$[I] + [T] + [TI]$	0.372	$22.78(7,250) \, p < 0.0001$
Anxiety	$[I]$	0.409	$179.22(1,257) \, p < 0.00005$
Inward directed irritability	$[I] + [T] + [TI]$	0.320	$18.30(7,250) \, p < 0.0001$
Outward directed irritability	$[I]$	0.432	$196.16(1,256) \, p < 0.00005$
Cognitive failures	$[I]$	0.482	$241.43(1,256) \, p < 0.00005$

Table A2.2   Results of analyses of the child behaviour variables for Hypothesis 1

Follow up measure	Model components	R^2	F Ratio
Total score	$[I]$	0.190	$61.10(1,256) \, p < 0.00005$
Eating problems subscore	$[I] + [T] + [TI]$	0.345	$18.99(7.252) \, p < 0.00005$
Sleep problems subscore	$[I]$	0.228	$76.15(1,258) \, p < 0.00005$
Bowel and bladder problems subscore	$[I] + [T] + [TI]$	0.120	$4.91(7,252) \, p < 0.00005$
Attention problems subscore	$[I]$	0.094	$27.87(1,258) \, p < 0.00005$
Relationship and temper problems subscore	$[I]$	0.244	$55.63(1,168) \, p < 0.00005$
Anxiety problems subscore	$[I]$	0.146	$45.29(1,258) \, p < 0.00005$

Table A2.3 Results of analyses of the marriage ratings variables for Hypothesis 1

Follow up measure	Log-linear model	Chi-square goodness of fit	Residual degrees of freedom	p value
Irritability wife to husband	[IF][T]	91.52	72	0.060
Irritability husband to wife	[IF][T]	73.68	72	0.423
Quarrels and bickering	[IF][T]	24.45	24	0.436
Nagging of wife by husband	[IF][T]	25.04	27	0.572
Nagging of husband by wife	[IF][IT][FT]	20.11	12	0.065
Overall quality of marriage	[IF][T]	4.54	9	0.873

Table A2.4 Results of analyses of the psychometric qualities of the child for Hypothesis 1

Follow up measure	Model components	R^2	F Ratio
Developmental Quotient	[I] + [T] + [TI]	0.373	$22.09(7,241)\ p < 0.00005$
Mean sentence length	[I]	0.199	$60.91(1,240)\ p < 0.00005$
Identifying shapes and objects	[I]	0.433	$187.12(1,243)\ p < 0.00005$
Direct observations	[I]	0.344	$136.52(1,258)\ p < 0.00005$

Table A2.5 Results of analyses of the mother's mental state variables for Hypothesis 2

Follow up measure	Model components	R^2	F Ratio
Depression	[I] + [A]	0.378	$79.09(2,255)\ p < 0.00005$
Anxiety	[I] + [A]	0.425	$96.28(2,256)\ p < 0.00005$
Inward directed irritability	[I]	0.301	$111.91(1,256)\ p < 0.0001$
Outward directed irritability	[I]	0.432	$196.16(1,256)\ p < 0.00005$
Cognitive failures	[I]	0.482	$241.43(1,256)\ p < 0.00005$

Table A2.6   Results of analyses of the child behaviour variables for Hypothesis 2

Follow up measure	Model components	R^2	F Ratio
Total score	$[I] + [A]$	0.198	32.77(2,255) $p < 0.00005$
Eating problems subscore	$[I]$	0.306	113.80(1,258) $p < 0.00005$
Sleep problems subscore	$[I]$	0.225	76.15(1,258) $p < 0.00005$
Bowel and bladder problems subscore	$[I] + [A] + [IA]$	0.083	8.76(3,256) $p < 0.00005$
Attention problems subscore	$[I] + [A]$	0.123	19.19(2,257) $p < 0.00005$
Relationship and temper problems subscore	$[I] + [A] + [IA]$	0.280	22.90(3,166) $p < 0.00005$
Anxiety problems subscore	$[I] + [A]$	0.167	18.32(3,256) $p < 0.00005$

Table A2.7   Results of analyses of the marriage ratings variables for Hypothesis 2

Follow up measure	Log-linear model	Chi-square goodness of fit	Residual degrees of freedom	p value
Irritability wife to husband	$[IF][IA]$	25.33	20	0.189
Irritability husband to wife	$[IF][IA][FA]$	10.11	16	0.861
Quarrels and bickering	$[IF][IA][FA]$	0.64	4	0.959
Nagging of wife by husband	$[IF][IA][FA]$	10.866	9	0.285
Nagging of husband by wife	$[IF][IA][FA]$	7.52	9	0.583
Overall quality of marriage	$[IF][IA]$	0.24	1	0.624

Table A2.8   Results of analyses of the psychometric qualities of the child for Hypothesis 2

Follow up measure	Model components	R^2	F Ratio
Developmental Quotient	$[I] + [A] + [IA]$	0.371	49.67(3,245) $p < 0.00005$
Mean sentence length	$[I]$	0.199	60.91(1,240) $p < 0.00005$
Identifying shapes and objects	$[I] + [A] + [IA]$	0.450	67.639(3,241) $p < 0.00005$
Direct observations	$[I]$	0.344	136.52(1,258) $p < 0.00005$

Table A2.9 Results of analyses of the child behaviour variables for Hypothesis 2, with sex of index child replacing the adversity score, and with S representing this variable in the models specified below

Follow up measure	Model components	R^2	F Ratio
Total score	[I]	0.189	61.100(2,255) $p < 0.00005$
Eating problems subscore	[I]	0.306	113.80(1,258) $p < 0.00005$
Sleep problems subscore	[I]	0.225	76.15(1,258) $p < 0.00005$
Bowel and bladder problems subscore	[I]	0.075	21.87(1,258) $p < 0.00005$
Attention problems subscore	[I]	0.094	27.87(1,258) $p < 0.00005$
Relationship and temper problems subscore	[I] + [S]	0.264	31.45(2,167) $p < 0.00005$
Anxiety problems subscore	[I] + [S] + [IS]	0.170	18.69(3,256) $p < 0.00005$

Table A2.10 Results of analyses of the psychometric qualities of the child for Hypothesis 2, with sex of index child replacing the adversity score, and with S replacing this variable in the models specified below

Follow up measure	Model components	R^2	F Ratio
Developmental Quotient	[I] + [S] + [IS]	0.376	50.85(3,245) $p < 0.00005$
Mean sentence length	[I]	0.199	60.91(1,240) $p < 0.00005$
Identifying shapes and objects	[I] + [S]	0.446	66.48(3,241) $p < 0.00005$
Direct observations	[I] + [S]	0.351	47.35(3,256) $p < 0.00005$

Table A2.11 Results of analyses of the mother's mental state variables for Hypothesis 3

Follow up measure	Model components	R^2	F Ratio
Depression	[I] + [A]	0.378	79.09(2,255) $p < 0.00005$
Anxiety	[I] + [A]	0.425	96.28(2,256) $p < 0.00005$
Inward directed irritability	[I] + [T] + [TI]	0.320	18.30(7,250) $p < 0.0001$
Outward directed irritability	[I]	0.432	196.16(1,256) $p < 0.00005$
Cognitive failures	[I]	0.483	241.43(1,256) $p < 0.00005$

Table A2.12   Results of analyses of the child behaviour variables for Hypothesis 3

Follow up measure	Model components	R^2	F Ratio
Total score	$[I] + [A] + [T] + [TI]$	0.211	9.59(8,249) $p < 0.00005$
Eating problems subscore	$[I] + [T] + [TI]$	0.345	18.99(7,252) $p < 0.00005$
Sleep problems subscore	$[I]$	0.228	76.15(1,258) $p < 0.00005$
Bowel and bladder problems subscore	$[I] + [T] + [TI]$	0.120	4.91(7,252) $p < 0.00005$
Attention problems subscore	$[I] + [A]$	0.123	19.19(2,257) $p < 0.00005$
Relationship and temper problems subscore	$[I] + [A] + [IA]$	0.280	22.90(3,166) $p < 0.00005$
Anxiety problems subscore	$[I] + [A]$	0.167	18.32(3,256) $p < 0.00005$

Table A2.13   Results of analyses of the child behaviour variables for Hypothesis 3, with sex of index child replacing the adversity score, and with S representing this variable in the models specified below

Follow up measure	Model components	R^2	F Ratio
Total score	$[I] + [T] + [TI]$	0.195	9.92(7,250) $p < 0.00005$
Eating problems subscore	$[I] + [T] + [TI]$	0.345	18.99(7,252) $p < 0.00005$
Sleep problems subscore	$[I]$	0.228	76.15(1,258) $p < 0.00005$
Bowel and bladder problems subscore	$[I] + [T] + [TI]$	0.120	4.91(7,252) $p < 0.00005$
Attention problems subscore	$[I]$	0.094	27.87(2,258) $p < 0.00005$
Relationship and temper problems subscore	$[I] + [S]$	0.264	31.45(2,167) $p < 0.00005$
Anxiety problems subscore	$[I] + [S] + [IS]$	0.170	18.69(3,256) $p < 0.00005$

Table A2.14   Results of analyses of the marriage ratings variables for Hypothesis 3

Follow up measure	Log-linear model	Chi-square goodness of fit	Residual degrees of freedom	p value
Irritability wife to husband	$[IF][IA][T]$	160.91	167	0.618
Irritability husband to wife	$[IF][IA][T]$	133.47	167	0.974
Quarrels and bickering	$[IF][IA][FA][T]$	46.973	55	0.771
Nagging of wife by husband	$[IF][FA][T]$	95.36	105	0.739
Nagging of husband by wife	$[IF][IA][FA][IT]$	101.29	93	0.261
Overall quality of marriage	$[IF][IA][T]$	23.925	23	0.408

Table A2.15   Results of analyses of the psychometric qualities of the child for Hypothesis 3

Follow up measure	Model components	R^2	F Ratio
Developmental Quotient	$[I] + [T] + [TI]$	0.373	$22.09(7,241)\ p < 0.00005$
Mean sentence length	$[I]$	0.199	$60.91(1,240)\ p < 0.00005$
Identifying shapes and objects	$[I] + [A] + [IA]$	0.450	$67.64(3,241)\ p < 0.00005$
Direct observations	$[I]$	0.344	$136.52(1,258)\ p < 0.00005$

Table A2.16   Results of analyses of the psychometric qualities of the child for Hypothesis 3, with sex of index child replacing the adversity score, and with S representing this variable in the models specified below

Follow up measure	Model components	R^2	F Ratio
Developmental Quotient	$[I] + [S] + [T] + [TI] + [IS]$	0.382	$18.07(9,239)\ p < 0.00005$
Mean sentence length	$[I]$	0.199	$60.91(1,240)\ p < 0.00005$
Identifying shapes and objects	$[I] + [S]$	0.446	$66.48(3,241)\ p < 0.00005$
Direct observations	$[I] + [S]$	0.352	$71.23(1,257)\ p < 0.00005$

Table A2.17   Results of analyses of third year follow up measures of the mother's mental state variables for Hypothesis 3

Follow up measure	Model components	R^2	F Ratio
Depression	$[I] + [A]$	0.455	$108.12(2,247) \, p < 0.00005$
Anxiety	$[I] + [A]$	0.444	$101.21(2,253) \, p < 0.00005$
Inward directed irritability	$[I] + [A]$	0.273	$47.35(2,252) \, p < 0.00005$
Outward directed irritability	$[I] + [A]$	0.299	$53.85(2,252) \, p < 0.00005$
Cognitive failures	$[I] + [A]$	0.388	$80.28(2,253) \, p < 0.00005$

Table A2.18   Results of analyses of third year follow up measures of the child behaviour variables for Hypothesis 3

Follow up measure	Model components	R^2	F Ratio
Total score	$[I] + [A] + [IA]$	0.037	$2.69(3,254) \quad p < 0.00005$
Eating problems subscore	$[I] + [T] + [TI] + [A]$ $+ [AT] + [IA] + [ITA]$	0.258	$5.64(15,243) \, p < 0.00005$
Sleep problems subscore	$[I] + [T]$	0.032	$2.39(4,254) \quad p < 0.05$
Aches and pains subscore	$[I]$	0.003	$1.78(1,256) \quad$ n.s.
Speech problems subscore	$[I]$	0.046	$13.36(1,256) \quad p < 0.0003$
Temper problems subscore	$[I] + [A] + [IA]$	0.207	$15.88(3,168) \quad p < 0.00005$
Anxiety problems subscore	$[I] + [T] + [TI]$	0.049	$2.88(7,251) \quad p < 0.007$

Table A2.19   Results of analyses of third year follow up measures of the child behaviour variables for Hypothesis 3, with sex of index child (S) replacing the overall measure of adversity as the background variable

Follow up measure	Model components	R^2	F Ratio
Total score	$[I]$	-0.003	$0.12(1,256)$ n.s.
Eating problems subscore	$[I]$	0.173	$54.92(1,257) \quad p < 0.00005$
Sleep problems subscore	$[I] + [T]$	0.032	$2.39(4,254) \quad p < 0.05$
Aches and pains subscore	$[I]$	0.003	$1.78(1,256)$ n.s.
Speech problems subscore	$[I] + [S]$	0.086	$10.00(2,255) \quad p < 0.0001$
Temper problems subscore	$[I] + [S] + [IS]$	0.253	$20.31(3,168) \quad p < 0.00005$
Anxiety problems subscore	$[I] + [T] + [TI]$	0.049	$2.88(7,251) \quad p < 0.007$

Table A2.20   Results of analyses of third year follow up measures of the marriage ratings variables under Hypothesis 3

Follow up measures	Log-linear model	Chi-square goodness of fit	Residual degrees of freedom	p value
Irritability wife to husband	$[IF][IA][FA][T]$	97.89	163	0.999
Irritability husband to wife	$[IF][IA][FA][T]$	117.89	163	0.997
Quarrels and bickering	$[IF][IA][FA][T]$	48.41	55	0.723
Nagging of wife by husband	$[IF][FA][T]$	99.51	105	0.633
Nagging of husband by wife	$[IF][IA][FA][T]$	97.27	102	0.614
Overall quality of marriage	$[IF][IA][T]$	21.57	23	0.546

Table A2.21   Results of analyses of third year follow up measures of the psychometric qualities of the child for Hypothesis 3

Follow up measure	Model components	R^2	F Ratio
Verbal IQ	$[I] + [A]$	0.347	$67.45(2,248)\ p < 0.00005$
Performance IQ	$[I] + [A]$	0.218	$35.78(2,248)\ p < 0.00005$
Full-scale IQ	$[I] + [A]$	0.346	$67.26(2,248)\ p < 0.00005$
Language skills	$[I]$	0.075	$21.12(1,249)\ p < 0.00005$
Number skills	$[I]$	0.038	$10.92(1,249)\ p < 0.0015$
Direct observations	$[I]$	0.242	$83.21(1,257)\ p < 0.00005$

Table A2.22   Results of analyses of first year follow up for the mother's mental state variables for Hypothesis 4

Follow up measure	Model components	R^2	F Ratio
Depression	$[I] + [P]$	0.343	$34.71(2,127)\ p < 0.00005$
Anxiety	$[I] + [P]$	0.448	$53.26(2,127)\ p < 0.00005$
Inward directed irritability	$[I]$	0.243	$42.46(1,128)\ p < 0.00005$
Outward directed irritability	$[I] + [P]$	0.430	$49.614(2,127)\ p < 0.00005$
Cognitive failures	$[I]$	0.548	$157.63(1,128)\ p < 0.00005$

Table A2.23 Results of analyses of third year follow up measures of the mother's mental state variables for Hypothesis 4

Follow up measure	Model components	R^2	F Ratio
Depression	[I] + [P]	0.339	33.86(2,126) $p < 0.00005$
Anxiety	[I]	0.347	69.15(1,127) $p < 0.00005$
Inward directed irritability	[I]	0.173	27.74(1,127) $p < 0.00005$
Outward directed irritability	[I]	0.204	33.73(1,127) $p < 0.00005$
Cognitive failures	[I]	0.421	94.09(1,127) $p < 0.00005$

Table A2.24 Results of analyses of first year follow up measures of the child behaviour variables for Hypothesis 4

Follow up measure	Model components	R^2	F Ratio
Total score	[I]	0.353	71.99(1,129) $p < 0.00005$
Eating problems subscore	[I]	0.270	49.53(1,130) $p < 0.00005$
Sleep problems subscore	[I]	0.249	44.41(1,130) $p < 0.00005$
Bowel and bladder problems subscore	[I]	0.099	15.39(1,130) $p < 0.0001$
Attention problems subscore	[I]	0.136	21.60(1,130) $p < 0.00005$
Relationship and temper problems subscore	[I]	0.355	53.87(1,95) $p < 0.00005$
Anxiety problems subscore	[I]	0.299	56.89(1,130) $p < 0.00005$

Table A2.25 Results of analyses of third year follow up measures of the child behaviour variables for Hypothesis 4

Follow up measure	Model components	R^2	F Ratio
Total score	[I]	0.0002	1.03(1,130) n.s.
Eating problems subscore	[I]	0.170	27.92(1,130) $p < 0.00005$
Sleep problems subscore	[I]	−0.002	0.74(1,130) n.s.
Aches and pains subscore	[I] + [P]	0.085	3.01(2,129) $p < 0.05$
Speech problems subscore	[I]	0.144	23.00(1,130) $p < 0.00005$
Temper problems subscore	[I]	0.218	27.49(1,94) $p < 0.00005$
Anxiety problems subscore	[I]	0.018	3.36(1,130) n.s.

Table A2.26   Results of analyses of first year follow up measures of the psychometric qualities of the child for Hypothesis 4

Follow up measure	Model components	R^2	F Ratio
Developmental Quotient	[I]	0.288	52.36(1,126) $p < 0.00005$
Mean sentence length	[I]	0.118	17.70(1,124) $p < 0.00005$
Identifying shapes and objects	[I]	0.378	77.44(1,125) $p < 0.00005$
Direct observations	[I] + [P] + [IP]	0.324	21.89(3,128) $p < 0.00005$

Table A2.27   Results of analyses of third year follow up measures of the psychometric qualities of the child for Hypothesis 4

Follow up measure	Model components	R^2	F Ratio
Verbal IQ	[I] + [P] + [IP]	0.166	9.47(3,125) $p < 0.00005$
Performance IQ	[I]	0.224	37.99(1,127) $p < 0.00005$
Full-scale IQ	[I] + [P]	0.211	18.10(2,126) $p < 0.00005$
Language skills	[I]	0.003	1.41(1,127) n.s.
Number skills	[I]	0.002	1.21(1,127) n.s.
Direct observations	[I] + [P] + [IP]	0.218	13.24(3,128) $p < 0.00005$

Consumer Response Questionnaire

We are trying to get a general picture of the ways in which families have found our work useful. It would be very helpful if you could give us an idea of your impressions. You can remain anonymous but we need to know what type of visits you had.

Type of visit (Health Visitor, family meetings or group discussions)

1+	It helped me think out ways of coping with my child.	No	Possibly	Yes	N/A
2−	It was just talk and not really useful.	No	Possibly	Yes	N/A
3+	It helped me to understand my child more.	No	Possibly	Yes	N/A
4−	I would have liked more advice.	No	Possibly	Yes	N/A
5+	It helped me to think of ways to cope with my child's sleep or eating problems.	No	Possibly	Yes	N/A
6−	There were not enough visits to be really useful.	No	Possibly	Yes	N/A
7+	It helped to have someone to talk to.	No	Possibly	Yes	N/A
8−	Too many questions were asked.	No	Possibly	Yes	N/A
9+	It helped me to understand myself more than before.	No	Possibly	Yes	N/A
10+	It was very easy to talk to the worker (social worker or health visitor).	No	Possibly	Yes	N/A
11−	Fewer visits would have been better.	No	Possibly	Yes	N/A
12−	It was difficult to see the point of some of the things brought up.	No	Possibly	Yes	N/A
13+	It helped me to understand things about the whole family.	No	Possibly	Yes	N/A
14+	It helped me to think of ways to cope with behaviour difficulties in my child.	No	Possibly	Yes	N/A
15−	Discussions like that are just a waste of time.	No	Possibly	Yes	N/A
16−	I found the visits inconvenient.	No	Possibly	Yes	N/A
17−	Other family members should have had a chance to join in the discussions.	No	Possibly	Yes	N/A
18+	It helped me to understand my child better.	No	Possibly	Yes	N/A

19−	I sometimes felt upset after the discussions.	No	Possibly	Yes	N/A
20−	I would like to have been told more about handling my children.	No	Possibly	Yes	N/A
21−	I worried over what had been discussed.	No	Possibly	Yes	N/A
22+	The meetings were useful to us as a family group.	No	Possibly	Yes	N/A
23+	The meetings were useful to me in seeing that other people may have similar difficulties to me.	No	Possibly	Yes	N/A
24−	The visits would have been more useful if they had been more frequent.	No	Possibly	Yes	N/A
25+	It helped me to understand my own reactions to things better.	No	Possibly	Yes	N/A
26+	I found it helpful on the whole.	No	Possibly	Yes	N/A

Thank you very much for your help.

Scoring Note: Each item was scored +1 or −1 as indicated in the left hand column.

© Not to be used without permission of the authors.

References

Abernathy, V. (1973) Social network and the response to the marital role. *International Journal of the Sociology of the Family*, **3**, 86–92.

Achenbach, T.M., Edelbock, C.S. and Howell, C.T. (1987) Empirically based assessment of the behavioral/emotional problems of 2 and 3 year old children. *Journal of Abnormal Child Psychology*, **15**, 629–650.

Adams, L.A. and Rickert, V.I. (1989) Reducing bedtime tantrums: comparison between positive routines and graduated extinction. *Pediatrics*, **84**, 756–761.

Ainsworth, M.D.S., Blehar, M.C., Waters, E. and Wall, S. (1978) *Patterns of Attachment: A Psychological Study of the Strange Situation*. Hillsdale, NJ: Erlbaum.

Aldous, J. (1978) *Family Careers: Development Change in Families*. New York: Wiley.

Allen, D.V. and Oliver, J.M. (1982) The effects of child maltreatment on language development. *Child Abuse and Neglect*, **6**, 299–305.

Anastasi, A. (1982) *Psychological Testing*, 5th edn. New York: Macmillan.

Andersson, B.E. (1992) Effects of day-care on cognitive and socioemotional competence of thirteen year old Swedish schoolchildren. *Child Development*, **63**, 20–36.

Andrews, B. and Brown, G.W. (1988) Social support, onset of depression and personality. *Social Psychiatry and Psychiatric Epidemiology*, **23**, 99–108.

Andrews, S.R., Blumenthal, J.B., Johnson, D.L., Kahn, A.J., Ferguson, C.J., Lasater, T.M., Malone, P.E. and Wallace, D.B. (1982) The skills of mothering: a study of parent child development centres. *Monographs of the Society for Research in Child Development*, vol 47, no 6.

Appleton, P.L. (1990) Interventions by health visitors. In J. Stevenson (ed) *Health Visitor Based Services for Pre-school Children with Behaviour Problems*. Occasional papers No. 2. London: The Association of Child Psychology and Psychiatry.

Archbishop of Canterbury's Commission on Urban Priority Areas (1985) *Faith in the City*. London: Church House Publishing.

Balleyguier, G. (1991) French research on day care. In E.C. Melhuish and P. Moss (eds) *Day Care for Young Children*. London: Routledge.

Bandura, A. and Walters, R.H. (1963) *Social Learning and Personality Development*. New York: Holt, Rinehart & Winston.

Barkley, R. (1988) Child behavior rating scales and checklists. In M. Rutter, A.H. Tuma and I.S. Lann (eds) *Assessment and Diagnosis in Child Psychopathology*. London: David Fulton.

Bates, J.E. (1989) Applications. In G.A. Kohnstramm, J.E. Bates and M.K. Rothbart (eds) *Temperament in Childhood*. Chichester: Wiley.

Beck, A.T., Rush, A.J., Shaw, B.F. and Emery, G. (1979). *Cognitive Therapy for Depression*. New York: Wiley.

Behar, L. and Stringfield, S. (1974) A behavior rating scale for the preschool child. *Developmental Psychology*, **10**, 601–610.

Belsky, J. (1988) Infant day care and socioemotional development: the United States. *Journal of Child Psychology and Psychiatry*, **29**, 397–406.

Bene, E. and Anthony, J. (1957) *The Manual of the Family Relations Test*. Slough, Berks: National Foundation for Educational Research.

Bereiter, C. (1963) Some persisting dilemmas in the measurement of change. In C. Harris (ed) *Problems in Measuring Change*. Madison, Wis: University of Wisconsin Press.

Bibring, G.L. (1959) Some considerations of the psychological processes of pregnancy. *Psychoanalytic Study of the Child*, **145**, 113–121.

Birch, H.G. and Gussow, J.D. (1970) *Disadvantaged Children: Health, Nutrition and School Failure*. New York: Harcourt Brace & World/Grune & Stratton.

Bishop, D. and Rosenbloom, L. (1987) Childhood language disorders: classification and overview. In W. Yule and M. Rutter (eds) *Language Development and Disorders*. Clinics in Developmental Medicine, McKeith Press, Oxford: Blackwell.

Bishop, D.V.M. (1979) Comprehension in developmental language disorders. *Developmental Medicine and Child Neurology*, **21**, 225–238.

Bishop, Y.M.M., Fienberg, S.E. and Holland, P.W. (1975) *Discrete Multivariate Analysis: Theory and Practice*. Cambridge, Mass: MIT Press.

Boulton, M.G. (1983) *On Being a Mother: A Study of Women with Pre-school Children*. London: Tavistock.

Bradley, R.H. and Caldwell, B.M. (1984) *HOME Inventory*. Little Rock, Ark.: University of Arkansas.

Bricker, D. and Veltman, M. (1990) Early intervention programs: child focused approaches. In S.J. Meisels and J.P. Shonkoff (eds) *Handbook of Early Childhood Intervention*. Cambridge: Cambridge University Press.

Brim, O.G. (1962) *Personality and Thinking Processes: Studies in the Psychology of Thinking*. Stanford, Calif.: Stanford University Press.

Broadbent, D.E., Cooper, P.F., Fitzgerald, P. and Parkes, K.R. (1982) The cognitive failures questionnaire and its correlates. *British Journal of Clinical Psychology*, **21**, 1–16.

Broberg, A. (1988) The Swedish child care system. *Göteborg Psychological Reports*, vol 18, no 6.

Brody, G.H. and Forehand, R. (1985) The efficacy of parent training with maritally distressed and nondistressed mothers: a multimethod assessment. *Behaviour Research and Therapy*, **23**, 291–296.

Bronfenbrenner, U. (1974) *Is Early Intervention Effective? A Report on Longitudinal Evaluations of Preschool Programs*, vol 2, DHEW publication no (OHD) 74–25. Washington, DC: US Department of Health Education and Welfare.

Brown, G.W. and Harris, T. (1978) *Social Origins of Depression*, London: Tavistock.

Brown, G.W. and Harris, T. (1989) *Life Events and Illness*, London: Unwin & Hyman.

Brown, G.W., Harris, T.O. and Bifulco, A. (1986) Long term effects of loss of parent. In M. Rutter, C.E. Izard and P.B. Read (eds) *Depression in Young People*. New York: Guilford Press.

Brown, G.W., Ni Bhrolchain, M. and Harris, T. (1975) Social class and psychiatric disturbance among women in an urban population. *Sociology*, **9**, 225–254.

Brown, M. and Madge, N.J. (1982) *Despite the Welfare State*. London: Heinemann.

Bryant, D.M. and Ramey, C.T. (1987) An analysis of the effectiveness of early intervention programs for environmentally at risk children. In M.J. Guaralnick and F.C. Bennett (eds) *The Effectiveness of Early Intervention for At-risk and Handicapped Children*. Orlando, Fla: Academic Press.

Bukowski, W.M. and Hoza, B. (1989) Popularity and friendship. In T.J. Berndt and G. Ladd (eds) *Peer Relationships and Child Development*. New York: Wiley.

Burchinal, M., Lee, M. and Ramey, C. (1989) Type of day care and preschool intellectual development in disadvantaged children. *Child Development*, **60**, 128–137.

Caldwell, B.M. and Bradley, R.H. (1979) *HOME Observation for Measurement of the Environment*. Little Rock, Ark.: University of Arkansas.

Calvert, S.C. and McMahon, R.J. (1987) The treatment applicability of a behaviour parent training program and its components. *Behaviour Therapy*, **18**, 165–180.

Campbell, S.B. (1987) Parent referred problem three-year-olds: developmental changes in symptoms. *Journal of Child Psychology and Psychiatry*, **28**, 835–845.

Campbell, S.B. and Ewing, L.J. (1990) Follow up of hard to manage preschoolers: adjustment at age 9 and predictors of continuing symptoms. *Journal of Child Psychology and Psychiatry*, **31**, 871–890.

Campos, J.J., Barrett, K.C., Lamb, M.E., Goldsmith, H.H. and Stenberg, C. (1983) Socioemotional development. In M.M. Haith and J.J. Campos (eds) *Mussen's Handbook of Child Psychology*, 4th edn, vol 2. New York: Wiley.

Cantwell, D.P. (1988) DSM-III studies. In M. Rutter, A.H. Tuma and I.S. Lann (eds) *Assessment and Diagnosis in Child Psychopathology*. London: David Fulton.

Caplan, G. (1964) *Principles of Preventive Psychiatry*. London: Tavistock.

Caplan, G. (1970) *The Theory and Practice of Mental Health Consultation*. New York: Basic Books.

Caplan, H.L., Alexandra, H., Robson, K.M., Katz, R. and Kumar, R. (1989) Maternal depression and the emotional development of children. *British Journal of Psychiatry*, **154**, 818–822.

Casey, R.J. and Berman, J.S. (1985) The outcome of psychotherapy with children. *Psychological Bulletin*, **98**, 388–400.

Clark, M.M. (1988) *Children Under Five: Educational Research and Evidence*. Final report to the Department of Education and Science. New York: Gordon & Breach Science Publishers.

Clarke-Stewart, K.A. and Fein, G. (1983) Early childhood programs. In M.M. Haith and J.J. Campos (eds) *Infancy and Developmental Psychobiology*, vol 2, *Mussen's Handbook of Child Psychology*, 4th edn. New York: Wiley.

Cleghorn, J. and Levin, S. (1973) Training family therapists by setting learning objectives. *American Journal of Orthopsychiatry*, **43**, 439–446.

Cohen, B. (1988) Report of the UK representative on the European Commission's Childcare Network. House of Commons Education Science and Arts. First Report. Volume 2, Appendix 2 in *Educational Provision for the Under Fives*. London: HMSO.

Cohen, H.J. (1990) Paper given at the 44th Annual Meeting of the American Academy for Cerebral Palsy and Developmental Medicine, October. Orlando, Florida.

Cohen, R., Coxall, J., Craig, G. and Sadiq-Sangster, A. (1992) *Hardship Britain*. London: Child Poverty Action Group.

Cohn, J.F. and Tronick, E. (1989) Specificity of infants' response to mother's affect. *Journal of the American Academy of Child and Adolescent Psychiatry*, **28**, 242–248.

Coie, J.D. and Kupersmidt, J.B. (1983) A behavioral analysis of emerging social status in boys' groups. *Child Development*, **54**, 1400–1416.

Coleman, J., Wolkind, S. and Ashley, L. (1977) Symptoms of behaviour disturbance and adjustment to school. *Journal of Child Psychology and Psychiatry*, **18**, 201–210.

Conners, C.K. (1969) A teacher rating scale for use in drug studies with children. *American Journal of Psychiatry*, **126**, 884–888.

Coombs, C.H. (1983) *Psychology and Mathematics*. Ann Arbor, Mich: University of Michigan Press.

Coombs, C.H. (1984) Theory and experiment in psychology. Transcript of talk presented to the European Experimental Psychology Group, 29 March 1983 meeting at the University of Hamburg, Germany.

Cooper, P.J., Campbell, E.A., Day, A., Kennerley, H. and Bond, A. (1988) Non psychotic psychiatric disorder after childbirth. *British Journal of Psychiatry*, **152**, 799–806.

Cornely, P. and Bromet, E. (1986) Prevalence of behavior problems in three-year-old children living near Three Mile Island: a comparative analysis. *Journal of Child Psychology and Psychiatry*, **27**, 489–498.

Court Report (1976) *Fit for the Future? Report of the Health and Social Security Committee on Child Health Services*. Chairman Professor S.D.M. Court. London: HMSO CMND 6684.

Cox, J.L. (1976) Psychiatric morbidity and childbirth: a prospective study from Kansagati Health Centre, Kampala. *Proceedings of the Royal Society of Medicine*, **69**, 221–222.

Cox, J.L., Connor, Y. and Kendell, R.E. (1982) Prospective study of the psychiatric disorders of childbirth. *British Journal of Psychiatry*, **140**, 111–117.

Creighton, S.J. (1988) The incidence of child abuse and neglect. In K. Browne, C. Davies and P. Stratton (eds) *Early Prediction and Prevention of Child Abuse*. Chichester: Wiley.

Crowe, B. (1973) *The Playgroup Movement*. London: George Allen & Unwin.

Crowell, J.A., Feldman, S.S. and Ginsberg, N. (1988) Assessment of mother child interaction in preschoolers with behaviour problems. *Journal of the American Academy of Child and Adolescent Psychiatry*, **27**, 303–311.

Dadds, M.R., Schwartz, S. and Sanders, M.R. (1987) Marital discord and treatment outcome in behavioral treatment of child conduct disorders. *Journal of Consulting and Clinical Psychology*, **55**, 396–403.

De Mulder, E.K. and Radke-Yarrow, M. (1991) Attachment to affectively ill and well mothers: concurrent behavioral correlates. *Development and Psychopathology*, **3**, 227–242.

Delamothe, T. (1992) Poor Britain. *British Medical Journal*, **305**, 263–264.

Denham, S.A. (1989) Maternal affect and toddlers' social emotional competence. *American Journal of Orthopsychiatry*, **59**, 368–376.

Deutch, H. (1947) *The Psychology of Women*. New York: Grune & Stratton.

Dodge, K.A. (1990) Developmental psychopathology in children of depressed mothers. *Developmental Psychology*, **26**, 3–6.

Douglas, J. (1990) Frameworks for providing in-service training to health visitors in behavioural treatment techniques. In J. Stevenson (ed) *Health Visitor Based Services for Pre-School Children with Behaviour Problems*. Occasional papers No. 2. London: Association of Child Psychology and Psychiatry.

Douglas, J. and Richman, N. (1984) *My Child Won't Sleep*. Harmondsworth: Penguin Books.

Draper, N. and Smith, H. (1981) *Applied Regression Analysis*, 2nd edn. New York: Wiley.

Duman, J.E., Ibson, J.A. and Albin, J.B. (1989) Behavioural correlates of maternal depressive symptomatology in conduct-disorder children. *Journal of Consulting and Clinical Psychology*, **57**, 516–521.

Dunn, J. (1987) The beginnings of moral understanding: development in the second year. In J. Kagan and S. Lamb (eds) *The Emergence of Morality in the Second Year*, Chicago, Ill: University of Chicago Press.

Dunn, J. (1988) Sibling influences on child development. *Journal of Child Psychology and Psychiatry*, **29**, 119–127.

Dunn, J. and Kendrick, C. (1982) *Siblings: Love, Envy and Understanding*. Oxford: Blackwell.

Dunn, J. and McGuire, S. (1992) Sibling and peer relationships in childhood. *Journal of Child Psychology and Psychiatry*, **33**, 67–100.

Dunn, J. and Munn, P. (1986) Sibling quarrels and maternal intervention: individual differences in understanding and aggression. *Journal of Child Psychology and Psychiatry*, **27**, 583–595.

Earls, F. (1980) The prevalence of behavior problems in three-year-old children: a cross national replication. *Archives of General Psychiatry*, **37**, 1153–1157.

Earls, F. and Jung, K.G. (1987) Temperament and home environment characteristics as causal factors in the early development of childhood psychopathology. *Journal of the American Academy of Child and Adolescent Psychiatry*, **26**, 491–498.

Easterbrooks, M.A. and Emde, R.N. (1988) Marital and parent child relationships: the role of affect in the family system. In R.A. Hinde and J. Stevenson-Hinde (eds) *Relationships within Families: Mutual Influences*. Oxford: Oxford University Press.

Egan, K.J. (1983) Stress management and child management with abusive parents. *Journal of Clinical Child Psychology*, **12**, 292–299.

Elkin, I., Shea, T., Watkins, J.T., Imber, S.D., Sotsky, S.M., Collins, J.F., Glass, D.R., Pilkonis, P.A., Leber, W.R., Docherty, J.P., Fiester, S.J. and Parloff, M.B. (1989) National Institute of Mental Health Treatment of Depression Collaborative Research Program. *Archives of General Psychiatry*, **46**, 971–982.

Elliott, B.J. and Richards, M.P.M. (1991) Effects of parental divorce on children. *Archives of Disease in Childhood*, **66**, 915–916.

Engfer, A. (1988) The interrelatedness of marriage and the mother child relationship. In R.A. Hinde and J. Stevenson-Hinde (eds) *Relationships within Families: Mutual Influences*. Oxford: Oxford University Press.

Epstein, N.B. and Bishop, D. (1981) Problem-centered systems therapy of the family. In A.S. Gurman and D.P. Kniskern (eds) *Handbook of Family Therapy*. New York: Brunner Mazel.

Epstein, N.B., Sigal, J.J. and Rakoff, V. (1962) Family categories schema. Unpublished manuscript. Family Research Group Department of Psychiatry, University of McGill, Montreal.

Eysenck, H.J. (1952) The effects of psychotherapy: an evaluation. *Journal of Consulting Psychology*, **16**, 319–324.

Farren, D.C. (1990) Effects of intervention with disadvantaged and disabled children: a decade review. In S.J. Meisels and J.P. Shonkoff (eds) *Handbook of Early Childhood Intervention*, Cambridge: Cambridge University Press.

Faull, C. and Nicol, A.R. (1986) Abdominal pain in a new town: an epidemiological study of six year olds. *Journal of Child Psychology and Psychiatry*, **27**, 251–260.

Fendrich, M., Warner, V. and Weissman, M.M. (1990) Family risk factors, parental depression and psychopathology in offspring. *Developmental Psychology*, **26**, 40–50.

Field, T., Healy, B., Goldstein, S. and Guthertz, M. (1990) Behavior state matching and synchrony in mother–infant interactions of nondepressed versus depressed dyads. *Developmental Psychology*, **26**, 7–14.

Fienberg, S.E. (1977) *The Analysis of Cross-classified Categorical Data*. Cambridge, Mass: MIT Press.

Fleiss, J.L. (1986) *The Design and Analysis of Clinical Experiments*. New York: Wiley.

Fleming, A.S., Klein, E. and Corter, C. (1992) The effect of a social support group on depression, material attitudes and behaviour in new mothers. *Journal of Child Psychology and Psychiatry*, **33**, 685–698.

Fries, C.L. and Simons, C. (1985) Training preschool children in interpersonal cognitive problem solving skills: a replication. *Prevention in Human Services*, **4**, 59–70.

Fundudis, T., Kolvin, I. and Garside, R.F. (1979) *Speech Retarded and Deaf Children: Their Psychological Development*. London: Academic Press.

Furey, W.M. and Basili, L. (1988) Predicting consumer satisfaction in parent training for non compliant children. *Behaviour Therapy*, **19**, 555–564.

Furman, W., Rahe, D.F. and Hartup, W.W. (1979) The rehabilitation of socially withdrawn preschool children through mixed age and same age socialization. *Child Development*, **50**, 915–922.

Garber, H.L. and Heber, R. (1981) The efficacy of early intervention with family rehabilitation. In M. Begab, H.C. Haywood and H.L. Garber (eds) *Psychosocial Influences in Retarded Performance*, vol 2, *Strategies for Improving Competence*. Baltimore, Md: University Park Press.

Gardner, M.J. and Altman, D.G. (eds) (1989) *Statistics with Confidence: Confidence Intervals and Statistical Guidelines*. London: British Medical Journal.

Garrison, W. and Earls, F. (1985) Change and continuity in behaviour problems from the preschool period through school entry: an analysis of mothers' reports. In J. Stevenson (ed) *Recent Research in Developmental Psychopathology*. Supplement to *Journal of Child Psychology and Psychiatry*, no. 4. Oxford: Pergamon.

Gath, A. (1988) Mentally handicapped people as parents. *Journal of Child Psychology and Psychiatry*, **29**, 739–744.

Gesten, E.L., Weissberg, R.P., Amish, P.L. and Smith, J.K. (1987) Social problem solving training: a skills based approach to prevention and treatment. In C.A. Maher and J.E. Zins (eds) *Psychoeducational Interventions in the Schools*. New York: Pergamon.

Ghodsian, M., Zajicek, E. and Wolkind, S. (1984) A longitudinal survey of maternal depression and child behaviour problems. *Journal of Child Psychology and Psychiatry*, **25**, 91–111.

Goldberg, D.P. (1972) *The Detection of Psychiatric Illness by Questionnaire*. Maudsley Monographs 21. London: Oxford University Press.

Goldberg, D. and Huxley, P. (1980) *Mental Illness in the Community: The Pathways to Psychiatric Care*. London: Tavistock.

Goldberg, D., Cooper, B., Eastwood, M.R., Kedward, M.B. and Shepherd, M. (1970) Standardized psychiatric interview for use in community surveys. *British Journal of Preventive and Social Medicine*, **24**, 18–23.

Goldberg, D.P. (1978) *Manual for the General Health Questionnaire*, Slough, Berks: National Foundation for Educational Research.

Goldsmith, H.H. and Gottesman, I.I. (1981) Origins of variation in behavioural style: a longitudinal study of temperament in young twins. *Child Development*, **52**: 91–103.

Goldstein, A.P. and Simonson, N.R. (1971) Social psychological approaches to psychotherapy research. In A.E. Bergin and S.L. Garfield (eds) *Handbook of Psychotherapy and Behavior Change*, vol 1, New York: Wiley.

Goldstein, H. (1979) *The Design and Analysis of Longitudinal Studies: Their Role in the Measurement of Change*. London: Academic Press.

Goodman, S.H. and Brumley, H.E. (1990) Schizophrenia and depressed mothers: relational deficiencies in parenting. *Developmental Psychology*, **26**, 31–39.

Goodyer, I., Nicol, A.R., Eavis, D. and Pollinger, G. (1982) The application and utility of a family assessment procedure in a child psychiatry clinic. *Journal of Family Therapy*, **4**, 373–395.

Gordon, D.A. and Forehand, R. (1972) The relative efficiency of abbreviated forms of the Stanford–Binet. *Journal of Clinical Psychology*, **28**, 86–87.

Gray, J.A. (1982) *The Neuropsychology of Anxiety*. Oxford: Oxford University Press.

Gray, S.W. and Ruttle, K. (1980) The Family Oriented Home Visiting Program. *Genetic Psychology Monographs*, **102**, 299–316.

Gray, S.W. and Ramsey, B.K. (1985) Adolescent childbearing and high school completion. *Journal of Applied Developmental Psychology*, **1**, 167–179.

Greenwood, C.R. and Hops, H. (1981) Group oriented continuencies and peer behaviour change. In P. Strain (ed) *The Utilization of Peers as Behavior Change Agents*. New York: Plenum.

Grosskurth, P. (1985) *Melanie Klein*. London: Maresfield Library.

Gurman, A.S., Kniskern, D.P. and Pinsof, W.M. (1986) Research on marital and family therapies. In S.L. Garfield and A.E. Bergin (eds) *Handbook of Psychotherapy and Behavior Change*. New York: Wiley.

Gutelius, M.F., Kirsch, A.D., MacDonald, S., Brooks, M.R. and McErlean, T. (1977) Controlled study of child health supervision: behavioral results. *Pediatrics*, **60**, 294–304.

Guttman, H.A., Spector, R.M., Sigal, J., Rakoff, V. and Epstein, N.B. (1971) Reliability of coding affective communication in family therapy sessions: problems of measurement and interpretation. *Journal of Consulting and Clinical Psychology*, **37**, 397–402.

Hall, D.M.B. (1989) *Health for All Children: A Programme for Child Health Surveillance*. Oxford: Oxford Medical Publications.

Halsey, A.H. (ed) (1972) *Educational Priority*. Report of a research project sponsored by the Department of Education and Science and SSRC, vol 1, *EPA Problems and Policies*. London: HMSO.

Harris, C. (ed) (1963) *Problems in Measuring Change*. Madison, Wis: University of Wisconsin Press.

Haskins, R. (1985) Public school aggression among children with varying day care experience. *Child Development*, **56**, 689–703.

Heinicke, C.M., Beckwith, L. and Thomson, A. (1988) Early intervention in the family system: as framework and review. *Infant Mental Health Journal*, **2**, 111–141.

Heinicke, C.M., Ramsey, K. and Lee, D.M. (1986) Outcome of child psychotherapy as a function of frequency of session. *Journal of the American Academy of Child Psychiatry*, **25**, 247–253.

Herbert, M. (1987) *Conduct Disorders of Childhood and Adolescence*, 2nd edn. Chichester: Wiley.

Hetherington, E.M. (1988) Parents, siblings and children: six years after divorce. In R.A. Hinde and J. Stevenson-Hinde (eds) *Relationships within Families: Mutual Influences*. Oxford: Oxford Scientific Publications.

Hetherington, E.M., Cox, M. and Cox, R. (1979) Play and social interaction in children following divorce. *Journal of Social Issues*, **35**, 26–49.

Hewitt, K.E. and Crawford, W.V. (1988) Resolving behavior problems in pre-school children: evaluation of a workshop for health visitors. *Child Care Health and Development*, **14**, 1–9.

Hewitt, L.E. and Jenkins, R.L. (1949) *Fundamental Patterns of Adjustment: Dynamics of their Origin*. Michigan Child Guidance Institute, Illinois.

Hill Goldsmith, H. (1989) Behavior-genetic approaches in temperament. In G.A. Kohnstramm, J.E. Bates and M.K. Rothbart (eds) *Temperament in Childhood*. Chichester: Wiley.

Hinde, R.A. (1989) Temperament as an intervening variable. In G.A. Kohnstramm, J.E. Bates and M.K. Rothbart (eds) *Temperament in Childhood*. Chichester: Wiley.

Hinde, R.H. (1979) *Towards Understanding Relationships*. London: Academic Press.

Hindley, C.B. and Owen, C.F. (1978) The extent of individual changes in I.Q. for ages between six months and 17 years in a Bristol Longitudinal Sample. *Journal of Child Psychology and Psychiatry*, **19**, 329–350.

Hobbs, D.F. and Cole, S.P. (1976) Transition to parenthood: a decade replication. *Journal of Marriage and the Family*, **38**, 723–731.

Hoffman, M.L. (1981) The role of father in moral internalization. In M. Lamb (ed) *The Role of Father in Child Development*. New York: Wiley Interscience.

Hollon, S.D. and Emerson, M.G. (1985) Negative outcome: treatment of depressive disorders. In D.T. Mays and C.M. Franks (eds) *Negative Outcome in Psychotherapy*. New York: Springer.

Howes, C. (1988) Relations between early child care and schooling. *Developmental Psychology*, **24**, 53–57.

Howes, C., Phillips, D.A. and Whitebook, M. (1992) Thresholds of quality: implications for the social development of children in center-based child care. *Child Development*, **63**, 449–460.

Hunt, J. McV. (1961) *Intelligence and Experience*. New York: Ronald Press.

Hymel, S. (1986) Interpretations of peer behaviour: affective bias in childhood and adolescence. *Child Development*, **57**, 431–445.

Infant Health and Development Program (1990) Enhancing outcomes of low birthweight premature infants: a multisite randomized trial. *Journal of the American Medical Association*, **263**, 3035–3042.

Jenkins, S., Bax, M. and Hart, H. (1984) Continuities of common behavioural problems in pre-school children. *Journal of Child Psychology and Psychiatry*, **25**, 75–89.

Kagan, J. (1982) The emergence of self. *Journal of Child Psychology and Psychiatry*, **23**, 363–382.

Kataria, S., Swanson, M.S. and Trevathan, G.E. (1987) Persistence of sleep disturbances in preschool children. *Journal of Pediatrics*, **110**, 642–646.

Kazdin, A.E. (1988) *Child Psychotherapy: Developing and Identifying Effective Treatments*. New York: Pergamon.

Kearns, N.P., Cruickshank, C.A., Mcguigan, K.J., Riley, S.A., Shaw, S.P. and Snaith, R.P. (1982) A comparison of depression rating scales. *British Journal of Psychiatry*, **141**, 45–49.

Keenan, E.O. (1974) Conversational competence in children. *Journal of Child Language*, **1**, 163–183.

Kendall, P.C. and Braswell, L. (1985) *Cognitive Behavioral Therapy for Impulsive Children*. New York: Guilford Press.

Kendell, R.E., Wainwright, S., Hailey, A. and Shannon, N. (1976). The influence of childbirth on psychiatric morbidity. *Psychological Medicine*, **6**, 297–302.

Kenny, D.A. (1979) *Correlation and Causality*. New York: Wiley.

Kiloh, L.G., Andrews, G. and Neilson, M. (1988) The long term outcome of depressive illness. *British Journal of Psychiatry*, **153**, 752–757.

King, R.S., Raynes, N.V. and Tizard, J. (1971) *Patterns of Residential Care*. London: Routledge & Kegan Paul.

Klackenberg, G. (1982) Sleep behaviour studied longitudinally. *Acta Paediatrica Scandinavica*, **71**, 501–506.

Klerman, G.L., Weissman, M.M., Rounsaville, B.J. and Chevron, E.S. (1984) *Interpersonal Therapy for Depression*. New York: Basic Books.

Kniskern, D.P. and Gurman, A.S. (1985) A marital and family perspective on deterioration in psychotherapy. In D.T. Mays and C.M. Franks (eds) *Negative Outcome in Psychotherapy*. New York: Springer.

Kochanska, G. (1991) Socialization and temperament in the development of guilt and conscience. *Child Development*, **62**, 1379–1392.

Kochanska, G., Kucznski, L., Radke-Yarrow, M. and Welsh, J. (1987) Resolutions of control episodes between well and affectively ill mothers and their young children. *Journal of Abnormal Child Psychology*, **15**, 441–56.

Kohn, M. and Rosman, B.L. (1973) A two factor model of emotional disturbances in the young child: validity and screening efficiency. *Journal of Child Psychology and Psychiatry*, **14**, 31–56.

Kohn, M. and Rosman, B.L. (1982) A social competence scale and symptom checklist for the preschool child: factor dimensions, their cross-instrument generality and longitudinal persistence. *Developmental Psychology*, **6**, 430–444.

Kolvin, I., Wolff, S., Barber, L.M., Tweddle, E.G., Garside, R., Scott, D. McI. and Chambers, S. (1975) Dimensions of behaviour in infant school children. *British Journal of Psychiatry*, **126**, 114–126.

Kolvin, I., Garside, R.F., Nicol, A.R., Macmillan, A., Wolstenholme, F. and Leitch, I. (1981) *Help Starts Here: The Maladjusted Child in Ordinary School*. London: Tavistock.

Kolvin, I., Miller, F.J.W., Scott, D. McI., Gatzanis, S.R.M. and Fleeting, M. (1990) *Continuities of Deprivation? The Newcastle 1000 Family Study*. Aldershot: Avebury.

Krantz, D.H., Luce, R.D., Suppes, P. and Tversky, A. (1971) *Additive and Polynomial Representations*, 1st edn, vol 1, *Foundations of Measurement*. New York: Academic Press.

Kumar, R. and Robson, K. (1978) Neurotic disturbance during pregnancy and the puerperium. In M. Sandler (ed) *Mental Illness in Pregnancy and the Puerperium*. Oxford: Oxford University Press.

Kumar, R. and Robson, K.M. (1984) A prospective study of emotional disorders in childbearing women. *British Journal of Psychiatry*, **144**, 35–47.

Kumar, R., Brant, H.A. and Robson, K.M. (1981) Childbearing and maternal sexuality: a prospective study of 119 primiparae. *Journal of Psychosomatic Research*, **25**, 373–383.

Lally, J.R., Mangione, P.L. and Honig, A.S. (1988) *Parent Education as Early Intervention: Emerging Directions in Theory, Research and Practice*. Norwood, NJ: Ablex.

Lambert, M.J., Shapiro, D.A. and Bergin, A.E. (1986) The effectiveness of psychotherapy. In S.L. Garfield and A.E. Bergin (eds) *Handbook of Psychotherapy and Behavior Change*. New York: Wiley.

Larson, C.P., Pless, I.B. and Miettinen, O. (1988) Preschool behavior disorders: their prevalence in relation to determinants. *Journal of Pediatrics*, **113**, 278–285.

Lazar, I. and Darlington, R. (1982) Lasting effects of early education. *Monographs of the Society for Research in Child Development*, **47**, (2–3 serial 195).

Le Prince, F. (1991) Day care for young children in France. In E.C. Melhuish and P. Moss (eds) *Day Care for Young Children*. London: Routledge.

Lee, A.S. and Murray, R.M. (1988) The long term outcome of Maudsley depressives. *British Journal of Psychiatry*, **153**, 741–751.

Lee, P.M. (1989) *Batesian Statistics: An Introduction*. London: Edward Arnold.

Lee, V.E., Brooks-Gunn, J. and Schuur, E. (1988) Does Head Start Work? A 1-year follow up comparison of disadvantaged children attending Head Start, no preschool and other preschool programs. *Developmental Psychology*, **24**, 210–222.

Leff, J. and Vaughn, C. (1985) *Expressed Emotion in Families*. London: Guilford Press.

Lerner, J.A., Trupin, E.W. and Douglas, E. (1985) Preschool behaviour can predict future psychiatric disorders. *Journal of the American Academy of Child Psychiatry*, **24**, 42–48.

Levenstein, P. (1970) Cognitive growth in preschoolers through verbal interaction with mothers. *American Journal of Orthopsychiatry*, **40**, 426–432.

Levitt, E.E. (1971) Research on psychotherapy with children. In A.E. Bergin and S.L. Garfield (eds) *Handbook of Psychotherapy and Behavior Change*. New York: Wiley.

Levy, P. (1981) On the relation between method and substance in psychology. *Bulletin of the British Psychological Society*, **34**, 265–270.

Lewinsohn, P.M., Zeiss, A.M., Duncan, E.M. (1989) Probability of relapse after recovery from an episode of depression. *Journal of Abnormal Psychology*, **98**, 107–116.

Lieberman, S. (1979) *Transgenerational Family Therapy*. London: Croom Helm.

Locke, H.J. and Wallace, K.M. (1959) Short marital adjustment and prediction tests: their reliability and validity. *Marriage and Family Living*, **21**, 251–255.

Luce, R.D., Krantz, D.H., Suppes, P. and Tversky, A. (1990) *Representation, Axiomatization, and Invariance*, 1st edn, vol 3, *Foundations of Measurement*. San Diego, Calif: Academic Press.

McAuley, R. and McAuley, P. (1977) *Child Behaviour Problems: An Empirical Approach to Management*. London: Macmillan.

McCall, R.B., Eichorn, D.H. and Hogarty, P.S. (1977) *Transitions in Early Development*. Monographs of the Society for Research in Child Development 42, No. 3 (Serial No. 171).

Maccoby, E.E. and Martin, J.A. (1983) Socialization in the context of the family: parent child socialization. In E.M. Hetherington (ed) *Mussen's Handbook of Child Psychology*, 4th edn. New York: Wiley.

McCullagh, P. and Nelder, J.A. (1983) *Generalized Linear Models*. Monographs on Statistics and Applied Probability. London: Chapman and Hall.

McGee, R., Partridge, F., Williams, S. and Silva, P.A. (1991) A twelve year follow up of preschool hyperactive children. *Journal of the American Academy of Child and Adolescent Psychiatry*, **30**, 224–232.

McGuire, J. and Richman, N. (1986) The prevalence of behaviour problems in three types of preschool group. *Journal of Child Psychology and Psychiatry*, **27**, 455–472.

Mackenzie, E. (1827) *A Descriptive and Historical Account of the City and County of Newcastle upon Tyne*. Newcastle upon Tyne: Mackenzie & Dent.

MacRae, A.W. (1988) Measurement scales and statistics: what can significance tests tell us about the real world? *British Journal of Psychology*, **79**, 161–171.

Mattinson, J. and Sinclair, I.A. (1979) *Mate and Stalemate: Working with Marital Problems in a Social Services Department*. London: Blackwell.

Miller, L.B. and Dyer, J.L. (1975) Four preschool programs: their dimensions and effects. *Monographs of the Society for Research in Child Development*, **40**, nos 5–6.

Mills, M., Puckering, C., Pound, A. and Cox, A. (1985) What is it about depressed mothers that influences their children's functioning? In J.E. Stevenson (ed) *Recent Research in Developmental Psychopathology*. Oxford: Pergamon.

Minde, R. and Minde, K. (1977) Behavioural screening of pre-school children: a new approach to mental health? In P.J. Graham (ed) *Epidemiological Approaches to Child Psychiatry*. London: Academic Press.

Minuchin, S. (1974) *Families and Family Therapy*. London: Tavistock.

Mitchell, K.M., Bozarth, J.D. and Kraft, C.C. (1977) A reappraisal of the therapeutic effectiveness of accurate empathy, non possessive warmth and genuineness. In A.S. Gurman and A.S. Razin (eds) *Effective Psychotherapy: A Handbook of Research*. New York: Pergamon.

Moos, R.H. (1975) *Evaluating Correctional and Community Settings*. New York: Wiley.

Morris, J.B. and Beck, A.T. (1974) The efficacy of antidepressant drugs. *Archives of General Psychiatry*, **30**, 667–674.

Moss, P. (1991) Day care for young children in the United Kingdom. In E.C. Melhuish and P. Moss (eds) *Day Care for Young Children*. London: Routledge.

Moss, P. and Plewis, I. (1977) Mental distress in mothers of preschool children in Inner London. *Psychological Medicine*, **7**, 641–652.

Myers, J.L. (1979) *Fundamentals of Experimental Design*, 3rd edn. Boston, Mass: Allyn & Bacon.

Nebylitsyn, V.D. (1972) The general and partial properties of the nervous system. In V.D. Nebylitsyn and J.A. Gray (eds) *Biological Bases of Individual Behaviour*. New York: Academic Press.

Nettelbladt, P., Uddenberg, N. and Englesson, I. (1985) Marital disharmony four and a half years post partum. *Acta Psychiatrica Scandinavica*, **71**, 392–401.

Newson, J. and Newson, E. (1968) *Four Years Old in an Urban Community*. London: Allen & Unwin.

Nicol, A.R. (1988) The treatment of child abuse in the home environment. In K. Browne, C. Davies and P. Stratton (eds) *Early Prediction and Prevention of Child Abuse*. Chichester: Wiley.

Nicol, A.R., Stretch, D.D., Fundudis, T., Smith, I. and Davison, I. (1987) The nature of mother and toddler problems, 1: Development of a multicriterion screen. *Journal of Child Psychology and Psychiatry*, **28**, 739–754.

Nicol, AR., Koziarski, M. and Hodgson, S. (1986) A short family assessment interview based on the McMaster Model of Family Functioning. Unpublished.

Nicol, A.R., Smith, J., Kay, B., Hall, D., Barlow, J. and Williams, B. (1988) Controlled comparison of two interventions for child abuse. *Journal of Child Psychology and Psychiatry*, **29**, 703–712.

Nott, P.N. (1987) Extent, timing and persistence of emotional disorders following childbirth. *British Journal of Psychiatry*, **151**, 523–527.

Oakley, A. (1974) *The Sociology of Housework*. Oxford: Martin Robertson.

O'Hara, M.W. and Zekoski, E.M. (1988) Postpartum depression: a comprehensive review. In R. Kumar and I.F. Brockington (eds) *Motherhood and Mental Illness*. London: Wright.

O'Hara, M.W., Zekoski, E.M., Philipps, L.H. and Wright, E.J. (1990) Controlled prospective study of postpartum mood disorders: comparison of childbearing and nonchildbearing women. *Journal of Abnormal Psychology*, 99, 3–15.

Olexa, D.F. and Forman, S.G. (1984) Effects of social problem solving training on classroom behaviour of urban disadvantaged children. *Journal of School Psychology*, 22, 165–175.

Olson, D.H. and McCubbin, H.I. (1983) *Families: What Makes Them Work*. Beverly Hills, Calif: Sage.

Olson, D.H., Lavee, Y. and McCubbin, H.I. (1988) Types of families and family response to stress across the family life cycle. In D.M. Klein and J. Aldous (eds) *Social Stress and Family Development*. New York: Guilford Press.

Oppenheim, C. (1990) *Poverty: The Facts*. London: Child Poverty Action Group.

Osborne, A.F. and Milbank, J.E. (1987) *The Effects of Early Education*. Oxford: Clarendon Press.

Owen, G.M. (1977) The health visitor today. In G.M. Owen (ed) *Health Visiting*. London: Macmillan.

Palmer, F.H. and Anderson, L.W. (1981) Early intervention treatments that have been tried, documented and assessed. In M.J. Begab, H.C. Haywood and H.L. Garber (eds) *Psychosocial Influences on Retarded Performance*, vol 2. Baltimore, Md: University Park Press.

Palmer, F.H., Semlear, T. and Fischer, M.A. (1981) One to one: the Harlem Study. In M.J. Begab, H.C. Haywood and H.L. Garber (eds) *Psychosocial Influences on Retarded Performance*, vol 2. Baltimore, Md: University Park Press.

Patterson, G.R. (1975) *Families: Applications of Social Learning to Family Life*. Champaign, Ill: Research Press.

Patterson, G.R. (1976) The aggressive child: victim and architect of a coercive system. In L.A. Hamerlynck, L.C. Handy and E.J. Mash (eds) *Behaviour Modification and Families: Theory and Research*, vol 1. New York: Brunner Mazel.

Patterson, G.R. (1980) Mothers: the unacknowledged victims. *Monographs of the Society of Research on Child Development*, 45 (5, serial 186).

Patterson, G.R. (1982) *Coercive Family Process*. Eugene, Oreg: Castalia.

Patterson, G.R. (1986) The contribution of siblings to training for fighting: a microsocial analysis. In D. Olweus, J. Block and M. Radke Yarrow (eds) *Development of Antisocial and Prosocial Behaviour: Research Theories and Issues*. New York: Academic Press.

Patterson, G.R. and Dishion, T.J. (1985) Contributions of families and peers to delinquency. *Criminology*, 23, 63–79.

Patterson, G.R. and Fleischman, M.J. (1979) Maintenance of treatment effects: some considerations concerning family systems and follow up data. *Behavior Therapy*, 10, 168–185.

Patterson, G.R., Chamberlain, P. and Reid, J.B. (1982) A comparative evaluation of a parent training program. *Behavior Therapy*, 13, 638–650.

Paykel, E.S., Emms, E.M., Fletcher, J. and Rassaby, E.S. (1980) Life events and social support in puerperal depression. *British Journal of Psychiatry*, 136, 339–346.

Philipps, L.H. and O'Hara, M.J. (1991) Prospective study of post partum depression:

$4\frac{1}{2}$ year follow up of women and children. *Journal of Abnormal Psychology*, **100**, 151–155.

Phillips, D. (1991) Day care for young children in the United States. In E.C. Melhuish and P. Moss (eds) *Day Care for Young Children*. London: Routledge.

Pilowsky, I. and Sharp, J. (1971) Psychological aspects of PET: a prospective study. *Journal of Psychosomatic Research*, **15**, 193–198.

Pistang, N. (1984) Women's work involvement and experience of new motherhood. *Journal of Marriage and the Family*, **46**, 433–447.

Pitt, B. (1968) Atypical depression following childbirth. *British Journal of Psychiatry*, **114**, 1325–1335.

Plewis, I. (1981a) *Analyzing change: using longitudinal data for the measurement and explanation of change in the social and behavioural sciences*. Final report to the SSRC on work carried out with an SSRC fellowship, March 1977–February 1981).

Plewis, I. (1981b) A comparison of approaches to the analysis of longitudinal categoric data. *British Journal of Mathematical and Statistical Psychology*, **34**, 118–123.

Plewis, I. (1985) *Analyzing Change*. Chichester: Wiley.

Pound, A. and Mills, M. (1985) A pilot evaluation of NEWPIN, a home visiting and befriending scheme in South London. *Association of Child Psychology and Psychiatry Newsletter*, **7**, 13–15.

Price, J.M. and Dodge, K.A. (1989) Peers' contribution to children's social maladjustment. In T.J. Berndt and G.W. Ladd (eds) *Peer Relationships in Child Development*. New York: Wiley Interscience.

Provence, S. and Lipton, R.C. (1962) *Infants in Institutions: A Comparison of their Development with Family Reared Infants during the First Year of Life*. New York: International Universities Press.

Puckering, C. (1989) Maternal depression. *Journal of Child Psychology and Psychiatry*, **30**, 807–817.

Pugh, G. (1988) *Services for Under Fives Developing a Coordinated Approach*. London: National Children's Bureau.

Quinton, D. and Rutter, M. (1985) Family pathology and child psychiatric disorder: a four year prospective study. In A.R. Nicol (ed) *Longitudinal Studies in Child Psychology and Psychiatry*. Chichester: Wiley.

Quinton, D. and Rutter, M. (1988) *Parenting Breakdown: The Making and Breaking of Intergenerational Links*. Aldershot: Avebury.

Quinton, D., Rutter, M. and Rowlands, O. (1976) An evaluation of an interview assessment of marriage. *Psychological Medicine*, **6**, 577–586.

Radke-Yarrow, M., Richters, J. and Elbert Wilson, W. (1988) Child development in a network of relationships. In R. Hinde and J. Hinde-Stevenson (eds) *Relationships within Families: Mutual Influences*. Oxford: Oxford Science Publications.

Rakoff, V., Sigal, J. and Epstein, N.B. (1975) Predictions of therapeutic process and progress in conjoint family therapy. *Archives of General Psychiatry*, **32**, 1013–1017.

Ramey, C.T. and Haskins, R. (1981) The causes and treatment of school failure: insights from the Carolina Abecedarian project. In M.J. Begab, H.C. Haywood and H.L. Garber (eds) *Psychosocial Influences on Retarded Performance*, vol 2. Baltimore, Md: University Park Press.

Ramey, C.T., Bryant, D., Sparling, J.J. and Wasik, B.H. (1985) Educational interventions to enhance intellectual development. In S. Harel and N.J. Anastasiow (eds) *The At Risk Infant: Psycho/Socio/Medical Aspects*. Baltimore, Md: Brookes.

Ramey, C.T., Yeates, K.O. and Short, E.I. (1984) The plasticity of intellectual development: insights from preventive intervention. *Child Development*, 55, 1913–1925.

Rees, W.D. and Lutkins, S.G. (1971) Parental depression before and after childbirth: an assessment with the Beck Depression Inventory. *Journal of the Royal College of General Practitioners*, 21, 26–31.

Registrar General's Office (1951) *Classification of Occupation*. London: HMSO.

Reid, W.J. (1979) *The Task Centred System*. New York: Columbia University Press.

Reid, W.J. and Shyne, A.W. (1969) *Brief and Extended Casework*. New York: Columbia University Press.

Rexroat, C. and Shehan, C. (1987) The family life cycle and spouse's time in housework. *Journal of Marriage and the Family*, 49, 737–750.

Richards, M.P.M. (1984) Children and divorce. In J.A. Macfarlane (ed) *Progress in Child Health*. Edinburgh: Churchill Livingstone.

Richman, N. (1977) Is a behaviour checklist useful? In P.J. Graham (ed) *Epidemiological Approaches in Child Psychiatry*. London: Academic Press.

Richman, N. and Graham, P. (1971) A behavioural screening questionnaire for use with three year old children. *Journal of Child Psychology and Psychiatry*, 12, 5–33.

Richman, N., Stevenson, J. and Graham, P.J. (1982) *Preschool to School: A Behavioural Study*. London: Academic Press.

Richman, N., Stevenson, J. and Graham, P.J. (1985) Sex differences in outcome of preschool behaviour problems. In A.R. Nicol (ed) *Longitudinal Studies in Child Psychology and Psychiatry*. Chichester: Wiley.

Rist, R.C. (1971) Student social class and teacher expectations: the self fulfilling prophecy in ghetto education. *Harvard Educational Review*, reprint series no 5: 70–110.

Robins, L.N. (1966) *Deviant Children Grown Up*. Baltimore, Md: Williams & Wilkins.

Rose, N.S. (1972) *Ten Therapeutic Play Groups: A Preliminary Study of the Children Attending and their Families*. London: National Society for the Prevention of Cruelty to Children.

Rothbart, M.K. (1989) Biological processes in temperament. In G.A. Kohnstramm, J.E. Bates and M.K. Rothbart (eds) *Temperament in Childhood*. Chichester: Wiley.

Royce, J.M., Darlington, R.B. and Murray, H.W. (1983) Pooled analyses: findings across studies. In Consortium for Longitudinal Studies (ed) *As the Twig is Bent . . . Lasting Effects of Preschool Programs*. Hillsdale, NJ: Erlbaum.

Rubin, K.L., Both, L., Zahn-Waxler Cummings, E.M. and Wilkinson, M. (1991) Dyadic play behaviors of children of well and depressed mothers. *Developmental Psychopathology*, 3, 243–251.

Russell, C.S. (1974) Transition to parenthood: problems and gratifications. *Journal of Marriage and the Family*, 33, 244–303.

Rutter, M. (1990) Commentary: some focus and process considerations regarding effects of parental depression on children. *Developmental Psychology*, 26, 60–67.

Rutter, M. and Giller, H. (1983) *Juvenile Delinquency: Trends and Perspectives*. Harmondsworth: Penguin.

Rutter, M. and Lord, C. (1987) Language disorders associated with psychiatric disturbance. In W. Yule and M. Rutter (eds) *Language Development and Disorders*. Clinics in Developmental Medicine, McKeith Press; Oxford: Blackwell.

Rutter, M. and Madge, N. (1976) *Cycles of Disadvantage*. London: Heinemann.

Rutter, M., Quinton, D. and Hill, J. (1990) Adult outcome of institution reared children: males and females compared. In L. Robins and M. Rutter (eds) *Straight and Devious Pathways from Childhood to Adulthood*. Cambridge: Cambridge University Press.

Rutter, M., Tizard, J. and Whitmore, K. (1970) *Education Health and Behaviour*. London: Longman.

Rutter, M., Maughan, B., Mortimore, P., Ouston, J. and Smith, A. (1979) *Fifteen Thousand Hours: Secondary Schools and their Effects on Children*. London/Boston, Massachusetts: Open Books/Harvard University Press.

Ryan, S. (1974) Overview. In S. Ryan (ed) *A Report on Longitudinal Evaluations of Preschool Programs*, vol 1, *Longitudinal Evaluations*. DHEW publication no (OHD) 74–24. Washington, DC: US Department of Health Education and Welfare.

Sachs, J.S. (1983) Negative effects in brief psychotherapy: an empirical assessment. *Journal of Consulting and Clinical Psychology*, **51**, 557–564.

Sameroff, A.J. and Chandler, M.J. (1975) Reproductive risk and the continuum of caretaking casualty. In F.D. Horowitz (ed) *Review of Child Development Research*, vol 4. Chicago, Ill: University of Chicago Press.

Sanger, S., Weir, K. and Churchill, E. (1981) Treatment of sleep problems: the use of behaviour modification techniques by health visitors. *Health Visitor*, **54**, 421–424.

Santa Barbara, J., Woodward, C., Levin, S., Steiner, D., Goodman, J. and Epstein, N.B. (1977) Interrelationships among measures in the McMaster Family Therapy Outcome Study. *Goal Attainment Review*, **3**, 47–58.

Santa Barbara, J., Woodward, C., Levin, S., Steiner, D., Goodman, J. and Epstein, N.B. (1978) The McMaster Family Therapy Outcome Study: an overview of methods and results. *Psychotherapy: Theory Research and Practice*, **15**, 1–12.

Scarr, S. (1992) Developmental theories for the 1990s: development and individual differences. *Child Development*, **63**, 1–19.

Scarr, S., Phillips, D. and McCartney, K. (1989) Working mothers and their families. *American Psychologist*, **44**, 1402–1409.

Schaffer, H.R. (1984) *The Child's Entry in the Social World*. London: Academic Press.

Schweinhart, L.J. and Weikart, D.P. (1980) *Young Children Grow Up: The Effects of the Perry Preschool Program on Youths through Age 15*. Monographs of the High/Scope Educational Research Foundation, no 7. Ypsilanti, Mich: High Scope Press.

Seitz, V., Rosenbaum, L.K. and Apfel, N.H. (1985) Effects of family support intervention: a ten year follow up. *Child Development*, **56**, 376–391.

Sheldon, W.H. and Stevens, S.S. (1942) *The Varieties of Human Temperament*. New York: Harper & Row.

Shepherd, M., Cooper, B., Brown, A.C. and Kalton, G.W. (1966) *Psychiatric Illness in General Practice*. London: Oxford University Press.

Shereshefsky, P.M. and Yarrow, L.J. (1973) *Psychological Aspects of a First Pregnancy and Early Post Natal Adaption*. New York: Raven Press.

Shure, M.B. and Spivack, G. (1978) *Problem-Solving Techniques in Child Rearing*. San Francisco, Calif: Jossey Bass.

Sigal, J., Rakoff, V. and Epstein, N.B. (1967) Indicators of therapeutic outcome in conjoint family therapy. *Family Process*, **6**, 215–226.

Slater, M. (1986) Modification of mother–child interaction processes in families with children at risk of mental retardation. *American Journal of Mental Deficiency*, **91**, 257–267.

Slaughter, D.T. (1983) Early intervention and its effects on maternal and child development. *Monographs of the Society for Research in Child Development* , 48 (serial no 202).

Snaith, R.P., Bridge, G.W.K. and Hamilton, M. (1976) The Leeds Scale for the self assessment of depression. *British Journal of Psychiatry*, **128**, 156–166.

Snaith, R.P., Constantopoulis, A.A., Jardine, M.Y. and McGuffin, P. (1978) A clinical scale for the self assessment of irritability. *British Journal of Psychiatry*, **132**, 164–171.

Spivack, G. and Shure, M.B. (1974) *Social Adjustment of Young Children*. San Francisco, Calif: Jossey Bass.

Spivack, G., Platt, J. and Shure, M.B. (1976) *The Problem Solving Approach to Adjustment*. San Francisco, Calif: Jossey Bass.

Sroufe, A. and Fleeson, J. (1988) The coherence of family relationships. In R. Hinde and J. Stevenson-Hinde (eds) *Relationships within Families: Mutual Influences*. Oxford: Oxford University Press.

Stein, A., Gath, D.H., Bucher, J., Bond, A., Day, A. and Cooper, P.J. (1991) The relationship between post natal depression and mother child interaction. *British Journal of Psychiatry*, **158**, 40–45.

Steinberg, D. and Yule, W. (1985) Consultative work. In M. Rutter and L. Hersov (eds) *Child and Adolescent Psychiatry: Modern Approaches*, 2nd edn. Oxford: Blackwell.

Stern, D.N. (1985) *The Interpersonal World of the Infant*. New York: Basic Books.

Stevenson, J. (1990) Introduction. In J. Stevenson (ed) *Health Visitor Based Services for Pre-school Children with Behaviour Problems*. Occasional Papers no. 2. London: Association of Child Psychology and Psychiatry.

Stevenson, J., Richman, N. and Graham, P. (1985) Behaviour problems and language abilities at three years and behavioural deviance at eight years. *Journal of Child Psychology and Psychiatry*, **26**, 215–230.

Stipek, D., Recchia, S. and McClintic, S. (1992) Self evaluation in young children. *Monographs of the Society for Research in Child Development*, series no 226, vol 57, no 1.

Strain, P.S., Shores, R.E. and Timm, M.A. (1977) Effects of peer social interactions on the behaviour of socially withdrawn children. *Journal of Applied Behavioral Analysis*, **10**, 289–298.

Stretch, D.D. and Stoker, A.J. (in preparation) Axiomatic measurement theory and mathematical psychology: their contribution to the debate about operational definitions.

Stretch, D.D., Nicol, A.R., Davison, I.D. and Fundudis, T. (1992) The prevalence of mother and toddler disturbance in a community prevention project. Submitted for publication.

Strupp, H.H. and Hadley, S.W. (1985) Negative effects and their determinants. In D.T. Mays and C.M. Franks (eds) *Negative Outcome in Psychotherapy*. New York: Springer.

Suppes, P., Krantz, D.H., Luce, R.D. and Tversky, A. (1989) *Geometrical Threshold and Probabilistic Representations*, 1st edn, vol 2, *Foundations of Measurement*. San Diego, Calif: Academic Press.

Taylor, E. and Sandberg, S. (1984) Classroom behaviour problems and hyperactivity: a questionnaire study in English schools. *Journal of Abnormal Child Psychology*, **12**, 143–156.

Teti, D.M. and Abland, K.E. (1989) Security of attachment and infant–sibling relationships: a laboratory study. *Child Development*, **60**, 1519–1528.

Thomas, A. and Chess, S. (1977) *Temperament and Development*. New York: Brunner Mazel.

Thomas, A. and Chess, S. (1981) The role of temperament in the contributions of individuals to their development. In R.M. Lerner and N.A. Busch-Rossnagel (eds) *Individuals as Producers of their Development*. New York: Academic Press.

Thomas, A., Chess, S. and Birch, H. (1968) *Temperament and Behavior Disorders in Children*. New York: New York University Press.

Tizard, B. and Hughes, M. (1984) *Young Children Learning: Talking and Thinking at Home and at School*. London: Fontana.

Townsend, P. and Davidson, N. (1982) *Inequalities in Health*. Harmondsworth: Penguin.

Tronick, E.Z., Als, H., Adamson, L., Wise, S. and Brazelton, T.B. (1978) The infant's response to contradictory messages in face-to-face interaction. *Journal of the American Academy of Child Psychiatry*, **17**, 1–13.

Truax, C.B. and Carkhuff, R.R. (1967) *Toward Effective Counseling and Psychotherapy*. Chicago: Aldine.

Uddenberg, N. and Englesson, I. (1978) Prognosis of post partum mental disturbance. *Acta Psychiatrica Scandinavica*, **58**, 201–212.

Upton, G.J.G. (1978) *The Analysis of Cross-tabulated Data*. Chichester: Wiley.

Van der Eyken, W. (1982) *Home Start: A Four Year Evaluation*. Leicester: Home Start Consultancy.

Van der Eyken, W. (1984) *Day Nurseries in Action: A National Study of Local Authority Day Nurseries in England 1975–1983*. Final Report. Department of Child Health Research Unit, University of Bristol.

Van Eerdewegh, M., Bieri, M., Parilla, R. and Clayton, P. (1982) The bereaved child. *British Journal of Psychiatry*, **140**, 23–29.

Vaughn, S.R. and Ridley, C.A. (1983) A preschool interpersonal problem solving program: does it affect behavior in the classroom? *Child Study Journal*, **13**, 1–11.

Vaughn, S.R., Ridley, C.A. and Bullock, B. (1984) Interpersonal problem solving training with aggressive young children. *Journal of Applied Developmental Psychology*, **5**, 213–223.

Vigotsky, L. (1962) *Thought and Language*. Boston, Mass: MIT Press.

Wagner, M.E., Schubert, H.J.P. and Schubert, D.S.P. (1985) Effects of sibling spacing on intelligence, intrafamilial relations, psychosocial characteristics and mental and physical health. In H.W. Reeve (ed) *Advances in Child Development and Behavior*. Orlando, Fla: Academic Press.

Wallerstein, J.S. and Kelly, J.B. (1980) *Surviving the Breakup: How Children and Parents Cope with Divorce*. London: Grant McIntyre.

Wallin, P. (1954) A Guttman Scale for measuring women's neighbourliness. *American Journal of Sociology*, **59**, 243–246.

Washington, V. (1985) Head Start: how appropriate for minority families in the 1980s? *American Journal of Orthopsychiatry*, **55**, 577–590.

Wasik, B.H., Ramey, C.T., Bryant, D.M. and Nurcombe, B. (1990) A longitudinal study of two early intervention strategies: project CARE. *Child Development*, **61**, 1682–1696.

Waskow, I. (1983) Presentation at Conference of the Society for Psychotherapy Research, Sheffield, July.

Watson, J.P., Elliott, S.A., Rugg, A.J. and Brough, D.I. (1984) Psychiatric disorder in pregnancy and the first post natal year. *British Journal of Psychiatry*, **144**, 453–462.

Watts, C.A. (1982) Depression in general practice. In E.S. Paykel (ed) *Handbook of Affective Depression*. Edinburgh: Churchill Livingstone.

Wedge, P. and Prosser, N. (1973) *Born to Fail?* London: Arrow Books.

Weick, K.E. (1971) Group processes, family processes and problem solving. In J. Aldous, T. Condon, R. Hill, M. Straus and I. Tallman (eds) *Family Problem Solving: A Symposium on Theoretical Methodological and Substantive Issues*. Hinsdale Ill: Dryden Press.

Weir, K. and Duveen, G. (1981) Further development and validation of the prosocial behaviour questionnaire for use by teachers. *Journal of Child Psychology and Psychiatry*, **22**, 357–373.

Weitz, J.R., Weiss, B., Alicke, M.D. and Klotz, M.L. (1987) Effectiveness of psychotherapy with children and adolescents: a meta-analysis for clinicians. *Journal of Consulting and Clinical Psychology*, **55**, 542–549.

Werner, E.E. (1985) Stress and protective factors in children's lives. In A.R. Nicol (ed) *Longitudinal Studies in Child Psychology and Psychiatry*. Chichester: Wiley.

West, D.J. (1982) *Delinquency: Its Roots, Careers and Prospects*. London: Heinemann.

Westley, W. and Epstein, N.B. (1969) *The Silent Majority*. San Francisco, Calif: Jossey Bass.

White, R., Carr, P. and Lowe, N. (1990) *A Guide to the Children Act 1989*. London: Butterworths.

Wolkind, S. and Everitt, B.S. (1974) A cluster analysis of the behaviour items in the preschool child. *Psychological Medicine*, **4**, 422–427.

Wolkind, S. and Zajicek, E. (1985) From child to parent: early separation and the adaption to motherhood. In A.R. Nicol (ed) *Longitudinal Studies in Child Psychology and Psychiatry*. Chichester: Wiley.

Wolkind, S.N., Zajicek, E. and Ghodsian, M. (1980) Continuities in maternal depression. *International Journal of Family Psychiatry*, **1**, 167–182.

Woodward, C., Santa Barbara, J., Levin, S. and Epstein, N.B. (1978) The roles of goal attainment scaling in evaluating family therapy outcome. *American Journal of Orthopsychiatry*, **48**, 464–476.

Wrate, R.M., Rooney, A.C., Thomas, P.F. and Cox, J.L. (1985) Postnatal depression and child development: a three year follow up study. *British Journal of Psychiatry*, **146**, 622–627.

Yalom, I.D. (1985) *The Theory and Practice of Group Psychotherapy*, 3rd edn. New York: Basic Books.

Zajicek, E. (1981) The experience of being pregnant. In S. Wolkind and E. Zajicek (eds) *Pregnancy: A Psychological and Social Study*. London: Academic Press.

Zuckerman, B., Stevenson, J. and Bailey, V. (1987) Sleep problems in early childhood: continuities, predictive factors and behavioural correlates. *Pediatrics*, **80**, 664–671.

Index